JACK

Jack Clemo was born in [...]
wall. The only son of working class parents, he left
school at an early age. Increasingly cut off by the onset
of deafness, and later blindness, Clemo's innate poetic
genius developed under the pressure of isolation. His
certainty in the integrity of his work was rewarded
when he won the Atlantic Prize for his first novel,
Wilding Graft. This success was swiftly followed by
Confession of a Rebel, his first volume of autobiography;
the second volume, *The Marriage of a Rebel*, appeared
thirty-one years later, after his marriage at the age of
fifty-two to Ruth Peaty. The intervening years saw
financial hardship and the disappointment of rejected
manuscripts, but his poetry was published widely, as
was his statement of faith, *The Invading Gospel*. A
semi-autobiographical novel written in the early years,
The Shadowed Bed was recently published for the first
time.

Alan Bold of *The Scotsman* has written, 'Clemo regards
himself as an ordinary man, with a dislike of artiness;
he is, in fact, an extraordinary poet.' J. C. Trewin of *The
Birmingham Post* describes the author as 'one of the
most remarkable living Cornishmen ... For all the
tumult of his life and work, Jack Clemo is a curiously
serene figure now ... he remains an extraordinary
original.' Tim Lenton of *The Church of England Newspaper* writes, 'His faith is a shining response to what an
outsider would judge to be long years of suffering.'

Jack Clemo lives with his wife in Weymouth, Dorset.
'There is a truer revelation of God in the least happiness,' he writes, 'than in years of misery.'

SPIRE

By the same author

Wilding Graft
The Invading Gospel
The Marriage of a Rebel
The Bouncing Hills
The Shadowed Bed
A Different Drummer
Selected Poems

Jack Clemo

CONFESSION OF A REBEL

SPIRE

Spire is an imprint of Hodder & Stoughton *Publishers*

British Library Cataloguing in Publication Data

Clemo, Jack, *1916–*
Confession of a rebel.
I. Title
823′.914

ISBN 0-340-48896-4

*Reproduced from the original setting by arrangement with
Chatto & Windus Limited.*

*Printed in Great Britain for Hodder and Stoughton Limited, Mill Road, Dunton
Green, Sevenoaks, Kent by Richard Clay Limited, Bungay, Suffolk.*

Hodder and Stoughton Editorial Office: 47 Bedford Square, London WC1B 3DP.

*Priests and schools may doubt
Who never have believed; but I have loved*
CHESTERTON

Let my low ground shame their high
BROWNING

Contents

Preface

Even before the publication of my novel *Wilding Graft* it was obvious to me that I am one of those writers whose creative work cannot be fully understood without reference to certain broken boundaries in their private lives. It is in fairness to sympathetic readers of my fiction and poetry, as well as to myself, that I have written this personal story—the story of a village proletarian who, with practically no schooling or literary ambitions, spent his teens and most of his twenties in writing dud novels in the mere instinctive effort to come to terms with abnormal circumstances, and then, after being sealed off from the world by physical handicaps, produced a novel which a dozen British reviewers compared with the work of Hardy. The experience has that touch of oddity and perversity which characterizes the misfit, and the work is so inseparable from its background that both were apparently meant to fuse in a challenge to the moods and processes of our time. I can see no other reason why, as the son of an illiterate clay-worker, I was denied the aid of contemporary culture in obtaining freedom of mind and spirit, or why my general waywardness and revolt produced rigid orthodoxy as I was forced to undergo an educational process that few people would think possible in twentieth-century England.

To educationists the book should have some value as a protest on behalf of a temperament—a grim warning that where there are no loopholes a vision may perish. It deals with a question which the modern social planners do not dare to raise: "What is to be done for the oddly-talented child whom the schools cannot teach?" All offers of educational help to deserving children are made on one condition only—that this help be received through the schools by means of scholarships and other inducements designed to suit a majority. And this book will provide disturbing proof that, even in the present state of our advance towards uniformity, there is at least one type of child who is thereby placed beyond human assistance— the moody, unsociable, non-competitive, mystic type, whose mental energies burn fiercely at one narrow point and cannot be spread over the field of general intelligence. This record of the strange growth and emergence of one of this type should be of interest as a psychological case-history: though it is only fair to point out that while psychologists theorize about the morbid causes of my faith I shall be enjoying the fruits of it, which are curiously lacking in morbidity.

The main uses of the book will, I trust, be found on the spiritual front. This age has had a surfeit of autobiographies written by men who, reared in some form of Christianity, have failed to retain that faith in later years. Most of these confessions have been so full of cynicism and disillusion that one could only infer from them that the loss of faith does not mark any real advance towards either happiness or maturity. But they fitted a period of decadence and strengthened the prejudice against Christian affirmation in the work of original and independent minds. It was this prejudice more than anything else that made my literary struggle such a long and hard one: even when I had succeeded as a novelist some reviewers complained that my characters were "fogged by mystical religiosity." Materialists may now accuse me of having fogged my own life-story in the same way. They are so accustomed to seeing life stripped of spiritual significance that any emphasis on that significance is regarded by them as a mere fog obscuring the facts. I can only say that this book is an uncompromising challenge to the "clarity" of materialism and humanism, which is a product of over-simplification and superficiality; that it is the challenge of a mind that has known the vagueness and woolliness of mysticism, but worked through it to a creed of sharp, rugged definitions.

My theological position is roughly that of modern Calvinists —particularly Karl Barth—but with personal idiosyncrasies and overtones that would not be shared by any group of believers in the organized Church. I would have called myself simply a Christian if that word still meant anything as a definition of doctrinal belief. As it now means nothing in that connection I have to state that throughout this book events and values are interpreted from the Calvinist-Barthian standpoint—i.e., on the premises that the human soul is darkened by original sin and needs a saving illumination of divine grace, distinct from the revelation of God's wisdom and power in Nature; that knowledge of this grace comes "vertically from above"—as Barth puts it—striking first the elect, as it struck St. Paul, and then spreading to such of the non-elect as choose to share the discipline of faith. Neither I nor, I think, any other modern Calvinist accepts Calvin's notion that the non-elect are predestined to be damned, though I have stressed (and with good reason) my own belief that the "natural religion" produced by art, poetry and idealism is not only inadequate but deadly apart from the grace revealed to the elect. This is *forced* only upon a few—those whose temperament and circumstances compel them to stress the Divine rather than the human side of suffering, love, and all other redemptive processes. These persons are by no means a "favoured" few: the Divine compulsion usually works through tragedy, and the predestined Christian would be as pathetic a figure as most predestined poets and artists were it not that his faith opens up to him the infinite resources of a "particular Providence." For in the process of conversion a man's spiritual life passes from the control of the general Mood of Providence, which operates only through the laws of Nature, to the control of the Galilean Mood, the Will of Christ which subdues or adapts the tendencies of Nature when they impede the purposes of grace. Such ideas are probably unfamiliar to most modern readers, even to many church-goers; and the way they are worked out in this book—through a primitive, sensuous approach to life that normally leads to paganism—will be even less familiar. But this unusual blend of Calvinism and erotic mysticism— the alternating stresses of dogma and sex from which all my education was derived—has brought much happiness into a life that would otherwise have been a very dark one, and the

PREFACE

record may perhaps throw some light on fundamental spiritual and moral problems to which materialism and "modernist" Christianity obviously have no answer.

This volume covers my life up to the age of thirty, when the acceptance of *Wilding Graft* marked the first stage of my emergence and proved that my peculiar education was valid on modern intellectual and artistic levels. I have tried to give an honest account of the education itself rather than of its ultimate personal rewards.

I acknowledge my indebtedness to Mr. C. Day Lewis, at whose suggestion the work was seriously undertaken at the present juncture, and whose literary counsel has saved me from many pitfalls. My thanks are due also to Mr. Harold Raymond and his partners of Chatto and Windus for their generosity and sympathy with my peculiar problems; and to Mr. Raymond Savage, without whose efficient handling of former manuscripts I should have no story of literary emergence to record.

JACK CLEMO

Goonamarris,
St. Stephen's,
September 1948

NOTE TO THIRD EDITION

This book remains virtually as it was in its original form. The rugged honesty and occasional belligerence of the record are best left to make their full impact: any attempt to dilute facts or opinions would smudge the true picture of my youth. The first half of my life was a winter of adversity, and my faith had to grope and develop in a severe climate which was later totally changed. From middle-age onward, except for brief and superficial shadows, I lived in the summer sunshine of fulfilled hopes and answered prayers, amid the ripening comforts of marriage, friendship, church fellowship and prosperity. I almost ceased to recognize the suffering misfit whose story is told in these pages. But the seemingly harsh discipline of that early phase must have had some purpose, and this account of it may challenge and encourage others, even though mature experience led me to feel – and document in *The Marriage of a Rebel* – the refining influence of pleasant circumstances rather than painful ones.

Weymouth   Jack Clemo
March 1988

CHAPTER ONE

Family Background

THIS record of an unusual approach to love may start conveniently with a marriage that resulted from a more common approach—the marriage of my grandmother, Esther Trudgian. She was a cousin of the Cornish novelists, Joseph and Silas K. Hocking, who were born at St. Stephen's, a bare village about six miles north-west of St. Austell, and within a mile or so of my own birthplace. The family, in both its branches, was respectable but poor, the novelists' father, James Hocking, being a tin miner and most of the male Trudgians connected obscurely with the china clay works that were then becoming the chief industry of the district. But if anything of the Hockings' mental qualities passed to Esther it was smothered and obliterated by the coarseness of her early union with John Clemo, a drunken lout from the Mitchell area a few miles east of Newquay. He came apparently of a branch of a family well-known in Cornwall. The name Clemo, with its variants, Clemow, Clemmow, Clymo, is, I believe, rarely found outside the Duchy, though I am not curious enough about etymology to know anything of its derivations. I have never bothered to trace the family further back than my grandfather, and can therefore say nothing of my ancestry or of any social tone that may have dignified or disgraced the name in former ages. Divine predestination so skilfully challenged my natural fate that it would be a waste of time looking for atavistic tendencies that might have controlled that fate had they been given the chance.

In the early 'eighties John and Esther settled in a cottage near St. Stephen's, one of a small group wedged between Trethosa clay-dump and a railway siding overshadowed by a long grim line of drying-sheds. There they soon took on the tone of their surroundings, the choking coal-dust and clay-dust and the jangling of shunted trucks. Clemo being now a clay-labourer, they endured wretched poverty, and his persistent drunkenness and cruelty cut them off from the help of respectable neighbours. The quality of their life is probably reflected pretty well in the more brutal type of working-class novel; but as I had no first-hand knowledge of it—Clemo died four years before I was born—and few details were passed on to me, I do not propose to dwell upon the squalid picture. The atmosphere of the place, my father's revolt against it, the Divine use of the social menace bred there—these are the only factors I care to select and interpret. The shell of the house in which this raw tragedy was lived is now buried under Trethosa sand-dump, and the main pyramidal tip has covered the level bush-tufted ridge that once barred off the cottage from Goonvean clay-pit. During my childhood that ridge held a strange fascination for me as I sometimes crossed it on my way to school. I had heard a little of those nights when John Clemo, returning from St. Stephen's pub in drunken fury, would drive his wife and children outdoors and on to the sand-dump, where they often remained till morning, sleeping in the rude huts. Eight children grew up in this fashion; few of them turned out well. One of the daughters, Hetty, became a nymphomaniac in her teens and was removed to Bodmin Lunatic Asylum. Another drifted to London and had a son by a German lover: later her French husband walked out of the house one morning and never returned. These incidents are sufficient to suggest the background of my father's life.

Little could be expected of that life, as he seems never to have felt a spiritual tide destructively at work on the false foundations. At school he was remarkable for nothing but a propensity to lie on the floor and kick in fits of ungovernable temper. He appears to have had no literary aptitude that was thwarted by circumstances, no love of reading or any trace of that wistful respect for education that is sometimes found in manual labourers; he possessed no abilities of any sort beyond the average. Yet the seed of vivid individual power was there, the sheer violent brutality that was to vitalize and deepen the sensitive spiritual qualities I inherited from my mother's family. That dangerous primitive drive was the real keynote of his character, though, like others who lack the strength and assurance to stand alone, he tried to conceal it, when too old to kick on the schoolroom floor, by a stylish conventionality. He developed in his teen years a love of colour and flashiness which is alien both to my mother's personality and mine. He wore a ring and dressed as smartly as his means would permit, his slight, small-boned figure taking on an elegance that belied its true life, its background, its destiny. In the many studio portraits of himself which he gave my mother, his clothes are correct and fashionable, the shirt-cuffs, bow tie and hat being arranged with the meticulous care of a young dandy who wants to be admired and flattered. This trait of swagger was probably a reaction against the squalid slovenliness of his home, a cheap substitute for the religious faith that would have given him true balance, a sense of wholeness and dignity in himself. The craving for respectability even led him to attend the village chapel at Trethosa and become a member of the choir. He was a fine singer and gained the respect of the homely, warm-hearted Methodists of the chapel, then dominated by John Polmounter, who was to become his father-in-law. But in all these gestures he was trying to build up a façade of manhood that was not truly his; he was desperately seeking an escape, not so much from the spiritual contamination as from the social stigma of the cottage down by the railway siding. He brought all his resources to the effort of emancipating himself; but he was forced at length to realize that victory could not be won in Cornwall among the neighbours who, almost any night, could see his father staggering homeward, drunk, from St. Stephen's, or brawling outside the public house.

At the age of eighteen Reginald Clemo decided to make a fresh start. He went to America—and was there betrayed by the quality of his ideals, the lack of a spiritual core in his attempt at liberation. He suffered the vague, bitter disillusion of the untutored humanist whose beliefs fail him before they are recognized as beliefs. The *dénouement* had a grim irony. He had borne the strain of frustration and resisted it with a measure of success among his own people; the collapse came when he was friendless in a strange country—the country in which he had expected to find a complete freedom and fulfilment. His dream of achieving equality with the well-bred specimens of his class turned to a sick nightmare. Suddenly, inexplicably as it seemed to him, he was only the equal of his father, feeling the grime of the claywork stacks as he sat, bewildered and humiliated, in Butte City.

Such was the tragedy of my father's life—a common tragedy in every age and one which, in our day, has led to general cynicism regarding moral effort. It is the simple tragedy of having sensitiveness in the wrong place, in the shallows of personal vanity instead of in the deeps of the spirit. Reginald Clemo frittered away his energies in his battle for self-esteem, and had no power left to handle situations that could only be mastered through humility and faith. Yet he had put up a brave fight, and his defeat raises the old problems of the religious thinker. In his life the predestination of heredity and environment was unchallenged by that other Mood which has so often intervened to modify and make fruitful the natural destiny of my own career. The matter is an insoluble mystery, in his case as in thousands of others. Even had my life been free from bitter proofs of the Divine irony, the knowledge of my father's fate would have made untenable to me the cheap optimism of the popular creeds, the Oxford Group type of religion. Stern and ugly facts compelled me to go deep, so that from the outset my faith existed against a sombre intellectual background of agnosticism and bafflement regarding the general mood of Providence.

My father's early love-life was another facet of his struggle towards self-respect. Apart from that dominant motive it would be difficult to see why he was attracted to Eveline Polmounter, to whom he had plighted his troth before leaving England. She lived half-a-mile away on a farm that stood, an oasis of beauty and fertility, in the centre of Goonvean claywork. Like the Clemos' home it was hemmed in on one

4

hand by drying-sheds and a railway siding, but instead of the gloom of a sand-dump pressing in on the other side, there were the fields sloping away like the top of a cliff to the pit-edge, a small orchard close to the farmhouse and a wide view to the west, of the moors around Meledor and the fringe of Treviscoe village, all framed against the tiny white cones of clay-refuse on the horizon. The farm was gradually stripped of its buildings, including—though this was during my childhood—the farmstead itself, as the pit expanded. Only a barn and a cart-shed are standing today, and these are roped off within a dozen yards of the chasm. The fields and trees have disappeared, broken into the pit or supplanted by long concrete channels for the settling mica. Goonvean pit became merged with Trethosa as the strip of moorland that once divided them was worked away, and the huge crater is still spreading, eating into the scene of my parents' ill-fated romance. The view from the farmyard now is uniformly harsh: one feels stranded and menaced by the curving wall of white precipices stretching almost to the skyline. This joint clay-pit is one of the largest in England, nearly four hundred feet deep, and the richness of its yield dictated the inevitable policy of evicting families and blowing up houses that had nestled snugly for years in the folds of pasture and downland.

In those days nearly every claywork had its small farm adjoining, the horses and carts being indispensable before modern machinery was introduced for haulage between the various sections of the works. Life on the land in these circumstances was queerly different from the agricultural life of the open country. The carts rattling about under puffing stacks were filled as often with coal and clay as with farm produce, manure or fodder. Nature's role was reduced to a minor one, and her hold was precarious. All round the ripening crops of summer and the ploughed fields of the darker months, was a hostile world of grey beauty, majestic as the land in its contours and more profound in its significance to the sensitive mind. It was a landscape of purgation in which the soil was thrown into tanks and kilns, and it brought to the human spirit more

poignantly than anything in the peaceful countryside the sense
of insecurity, the sudden pounce of the destroyer. There were
no rhythms about it, no recurrences; only a pitiless finality
in every change. Buildings were frequently altered or removed,
familiar nooks and hollows overrun by the sprawling refuse;
paths that had been used for years by lovers as well as workmen
were obliterated by dynamite in a moment. Nature might
promise further instalments of the glory of Spring, but the
clayworks told a different tale that was truer to human life.

There seemed to be something symbolic in this dual stress
of Nature and purgation on Eveline Polmounter's childhood;
a symbolism, too, in the presence of that rocky gulf between
the Clemos' home and hers. She must have looked out often
in her early years across those ribbed and blasted hollows to
the clay-dump that hid the cottage in which Reginald was
growing up. And after she had visited the house and come back
repelled and disgusted, she still looked, fascinated and
wondering. It was strange that she, the daughter of a Methodist
local preacher, reared amid the narrow and satisfying beauties
of Puritanism, should feel an overwhelming urge to bridge the
gulf and unite herself with a family untouched by such influences.

Her inheritance had fitted her for higher contacts. She had
been a dreamy, sensitive child, superior in character and taste
to her three sisters. She was much given to lonely brooding,
chiefly on religious questions, and was not without talent, for
she sometimes accompanied her father on preaching excursions
and recited pathetic ballads and doggerel verses against
intemperance to congregations that thought they were being
given a rendering of great poetry. She thought so, too, and
when, nearly twenty years later, she found that I had literary
leanings, she fetched from a trunk those old musty volumes of
The Prize Reciter in the serious belief that they contained real
literature that would develop my intellectual taste. This,
however, reflected no lack of perception; it simply proved
that her mind had been nurtured only by the books that could
be enjoyed in a Victorian working-class home.

Behind my mother's existence, no less than Reginald Clemo's, was the tale of a peculiar marriage. Jane Bullen, her mother, came of a family that had won some local distinction for its undoubted intellectual gifts. In Jane's brother George these gifts had been allied with a will that pitted itself against considerable odds. It is needless to say that all these families were poor in a sense that is practically unknown among rural dwellers today. Women as well as men were employed on the clayworks, the women earning as little as 5s. a week for carrying and scraping clay in the drying-sheds, while men's wages varied according to the nature of their work from 10s. to £1 a week. The Bullens were a tin-mining family, but conditions in that industry were scarcely better. George's hardships were exceptionally severe. His father was killed at Dowgas mine when George was seven, and shortly afterwards George started working there himself to help support his widowed mother. He received no formal education during childhood, but studied ardently in his spare time after taking some elementary lessons at the home of a local worthy. In his early teens he set himself with a fiery enthusiasm to fulfil his destiny in spite of all handicaps. Feeling himself called to the Methodist ministry he almost starved himself to procure the necessary training. An unknown, obscure labourer, he found ranged against him the forces of prejudice and snobbery. His humiliating struggle recalls that of Hardy's Jude. But Jude failed because he lost his faith— a calamity that often befalls Christians in pagan novels, but seldom in real life. George Bullen kept his faith and won through. Before he was twenty he became a student at Keswick College and could often be found in his bedroom at four a.m. studying Greek. He passed into the ministry and volunteered for missionary work in Newfoundland, going later to Michigan, where he died in 1917, a supernumerary of the Methodist Episcopal Church.

There is a symbolic hint of the shaping of my inheritance in the fact that while my father crossed the Atlantic to entangle himself in the grosser roots of materialism, George Bullen crossed it as a messenger of Christ; that while, in America, the Clemo strain was expressing itself much as it had done in the Trethosa cottage, the more sensitive traits on the maternal side were burning through George Bullen in passionate evangelism. An obituary notice of him in the annual Conference report of his Michigan church stated: "That Celtic temperament of his with its theological bent as to its mind, its exquisite sensitiveness, its unconquerable shyness, and its strong and subtle intellect, was both his crown and his cross." Some of these qualities I inherited, with a similar endowment from the Hocking family, and had not the Clemos been such a rough lot I should probably have become a clever man of the conventional sort, perhaps a writer of genial stories like the Hockings'; I might even have entered the ministry. But the stormy darkness and blinding undercurrents of vision are, I think, preferable to such a placid and useful career; anyway, I have had to put up with them.

Jane Bullen shared her brother's refinement of taste—she was a gentle and rather morbid woman with the shy reserved nature of the introvert, shunning all social contacts; yet, oddly enough, she married John Polmounter. John was illiterate; he could not write and signed the marriage register with a cross. Like his namesake of the Clemo family he had been a drunkard in his youth, but he had none of Clemo's sullen brutality. He was always jolly even when he was drunk. and carried his jollity into his religion when God led him that way. Even late in life when passing sometimes through the squalid "Raw" of Treviscoe, on the northern side of Goonvean clay-pit, he would reel and stagger about the road, throwing out his arms, pretending to be drunk, to amuse the children. Jane's standards were somewhat more dignified, and my mother has told me that when John came in "laughing like a pisky" to relate these antics, Jane would reprove him, though with the mildness of one who had abandoned all hope of curbing his exuberance. "For shame, father!" she would say. "People must think you'm a proper chiel." And at heart he was, knowing that in such childlike simplicity of heart was the kingdom that would outlive the shams and subtleties of the adult, self-conscious mind.

8

John had been something of a wrestler, too, in his early years, and never outgrew the physical gusto, the love of a romp. Whenever the occasion offered itself he would "wrastle the boys," and was seriously perturbed in his old age when one of these boys began to wrestle at local tournaments. John feared that his playful tacklings had encouraged the boy in this course—a thing he would not have done for the world. Like many of his sane and sensible generation, he regarded organized sport as sinful. What he and other robust-minded Puritans opposed was not the pleasure of any human activity, but the cankers which attacked that pleasure and drained it of vitality under the pretext of giving it a set of rules that enabled it to be exploited by baser instincts—greed, vanity and worldly ambition. These clear-sighted Christians hated commercialized games precisely because they loved fun and knew that nothing is more destructive of fun than the entirely solemn and technical routine of winning prizes and signing contracts. To call them killjoys is as silly as to call children killjoys because they prefer a spontaneous frolic to a strictly-regulated game.

In marrying John while he was still an unbeliever, Jane was no doubt guilty of a minor offence against religion, and by concentrating her feelings into prayer for his salvation she was violating the usual technique of sex. But Jane may be presumed to have known her man—John was a tender-hearted fellow; and she also knew God in a way that has unhappily gone out of fashion. She really believed in prayer as a force that brought results; and it is a mere matter of fact that within a few months of her marriage John was kneeling beside her, experiencing conversion. He had been broken down by the sight of Jane kneeling twice a day at his bedside, calling on God to have mercy on him. From the time that mercy arrived John became a teetotaller and non-smoker; very soon afterwards an evangelist and a father—fully the husband of her dreams. Whether such results would follow similar action today is perhaps doubtful, unless both parties were predestined Calvinists. A modern husband whose wife kept crying to Heaven for his salvation would probably seek a divorce on the ground of mental cruelty—an interesting comment on the progress of ideas, and possibly it throws some light on the problem of why so few modern marriages get anywhere near the Christian norm of happiness.

The Polmounters' marriage remained close to that norm for forty-five years—every one of them lived under economic conditions which, by every rule of eugenics, should have produced abject misery, physical and moral degradation. The harmony was never disturbed because it never depended on circumstances. While Hardy in his novels was blaming a pitiless First Cause for the squalor of the poor, indulging in bitter gibes about "Nature's holy plan," families less prosperous than the Durbeyfields were proving that there was a Plan beyond Nature's into which human love could fit and become holy. The Polmounters were one such group.

Twelve children came. Six of them died in childhood; some of the others had serious illnesses and got suddenly well after John had spent hours in prayer for their recovery. Always there was poverty, and with it the reckless generosity of those who gamble on God. Sometimes John gave away his last sixpence to relieve a neighbour's distress, and at one or two critical periods he did not know where the next meal was coming from. But prayer always brought the answer: whether he needed food or clothes or money, he had only to pray for the supply and it came. People who knew nothing of his need would arrive with help at the crucial hour. There on that claywork farm a humble Christian family were living the life of faith—a life so different from the Clemos' in quality that it was hard to realize that both were lived on the same economic level. The complete contrast between these two homes is a sufficient reply to the Communist gibe about the effect of Christianity on the working class. John Polmounter had pie at Goonvean farm as well as in the sky. It is doubtful whether John Clemo had pie in either world, but it was not the capitalist system that prevented him from getting it; it was his own pagan obstinacy, his refusal to submit to the discipline of faith.

The Christian life of faith is the only form of "primitive

revolt" that can be practised by law-abiding citizens. Its secret discipline at every material level preserves the balance of society. Those who choose this life—or are forced into it, as I was—are spared the weary and sterile investigation of Christianity as a philosophy, an ethical code, or a handy synthesis of ideals common to all good men. The idea of the "good life" had never occurred to the Polmounters to muddle them with a self-conscious regard for conduct; nor were they much concerned about "religion." The fact of Christ's deity, implying His control of the affairs of Goonvean farm, was accepted by them as a commonplace, non-ecclesiastical truth. Nothing could be further from vague sentimental piety. John and his wife wrestled their way through successive crises that would have swamped any faith that was not realistic and embittered any realism but that of the heart.

There was at Goonvean farm through all these years a source of trial that had no connection with family affairs. This was nothing less than the presence of a semi-lunatic, one Richard Best, commonly called "Maaster"—a title that expressed the odd respect due to a very singular character. During my childhood I heard many queer stories of this man. He had been born and reared on the farm, and when it passed into the Polmounters' hands he obstinately refused to leave. He was then middle-aged, unmarried, and with no taste for women. John agreed to his remaining there: indeed, there was no alternative but the Lunatic Asylum at Bodmin. Best's family would not be bothered further with his eccentricities, though their callous treatment had aggravated what was at first a harmless mental deficiency. They always excluded him from the house when entertaining their friends, and on one occasion, finding himself shut out in the farmyard while a party was being held, Richard seized a pick and hurled it through the window into the room where the company was gathered. Fortunately no one was hit, but it is rather surprising that he was still allowed to stay on the farm.

The Polmounters dealt with him more kindly, and he showed them a side of his nature that did something to justify the exalted idea he held of his importance. He spent much of his time in reading, and when educated persons visited the farm he would engage them in conversation, showing a lively vein of humour and a diversity of knowledge that astonished all who judged him by his appearance. This was indeed grotesque. He always went about in an old coat thrown over his shoulders; nothing could induce him to put his arms through the sleeves. He seldom washed, and usually, even at meal times, his hands were smeared with cow-dung from the stables. He helped with the farm work when it suited him, but sometimes in malicious moods he would damage the crops and impede the smooth working of the farm in any way he could think of. At such times John acted with firmness: Richard knew who was boss and soon became docile. He never got on well with my father, and there was considerable friction between the two after my mother married and Reginald settled at Goonvean. When John was ill my father would get up early and feed the livestock before going to work—a task that had always been "Maaster's"; so Best would creep out after him and snatch the bowl of grain from his hands, declaring shrilly that no son-in-law of Polmounter's was going to take *his* job. At first Reginald let him have his way, but John told him he "mus'n give in to Maaster—only 'is little crotchet." Thereafter Reginald stood firm; and the picture of those two—the old, half-crazed man and the young dare-devil—bickering childishly over the sacks of grain amid the morning shadows of Goonvean barn, has a touch of fantastic comedy about it. But the result might have been far from comic. On at least one occasion Best attacked my father with a shovel. There was a streak of violence in the man, flaring dangerously when he was opposed—except by John, whom he always obeyed meekly and with doglike devotion.

The central passion of John's life remained strangely steady amid all vicissitudes. Whatever the trouble at home, John went forth nearly every Sunday to some village Bethel, respectably dressed in a black suit, a venerable figure in later years with his long white hair and beard. His simple human fervour produced results and brought many new converts into membership of the local chapels. He knew no more of theological subtleties than he did of the scientific movements of his age that were gravely accumulating evidence to prove that a life such as his was rationally untenable. He lived that life with a gusto which infected his congregations as it infected and irradiated his family at home. My mother always spoke of her childhood as supremely happy.

It was fortunate that she was bred in the Nonconformist tradition. Had John Polmounter been an Anglican, passing on to me through my mother a formal Christianity, ornate, æsthetic, in its ritual appeal, my inevitable revolt against it might have led where such revolt has led many sceptics and immoralists of the past fifty years. The rough tang of spontaneity in John Polmounter's influence convinced me that what I wanted was not far from the Nonconformist springs, even though as I grew older Wesley's contribution became unpalatable to me.

I am glad, therefore, of the chance to place beside the well-known caricatures this brief sketch of a Methodist home during the period when Methodism was practically the only force that gave dignity and invigoration of soul to the Cornish working class. The Victorian Methodist one meets in fiction, the gloomy neurotic tortured between visions of hell-fire and half-smothered sexual lust, is very much a novelist's creation. with little truth in it. No doubt there were individual Methodists who had no sense of humour and were to that extent morbid, but they were probably less numerous than the modern thinkers who have no sense of humour and are therefore wholly morbid. Where there is faith, morbidity can never be complete, while for sceptics only a sense of humour can relieve the absolute drench of morbidity that is cynicism.

John Polmounter's faith, and his humour too, were sorely tested when he learnt that his youngest daughter had set her heart on one of the Clemos. He and Jane had desired and expected a very different fate for the girl. But they did not interfere: Eveline was then a mere child of fifteen, and it seemed likely that the attachment was an immature fancy that would soon pass. Their hope of this must have strengthened when home conditions became intolerable to Reginald and in a reckless mood he bolted to America. But love is apt to be perverse when it is fulfilling a destiny. The separation, so far from weakening Eveline's love, deepened it to a tragic hunger. She went into domestic service in the neighbouring village of Foxhole, but spent none of her leisure hours in the villages where other young men might try to capture her. She was happiest when at home, strolling about the broad fields bordering the clay-pit, sitting in the orchard, or indoors browsing among her father's stock of books, nearly a hundred volumes that he had somehow managed to accumulate—all religious works which gave her love a less sentimental background than Victorian novels would have done. She brooded much in solitude, casting her thoughts out to the far West, to Montana, where Reginald was feverishly seeking the means to return and marry her, working now on a ranch, now in the copper mines, of Anaconda. He sent the engagement ring across the Atlantic when she was sixteen, and knowing nothing of the world she was serenely confident that he was keeping the promises he had made her, that the shackles of his old home were now a dim memory that could never again threaten them.

Thus, cheating probability at every turn, life worked towards the bitter fulfilment. In 1912, being then twenty-two years of age, Reginald Clemo arrived back in Cornwall. The Polmounters remained passive; they saw that the thing they dreaded was inevitable. Eveline herself must have seen that Reginald had failed to realize the hopes and ambitions that had led him to emigrate, and that his swagger had lost something of its old innocence. But she seemed hypnotized for the next few months, until her awakening and revolt were powerless to thwart the Intention.

On July 5th, 1913, the pair were married at St. Austell. Within a year their first child was born, a girl, but it only lived a few weeks. In 1915, at the age of seventy, John Polmounter

died, feeling towards the end a grave concern for his daughter's
future, but spared the sight of domestic tragedy in full flood.
The old farm passed into other hands—Richard Best remaining
there under the new management, though he was disconsolate
at the change and died within a year or two. My parents, with
Jane and her unmarried daughter, Bertha, came to live in a
four-roomed granite cottage on Goonamarris Slip, a few
hundred yards east of Goonvean. It was a fitting birthplace for
me, being dwarfed under Bloomdale clay-dump, solitary,
grim-looking, with no drainage, no water or electricity supply,
and no back door; and there, on the 11th March, 1916, I was
born.

CHAPTER TWO

Foundations

HAVING fulfilled some obscure purpose and brought another misfit into existence, fate seemed to have no further use for my parents' marriage. I know very few details concerning the four years it endured, and even had my mother told me the whole story I should not pass it on to the public. I detest the exhibitionism that drags out and parades with morbid relish every squalid ghost of family and personal history. Had it been possible to give significance to this autobiography without reference to my father's tragic life, I would have done so. As it was not, I have said what must be said and no more. The evidence I have cited to show that the Clemos were something of a "problem" family will help to explain the qualities that make my personality, and my writings, individual and distinct. My foundations were roughly similar to D. H. Lawrence's, brutality and refinement warring in me through the conflicting natures of my parents, sharpened towards primitivism by the working-class, Nonconformist background. It was inevitable that the fundamental urge of my life, the central theme of my novels and poems, should be akin to his—the seeking of a balance between the sensual and the spiritual. That I found a solution where Lawrence denied that it exists—in orthodox Christianity—is the mystery I shall try to make intelligible in these pages.

Inherited experience is no doubt a part of my literary equipment, and as my life has flowered into something quite opposite to this inheritance, I have no need to fear, as idealists often do, that the Divine order is disturbed or disgraced by ignoble associations in the fashioning of a Christian life. The attitude which really disgraces God is that which minimizes the evil He has to subdue in His dealings with human personality. It is no credit to God that He succeeds with promising material;

human organizations can do that well enough. His power is most apparent when, as in my case, He succeeds with material so biassed and toned by Nature that educationists, even under the most enlightened and comprehensive social scheme, can do nothing with it.

There seemed no reason to expect anything extraordinary of the boy who appeared—so I am told—at two o'clock on that Saturday morning of 1916. The circumstances were normal, and I looked a healthy, full-sized child. My father is said to have been satisfied with me—sure proof that there were no abnormalities to suggest the presence of gifts that might take me beyond his own intellectual level. No doubt he believed that I would grow up to be a clay-worker like himself.

He had returned to this industry on settling again in Cornwall and was employed as a "dry"-man at Trethosa, engaged in heavy and oppressive work on the hot, steaming kilns. He took part in the clayworkers' strike of 1913, though he seems to have had little individual sense of social injustice. He was a good workman, content with the simple domestic comforts he had begun to enjoy. But gradually, after 1914, the war threat encroached upon the security of an occupation that was not essential to the killing of Germans, and within a few months of my birth he was conscripted. He had not volunteered—patriotism is a meaningless term to men of his type—and there was in his nature a curious undercurrent of sensitiveness, of recoil from the crude drama of bloodshed. The trait is, perhaps, best illustrated in a trifling incident of which my mother often spoke, as if she had seen in it the hint of a tenderness thwarted by grosser elements.

On one occasion he had agreed to shoot a dog on Goonvean farm, a sheepdog that had become old and diseased; but when he took the creature out into the field and levelled the gun at it, the puzzled, trustful look in its eyes had drained the resolution out of him. He returned to the house, looking shame-faced, the dog trotting at his heels. It was later shot by my uncle.

This may be another sign of a weak, vacillating character, but it indicates that the combination of brutality and sentimental moodiness is not exclusively a German attribute. It was strongly marked in my father, and I fear it is even more strongly marked in his son, though disciplined by Christianity. As he could not even kill a dog in cold blood it is easy to understand that he could not kill Germans in cold blood, though he could have killed his best friend in hot blood. I possess a photograph of him taken on a Montana ranch in which he is wearing cowboy garb and holding a revolver. The latent violence of character is unmistakable in the uneasy smile, the sleepy, enigmatic eyes. The gusts of cerebral sadism that were among my inherited morbidities can be traced to no other source than my father's divergence—slight but obvious enough—from normal feeling. At no period of his life does he seem to have been normally affectionate. He could be callous and cruel; he could wallow in sentiment; but of the ordinary tendernesses of simple innocent love he knew nothing. My mother's courtship had brought her more heartache than joy because of her bewilderment, the inability to understand his habitual repulse of any open demonstration of their attachment. He never liked her to put her arm round him or even to hold his arm; such touches appeared to rouse a deep-lying malice and antagonism in him. A full probing of his sexual disharmony would reveal the origin of certain traits in my own attitude to love which, but for the transformation of religious faith, would be monstrous.

Reginald had no conscientious objection to war as such; in his violent moments he had no conscientious objection to murder. It was the lack of a personal hatred for the enemy that kept him out of the conflict until he was forced into it, and that made him then try to escape combatant service. He spent a year at Woolwich Arsenal, and was later transferred to Devonport Dockyard. During this period he led an exemplary moral life, and while at Devonport his old daredevil spirit broke out in an audacious attempt to hoodwink the naval authorities in the interests of domestic virtue. At week-ends the dockyard workers were allowed to visit friends and relatives who lived within ten miles of the port; longer journeys were strictly forbidden. The ten-mile limit enabled my father to cross the Tamar and proceed as far as St. Germans, where it was supposed he stayed. But, unknown to the dockyard officials, he always borrowed a bicycle there and rode thirty miles westwards through Cornwall to Goonamarris. He would arrive home on the Saturday night and return the next day to report, quite truly, that he had been to St. Germans! My mother must have been troubled in conscience about this flagrant breach of the law, though it was some comfort to her that he attended morning service at Trethosa chapel during these stolen week-ends, carrying me thither in his arms. The practice continued regularly for months. He was never found out.

This is one of the few incidents in my father's life that make me feel proud of him. It exhibits the sort of daredevilry I have always liked myself, and without this reckless spirit which I derived from him God would never have challenged my faith with the border-line experiences that made me a Calvinist.

Reginald's period of war-work closed early in 1917. He was compelled to join the fighting forces, and entered the Navy as a stoker. In the summer of that year he left port on active service aboard H.M.S. *Tornado*.

I do not know how often he came home on leave thereafter; only that, three weeks before Christmas, he returned to sea after his last visit to Goonamarris, and that on Christmas Day a telegram from the Admiralty informed my mother that H.M.S *Tornado* had been torpedoed off the Dutch coast and Reginald Clemo was not among the survivors.

Some years later a brother of his, a spiritualist, attended a séance in America at which, he declared, my father's spirit materialized and not only sang with him some of their old rowdy songs, but also gave him particulars of the *Tornado* disaster. According to this spiritualist account Reginald was not drowned but had his limbs blown off by the explosion and died instantly. I do not give much credence to the statement, because my uncle was not the kind of man to whom spirits are likely to tell the truth. It is odd that so many spiritualists, from the time of "Sludge" onward, have held in contempt the very qualities that make it worth while to be a spirit.

My father probably died without having the least idea of the kind of son he had left behind him at Goonamarris. He would have been bewildered—and perhaps a trifle exasperated—had he guessed my future; yet I think he would have approved of my uncompromising stand against the idealism he had found so inadequate. He seems, indeed, to have come deeply under John Polmounter's influence during the four years of his married life; he had begun to learn humility and loyalty in the Christian atmosphere of Goonvean farm. The old days of illusion, of the pathetic confidence in himself that had betrayed him in America, were past. He was seeking a basis for faith elsewhere than in himself.

It was in a spirit that foreshadowed my own discovery of such foundations that my mother turned away from the popular mood of remembrance. She paid no heed whatever to Armistice Day celebrations; parades and flag-wavings were alien to her temperament and even more anti-pathetic to mine. We never voluntarily observed the two minutes' silence. It seemed incongruous to associate the lonely pain, the massive dignity of our loss with the pageantry of a war in which Reginald had not wished to participate.

When the first shock and prostration had passed, my mother groped her way back to the security she had left, the source of strength and guidance that had never failed in the old home. While many women of her generation yielded their senses to the usage of disillusion and revolt, she turned aside—as I was to turn aside from my generation in the nineteen-thirties—to discover in a full surrender to Christ what His purpose might be, and to shrink from no sacrifice in co-operating with that purpose. My mother yielded everything—her hope of re-marriage, with all the pleasures and social contacts that make life bearable to the average woman. She renounced every human narcotic, choosing to suffer an unmitigated spiritual stress so that its creative power might have free access to my personality.

Psychologists may explain the matter in their own interesting fashion. They may state that my mother had been frustrated in her experience of marriage, and that when that marriage collapsed she sublimated her emotions and "escaped" into the sicklier kind of piety. But when I consider the practical results of her renunciation I can only rejoice at the way they prove the fallibility of human theories—especially Freudian ones.

This venture of faith was a gradual product, yet it was rooted from the outset in the revelation of those hours when my mother turned to the Bible, receiving its promises as literal statements of the Divine Will concerning us. She has often spoken of her discovery of these promises as the turning-point of her life. Her consciousness of the personal presence of God was very real: the veil that had thickened upon her spirit during her marriage was rent, and she saw for the first time clearly that behind the blindness of her choice there had been a predestination. Her choice had given my life a background of Nature and society at their worst: there was the glum squalor of the Clemos' cottage, the tawdry degradation of Butte saloons, the ward in Bodmin asylum where Hetty was tormented by the raving obscenity of nymphomania. And above all this, challenging it, was the Word of unconquered Purity with its promise to my mother: "Thou shalt forget the shame...thy children shall be taught of the Lord, and great shall be the peace of thy children..."*

My mother naturally supposed that this Divine teaching would be of the conventional type, coming to me through conventional channels. She had no knowledge of any revelation of God outside the narrow bounds of Methodism. She had seen on Goonvean farm the sufficiency of that revelation; all that was sweet in her life had grown spontaneously from it, and her religious faith, from childhood, had been defined only in its terms. She could think of no other soil fit to nurture the seed of vivid Christian perception in me. She had never heard of isolated mystics outside the organized churches, and would not have admitted the validity of their claims. "These be they who separate themselves, sensual, having not the Spirit."† This

* Isaiah liv, 4, 13.
† Jude, 19.

scriptural warning would have sufficed for her judgment, and she would have been staggered had she known then that the decisive phase of my spiritual emergence was to have all the outward appearances of such a bastard growth.

I had already been christened at Trethosa chapel, being given the names of Reginald John, names so dull that they required some rearrangement when I came to sign my literary work; and from early infancy I was taken there every Sunday, sometimes twice, though the gaunt building standing amid the fields above Trethosa village was more than a mile from our home. I have, of course, no recollection of this period, but I can guess with what fervent prayer my mother did her part in moulding my destiny by thus making the atmosphere of worship a part of the rhythm which my dawning consciousness had to accept as inevitable.

My mother was not kept long in suspense before realizing that it was scarcely an average child on whom she had set her hopes. Like many other writers, I was distressingly precocious. Before my father's death, when I was only eighteen months old, I could recite not only all the usual nursery rhymes but the Lord's Prayer, from beginning to end, without a mistake. Neighbours were astonished, and mother, naturally proud of these achievements, let me display my talent perhaps more often than was good for me. It was no uncommon thing, whether at home or in friends' or relatives' houses, for me to be held aloft in mother's arms or set on a chair, while an open-mouthed group listened to my fluent declamations. Some of the villagers, however, shook their heads in grave concern. "'E'll suffer for it, Mrs. Clema," they declared, eyeing me askance with pity for a creature so obviously fore-doomed. "'E's too forward 'e is—no 'ealthy sign, Mrs. Clema." (With the Cornish habit of turning terminal "o"'s' into "a's" our name was always pronounced Clema locally, and still is).

Another characteristic, showing the extraordinary zeal of my pursuit of knowledge, came somewhat later. When I was out for a walk and saw a scrap of newspaper lying in the ditch, I would break from mother's grasp, pick it up and read whatever might be visible through the dust that lay on it. There was usually a lot of paper lying about on the roads that branched off from our home, all claywork routes over which the horse-drawn waggons passed almost daily. The paper had wrapped the drivers' pasties, etc., and was often greasy. If a strong wind was blowing I would run after the scraps that might be whirling about, and I daresay I caused much amusement— an infant of four or so chasing torn newspapers and gravely reading them when caught, standing sometimes in the middle of the road, oblivious of danger from passing traffic. What sense I ever made of the items I perused I cannot imagine. No picture or headline stamped itself upon my memory. Nothing sufficiently dramatic was happening at that time—1920 or thereabouts.

But drama was stalking down upon that tiny cottage, my home: the orderly development of my mind was soon to be interrupted, shattered, my talent thrust into painful bypaths where it could unfold with scarcely a prompting touch from the hand of formal education.

Having granted mother these glimpses of promise, quickening her faith for my future (her main thought during those days was that I might become an evangelist—novelists she had never heard of except for some horrified whispers about the Hockings). Fate slipped down the curtain and life resumed its old filching processes. Jane became bedridden and gave much trouble, suffering from complete loss of memory: she was often calling downstairs for things she had just received. My mother became exhausted in nursing her and bearing with the strange moods that preceded her death in October, 1919. Oddly enough, I have no personal recollections of Jane, though I am told she was very fond of me.

Being now left without parents or husband, with very few friends—mainly class-mates at Trethosa chapel, where she attended the prayer and testimony meeting every Tuesday: these meetings were her chief support in the darkest days—my mother felt the strain becoming too great, threatening her with a nervous breakdown. She was ordered to Newquay to recuperate, and in March, 1920, we took lodgings in the town.

But there we ran into one of those ironies of Providence that are so useful in ridding the world of superficial faith. The immediate cause of mother's breakdown was the loss of Jane, but it was the undercurrent of horror at the fashion of Reginald's death that had broken through the fresh breach, mauling her defences. And within a month of our coming to Newquay there was a shipwreck in sight of the town, the rocket booming out one morning, the streets filled with grim-faced people, the lifeboat battling out through wild seas. My mother saw it all—with what thoughts it is easy to imagine. The result of this distressing occurrence was that she had to return immediately to Goonamarris, in a worse state than she had left it, driven more than ever to find consolation and healing in her hope that somehow through me the tragic tide might be turned back.

But that hope too was soon blighted. She had braced herself to bear the lonely days that must come when I started to attend school, but that was a trifling shadow compared with the crisis that developed shortly after our return from Newquay.

Just before I was five years old I began to complain about my eyes, that strong sunlight, even lamplight if I directly faced it, gave me such pain that I had to squeeze the lids shut. Inflammation set in and grew worse, so that I could not look at books and was compelled to sit in the darkest corners of the room, very still and unlike myself, wondering what had happened. Mother took me to the local doctor, Manson of St. Dennis—a huge, genial Scotsman, probably the best-loved of mid-Cornwall's physicians—who found the case urgent and sent me to the Royal Cornwall Infirmary at Truro.

I remember dimly that first visit: the twelve miles' bus ride from St. Stephen's, the wooded slopes towering up beside the road below Ladock, heavy and terrifying to my distorted vision; the frightened feeling I had when we passed through the hospital entrance at Truro and under the high forbidding walls, the strange sounds and smells communicating to me the morbid atmosphere of the place; the long ordeal of suspense in the waiting-room with other children, some blindfolded, some wearing dark glasses, others celluloid shades: all tense and unnatural. When my turn came I received an X-ray examination, and the specialist declared that I must spend the next few weeks in darkness, having drops put into my eyes every night by the local doctor. Only this drastic treatment could save me from permanent blindness.

I remember that after we left the hospital my mother took me to the Waterfall Gardens on the northern outskirts of the city, and we sat upon a bench on the lower lawn—I staring at the arches of the viaduct with my left eye, the right being covered by a shade. I could not clearly see them, and they loomed threatening and fantastic among the trees. Neither mother nor I could have believed then that the next time I entered those Gardens it would be as a young man of twenty-six, healthy but moodily isolated, taking notes for the Truro scenes of *Wilding Graft*.

My subsequent visits to Truro hospital during that first attack of blindness are as a hazy nightmare in the remote depths of my mind. I could see nothing until I entered the doctor's consulting-room where the bandages were taken off and I discerned vague shapes of furniture, a stabbing blur of light, two indistinct figures, the specialist and my mother, talking about me. The doctor would pull my eyes wide open with his thumb and finger, rapping out a continuous "Look at me! Look at me!" while I struggled to face the light and stare into the strange flickering countenance, my mind blank and rigid between panic and stupor. Then the cloths were tied round my head again and in renewed darkness I would be led out and down into the city, to the bus, holding mother's hand desperately, knowing nothing of what she suffered. I would sit beside her on the homeward journey, tired and fretful, hearing the purring of the engines, the crisp chatter of voices outside the black wall that surrounded me. At home the days dragged so cloudily that I can recall no detail of my behaviour, nothing of the difficulty I must have had with meals, etc. The only thing I remember is the daily visit to St. Dennis, two miles north of our home, on the other side of Rostowrack Downs.

It became a familiar and pathetic sight to the people of St. Dennis, the solitary widow, dark, tight-lipped, with her sad, probing black eyes, wheeling down the hill from Rostowrack the sickly boy whose face was swathed in bandages: my mother and myself coming to the doctor's surgery for the prescribed treatment. It was part of the evening drama in a literal sense to those spectators and in a symbolic sense to us, and there can be little doubt that my mother feared the evening would deepen into midnight. Sometimes during those walks she wept silently to herself as she crossed the bleak tableland under the clay-dumps, the push-chair bumping along the rough tracks around the unfenced pits. She seldom spoke to me, who often whimpered on the homeward journey because the drops were making my eyes smart and the long weeks of darkness without a glimpse of a known face or of the earth and the friendly, open sunshine had become an incubus, fretting my nerves terribly.

My mother's life during her teens and early twenties had been scarcely less tragic than a Hardy novel. The blows had fallen upon her at intervals of two years, like the regular strokes of a hammer wielded by the grisly immortal President. In 1913 she had made her disastrous marriage and seen the death of her first child, in 1915 she had lost her father, in 1917 her husband, in 1919 her mother, and now, in 1921, another calamity had come, dashing her hope that I might grow up as healthy as I had seemed during infancy. As she looked forward to the years of my adolescence she must have seen them as Tess Durbeyfield saw her tomorrows, "very fierce and cruel, and as if they would say, "I'm coming. Beware of me! Beware of me!" Against these fears and probabilities she could set nothing but a few words in the Bible, a Divine promise—as she believed—that a special teaching and an ultimate peace should be the inheritance of the blind, tortured infant lying inert in the push-chair. The tension and irony of these evening walks were bitter things, and St. Dennis lay sprawled in sombre brooding indifference under Carne Hill as mother and child passed to and from it, like ghosts inhumanly detached from the normal pulse and texture of the village.

CHAPTER THREE

Early Schooling

Tʜɪꜱ story of my development is essentially, at levels which many people never look at, a love story. All other interests are either the background of that vision or the product of it ; and education in the formal sense does not fill much space even in the background. Had my talents been fashioned and empowered by the schools I could hardly have thought the experience worth recording. There is nothing very remarkable in a proletarian struggling free of his environment if his abilities are nurtured by conventional methods. If he is supported and trained from adolescence by the routine of secondary school, college and university, his achievement is different in kind from any that I have known. I do not say it is less real; and certainly I have never encountered any snobbery from those who have taken the academic way to emancipation. The most distinguished Cornishman of this type, A. L. Rowse, confessed to me on the publication of *Wilding Graft* that he was "astonished and fascinated" by the paradox of my position: that I had "emerged" intellectually while remaining physically, and to some extent spiritually, *inside* the world of working-class illiterates. The whole battle for independence and individuality was fought almost literally within the four walls of the cottage in which I was born and in which, throughout my later teens and twenties, I lived practically the life of a hermit, cut off from all social contacts and turning out my novels and poems by instinct, with the barest minimum of materials and with no encouragement except what I received from a few books, from my mother, and from those "subtle sanctities"—as Francis Thompson called them, referring to a child's caresses—

27

CONFESSION OF A REBEL

'wherein I viewed secure
The mirrored woman's fateful-fair allure,
The baréd limbs of the rebukeless mind."*

It was from such experiences that my highest education was derived.

I had almost completed my sixth year before that first attack of blindness passed off, and the child who survived it was scarcely recognizable to those who had known me in earlier years. Before the blindness came I was a plump, jolly, pink-faced little fellow, very lively, chattering and laughing all day long. Those few months of isolation, with the mental nightmare of inarticulate terrors and panics, a reality to which the fears of normal children are mere shadows, had changed me into a thin, pasty-faced brat, dull-eyed, silent and morbid. I shrank from beginning my attendance at school, although a year earlier I had anticipated it with the keenest excitement. I seemed to have lost all interest in life, all inquisitiveness, all desire to know anything or to be anything childlike or human. I groped towards a protective unconsciousness, a darkness of sleep. But as the doctor said that my sight would now bear such strain as would be put upon it in the infants' class, I was forced willy-nilly to submit myself to a system that could not possibly benefit a nature so warped and clouded as mine had become.

I made my first attendance in April, 1922, at Foxhole Council School, to which other Goonamarris children went. But as our home was not in the hamlet itself but on the Slip, a wild strip of downland on the ridge above, I was allowed to attend at Foxhole for only one day. The headmaster refused to put my name on the register—probably he thought I looked a dunce who would disgrace the school—and declared that Trethosa was the correct school for me. To this I was transferred—a rather stupid decision, as Foxhole was much nearer and the road thither sheltered under the Beacon, while to reach Trethosa I had to follow an exposed track through Goonvean claywork and the marshland beyond it, a journey of over a mile, and only the last few hundred yards of it was along a hedged road.

* *The Child-Woman.*

But I have realized since how fortunate was that seeming blunder. It ensured that, from the beginning, my attendance at school should be irregular, spasmodic, so that I never really came under its grip at all. During the winters of those early years I hardly ever put in a full week's attendance. The slightest exposure to rain or cold brought on a chill ; sometimes for weeks on end I was at home with illness. When passing through Goonvean claywork on winter mornings, my white pinched face muffled in scarves, my thin legs tottering under the gusts of wind blowing across the pit, I would notice the workmen shaking their heads and whispering together. Some of them told my mother in later years what they had usually said: "She'll never rear that boy." Such a view was generally held in the district: that I have become a novelist and poet is no greater miracle than the fact that, at thirty, I should find myself a healthy man who scarcely remembered what physical pain and weakness felt like.

A belief that I could not survive into adolescence may have caused the school authorities to be exceptionally lenient about my long absences. Whatever their motive, it was a profound blessing to me that the solitude for which I so passionately longed after my blindness was preserved under the intermittent shapings—faint touches, dreamlike, soon forgotten—that I received at school. I had no chance to develop the team spirit, the sense of co-operation, uniting with others engaged at the same time on the same tasks. I was never at the same point of tuition on a given subject as the other scholars. On the subject of English composition I soon overtook them, but at general studies, particularly arithmetic, I always lagged behind. I remember the sense of loneliness, of release and security that thrilled me from the infants' class onward as my mates were called to the blackboard while I remained at my desk, the only seated person in the room, busied with problems and points of instruction which they had passed weeks ago. The teacher's voice would be rapping out questions, giving information, but none of it was for me. I was apart, left to live my own life, not of their world.

CONFESSION OF A REBEL

I do not mean to imply that any of my teachers shirked their duty towards me. They gave me all the attention they could spare, certainly all that was due to me, and rather more than was useful to such a temperament as mine. The literary aptitude was recognized and encouraged from the start, and just after my seventh birthday I was awarded one of the book prizes allocated to Trethosa school by the National Canine Defence League for an essay on dogs. The teacher who had coached me thus far was no doubt proud of my success—Miss Liddicoat, a small sprightly woman, a local resident. I soon moved from the infants' class in to the care of another lady teacher, Miss Sarah, who was dark and burly, with thick eyebrows and a deep booming voice, and caused much excitement every morning when she arrived on her motor-cycle from Pentewan, nine miles away on the coast. Under her guidance I won further prizes for English, but my only clear memory of the period is of Miss Sarah's habit of snapping out at me during times of quiet study: "Don't frown so, Clemo!" This suggests that my broodings, even at that age, were beginning to mould my countenance in a way that did not commend itself to ladies. But I don't think I heeded these warnings: the dreamy intensity was essential to my growth. The teachers no doubt realized that I was an introspective type who was likely to make little headway along the normal competitive lines, but might achieve something on the creative side if I were given opportunity and encouragement. Miss Sarah went so far as to say that I might one day write a book—though her statement was made facetiously and, I believe, with a measure of sarcasm. It is pretty certain that all those faced with the task of educating me soon recognized that the obstacles were likely to prove insuperable. I daresay they pitied me, handicapped as I was by ill-health that seemed to be bogging me down and putting my talents beyond reach of any persistent, sympathetic culture.

It never occured to them that sympathetic nurture of my abilities was impossible in any Council school, and that the pressure of that system would have crippled me for life had it been exerted on me continuously for nine years as upon other children. They treated me as if I were a clever boy who needed training along practical, commonsense lines. I was expected to ripen in the same atmosphere as boys who have since become clerks, mechanics and shop assistants. It is this fundamental misconception of the material that was in me which prompts the satirical attitude to education so evident in my novels. I was a "problem child" in the deepest and least considered sense—in the sense that my talents were spiritual and mystical rather than intellectual. No system of education yet devised or envisaged can do anything with this type of child, because the first law of his nature is that the only way to help him is to let him alone. His faculties can develop only through solitary brooding. Throughout those years at Trethosa school my teachers were trying to impress me with facts I didn't want to know, to quicken my interest in subjects that bored me, and to hold out for my encouragement rewards and attainments which seemed to me not worth a moment's consideration. Worse still, they were trying to kindle my faculty of hero-worship by continual praise of persons towards whom I could feel nothing but antipathy—explorers, soldiers, statesmen, scientists and inventors. My taste and temperament were never consulted: all children were supposed to revere the same historic characters, and any divergence from the stock enthusiasms of the average extrovert was checked as an undesirable kink contrary to good taste and good citizenship. It is ironic to reflect that the men whose influence has done most to develop and liberate my personality were—with the exception of Browning—men whom I never heard of at school, men I should not have heard of there even had I attended school for years longer than I did. Great preachers like Spurgeon and Talmage, hymn-writers, obscure mystics of various centuries (some of them considered bawdy)—these are the men to whom I owe my ripening and balance, in so far as they were derived from books; and these are the very sources which an average schoolmaster would have tried to prevent me from reaching. He would have forbidden me to choose my own heroes, and in labouring to batter and twist my loyalties into line with the organized system he would have left me paralysed, broken between two worlds. My true world was spiritual with latent undercurrents of sensuality, and I can hardly blame my teachers for not understanding it. As Browning says in *Mr. Sludge the Medium*:

> "You must take
> A certain turn of mind for this—a twist
> In the flesh as well. Be lazily alive,
> Open-mouthed...."

It is the temperament of one who is vaguely aware of realities beyond normal consciousness, realities unfolding in spiritual light or breeding deep in the blood-darkness; and a State school is certainly not the place where such a personality can be matured.

The reports sent home to mother at the end of each term were full of irrelevant remarks like: "Must try to pull up on arithmetic. Homework would help." This reveals the fatuity of the modern educational system in its treatment of the Bunyan type. Homework, with special attention to arithmetic, would help the mind that was to make a synthesis of Calvinist dogma and sex mysticism! The incongruity tickles my sense of humour now; and I bear no grudge, because I didn't do the homework. But had such uncongenial studies been compulsory it is probable that I should never have become an author.

The range of my antipathies was so wide—covering not only arithmetic but history, geography, every branch of science, handicrafts, sports—that I had no common ground of sympathy with my teachers at all. On no subject could we truly co-operate, they to draw out, I to respond freely with confidence in their powers and gratitude for their interest. Even the literary power which so delighted them in my compositions was, in its essence, inseparable from that mystical life of which they knew nothing, and which would have repelled and exasperated them had they discovered it. I judged values instinctively by a standard to them incomprehensible. The religious items of the curriculum were the only parts that stirred me deeply. The brief service at the opening of the morning session, the hymns, the prayers and the private Bible-reading—these alone I really enjoyed. The rest of the day's routine was tedious, colourless, except for the English lessons in which I could escape somewhat into an imaginative world where spiritual values were not denied. Neither among teachers nor playmates could I find anyone who would share this preference for the element of worship or encourage me along that mystic path which my nature craved so vehemently. The Christian affirmations were regarded as merely formal, and are probably so regarded in primary and secondary schools today: some intellectuals would abolish them altogether. But they have to reckon with children who are destined for spiritual work, whether as evangelists, novelists or poets—a minority, but a potentially dangerous one under materialistic pressure.

H. G. Wells declared that he wrote *Kipps* "to show what the greatest and richest and proudest empire that the world has ever seen can do for one of its sons." It is time the Wellsian planners were shown what *their* world would do for the "sons" of the spirit. In a social Utopia run by materialists who demanded the active co-operation of every unit, there would be nothing but suicide or the madhouse for those of us who can be educated and freed for service only through the more anti-social instincts of religious faith.

The educationists, with such documents as this in their hands, must decide for themselves what course they intend to take with future mystics. That children of this type will continue to be born is certain: it is equally certain that the educational system, in striving towards "efficiency," is becoming less and less capable of dealing with spiritual talent. It is becoming increasingly an instrument of torture to the kind of child who regards "success" in the material, academic sense as a betrayal and a humiliation. If psychologists are brought in to try to "adjust" such children, they will either fail—I am sure they would have failed with me—or else impoverish and ultimately doom the world through the withdrawal of that spiritual fire which is essential to the welding and security of the social order.

As I look back I marvel that I came through that intermittent buffeting and repression with no mental kinks, no grievances: though I know what preserved me from such warping. Freud would have had to admit the "utility of illusion" in my case—if God were an illusion. The feeling that there was always One who understood, and that He was so important that it did not matter much if others misjudged me—this created an atmosphere in which no germs of bitterness could breed. It prevented me from ever feeling repulsed, unwanted; it saved me from disillusion—for I never *expected* my teachers and playmates to understand. Even in my childhood I adopted the attitude of the poet in Browning's *How it Strikes a Contemporary*—an alien among materialists, yet enjoying the isolation as a private joke between God and me: "How should the people know?" Quite right: how should they, with their aims and interests centred on things tangible and concrete? If the literary power they so misconstrued was busied secretly in writing letters (prayers and meditations) "to our Lord the King... Who reads them in His bedroom of a night," why expect attention from those who never read these mysterious letters, never guessed their existence? This was my position, though of course it was then vague, instinctive, not intellectually defined.

The resulting sense of peace and security was in great measure responsible for my complete freedom during childhood from those erotic perversions which usually attend a passionate and highly individual nature such as mine. In reading the autobiographies of other writers I have found an almost morbid insistence on their early enslavement to habits of masturbation and homosexuality. It was not until I read such books that I knew such things existed. No childhood could be healthier in this respect than mine was. My mother never gave me any sex instruction, and I did not mix with the type of boy who took a debased and sniggering interest in the subject. In consequence, my whole childhood was free from curiosity about sex which leads to those obsessions and practices that are so edifying to the Freudians. I sometimes overheard the little obscenities of schoolboy talk, but the bad words made no impression upon me at all; I did not recoil with disgust or find in them an erotic suggestion. Smut meant no more to me than the incomprehensible sports jargon about passes, tackles and hat tricks. My romantic imagination was satisfied with thoughts of God—humanized by a few little sweethearts—and these were so inexhaustible that I had no interest left even for the facts of generation in Nature. I never regarded springtime as mating time, and was always bored by lessons on the pollenation of flowers. I was throughout childhood, as I am still, rather stolid and insensitive to pure Nature. I preferred clay-dumps to woods, and under my trifling vexations and disappointments I sought and found solace not in flower-spangled fields but among old waggons and mica-beds. This idiosyncrasy was fundamental in my religious and emotional experience. It was not exactly an instance of the Puritan fear of sensuous beauty as an enemy of the soul: had it been that, I could never have known Christ as the "God of warm pulses and dishevelled hair, and panting bosoms bare" Whose activity is implied in much of my imaginative writing. But it was bound up with my life-long devotion to rawness and simplicity in all the media of worship—my preferring of ugly little chapels to ornate cathedrals, Sankey hymns to oratorios, the bleakness of Calvinistic theology to the more "poetic" interpretations of the Catholic and heterodox schools; and this notwithstanding the fact that my own nature is poetic, prone to Celtic romanticism and sentiment. The two elements may have conflicted at times, but I felt the duality only as a vague tension before adolescence. It never affected the spontaneity of my choice and enjoyment. The basic need of which I was always conscious was the need to tear aside the conventional mask, stripping everything back to the bare bones. Religion, literature and later, sex—all were approached in this way: not with my reason (for I remained credulous and superstitious) but through direct insight and intuition. It was well for me that the covering symbols were so meagre and scrappy that I was not forced to exhaust myself in the attempt to get rid of them. It would have been disastrous had I been compelled to tussle for years with impenetrable layers of ritual and sophistication. I was groping towards the world of dogma, a grey world of sharp outlines, but I was trying to apprehend it through fantasy, through sense-impressions on clay-works, never through the atmosphere of the study or the altar.

These qualities of my nature, and the simple contentment with crude heartiness, barred me from intellectual ambition, and created paradoxes that must have sadly perplexed my teachers, especially the headmaster who had to deal with me as I approached adolescence—Mr. W. S. Pellymounter, now headmaster of St. Dennis. I remember that on one occasion, apropos of a composition of mine, presumably a good one, he inquired hopefully what work I meant to adopt when I grew up. (I was then about eleven.) Obviously he expected a confession of lofty intellectual aims. I replied frankly and unhesitatingly that I meant to be a sky-tip worker—i.e. one who empties the refuse waggons at the top of the clay-dumps. Trethosa tip was visible from the schoolroom, only just across the road, and I often looked up at it from my studies, yearning for the sense of freedom, elevation and remoteness that must be felt up there on the ridge. My reply must have given the master a headache. Probably he had never before met a boy who seemed "bookish" yet wished to become a manual labourer. My habits showed clearly my antagonism to the student world, my determination to fight to the death against the "emancipation" which so often turns the proletarian into the prig with his pathetic, frustrated desire to fit in at the higher social levels. I was going to stay in my own world, the working-class world: there I could find all the education I wanted. In this matter there was, from the outset, a fundamental cleavage between my reactions and those of other writers bred in the working class. I did not feel, with D. H. Lawrence and A. L. Rowse, that because we originals cannot live in the same mental world as working-class folk we are necessarily stifled by contact with them. This may be true where the whole personality is sensitive and vulnerable, but I was sensitive only at the emotional and mystical points that were sympathetic to primitive vitality. The civilizing faculty of "intelligence" by which a child becomes aware that ugliness is repulsive, ignorance humiliating and poverty degrading was covered in my nature by a thick rind of stolidity, an instinctive taste for "commonness" which I cannot quite reconcile with my passion for individuality, though both were symptoms of my introvert preoccupations. It was the school atmosphere, with its attempts to reach and nourish that alien "intelligence," which I found stifling. I fought it all along the line, even in speech, using the Cornish dialect, the rough slipshod English of the working people, and never became self-conscious or ashamed of it. I simply would not adapt myself to "correct" manners, or bother about being clever or superior to anyone else. I think the headmaster perceived something of the true state of affairs before I left his hands, though he could have had little idea of the trend of my motives, the slow-moving, malicious insurgency that was vitalizing even those qualities of which he was proud. During my last year at school he told my mother: "Mrs. Clemo, your son is a born philosopher." Mother smiled and replied lamely that she " 'oped 'e might be one one day." "He *is* one," said Mr. Pellymounter; and I suppose that in some sense he was right.

But I can honestly say that it never occurred to me during childhood that I might become a novelist, or indeed a writer of any sort. I knew, of course, that the Hockings were my cousins, but this meant little, as I had never read any of their books. (I have read only one or two of them since.) Silas Hocking was a mere name to me—he had settled in London; and Joseph I saw only twice. I was present when he opened the St. Stephen's Recreation Ground in 1924, though I was extemely bored by the ceremony; and on another occasion my mother took me to hear him preach at St. Stephen's Methodist chapel. I have completely forgotten the service. I felt no pride or kinship of any kind: it was not the habit of the Clemo's to feel that. None of them attended St. Stephen's cemetery when his ashes were buried there in March 1937.

The inhibition regarding the literary streak in my family was no doubt strengthened by the fact that I so seldom heard the Hockings praised; there grew in me a vague feeling that they had done something to be ashamed of. The local gentry, of course, applauded their success, but I knew nothing of the gentry. The people who called at my home, and might casually mention the Hockings, were uneducated villagers, and the sturdy, chapel-going folk around St. Stephen's had never forgiven the Hockings for leaving the ministry in order to write story-books. I remember hearing Silas Hocking denounced from Trethosa chapel pulpit when, in his old age, he drifted so far from the Evangelical position as to champion Sunday cinemas and divorce law reforms. My mother scarcely ever mentioned these brothers: she strongly disapproved of novels, and though she let me borrow them from the school library she remarked that she would rather I read "good books."

These factors would have been influential on any sensitive child who had no other standards of comparison: the peculiarity in my case was that I did not chafe, I did not feel that I had been born into the wrong environment where I hadn't a chance to develop. I was quite happy and content that no one I trusted had the slighest knowledge of or sympathy with literature. The extreme anti-cultural attitude I found at my father's old home, the Clemos' cottage at the bottom of the lane under Trethosa clay-dump. My mother brought lunch there for me on several days a week, coming in along the claywork track over the dump from Goonvean, so that when I arrived early I would hang about the garden until I saw her appear, far up against the sky, with her basket, waving to me as she descended cautiously past the furze-clumps to the little gravel square below the house. By that time Esther was living alone there except for a grandson, the half-German William, who, after his mother's marriage, had been reared by Esther, hiding his dark London memories and growing into a moody, enigmatic character, unsociable and studious. All Esther's children were either married or dead, with the exception of Hetty, the idiot daughter in the asylum, and Horatio, a son who had emigrated to New Zealand. The atmosphere of the place had changed, become almost respectable, though Esther preserved something of the old barbaric fire. I recall her as a tall, vigorous old woman, scornful of men, cynical in her view of marriage, with frizzy hair dyed brown and a particularly harsh and strident voice that spoke always in broadest Cornish dialect. She was naturally contemptuous of the Hockings, who had ignored her from the time she married Clemo. Still to have admitted the relationship might have embarrassed them: it would have shown the incongruity of their choosing to write of Cornish life as a sweet romantic thing and Cornwall as a magic place in which baronets and millionaires are produced overnight through the discovery of buried Wills and even the servant-girls turn out to be heiresses. Esther ridiculed their literary efforts; she could scarcely read, she loathed books, and railed with bitter vehemence against the schools and churches, against all institutions that conveniently turned a blind eye to life as she had known it. It was not surprising that, with her experience, she had Spartan ideas on the training of children. My mother was constantly nagged about her folly in humouring my fastidious tastes, especially in matters of food. "Maake'n ate it, Eve, maake'n ate it," she would shout if my appetite failed me before my plate was cleared. Useless for mother to explain that my stomach was delicate. "Delicate is 'a ? Gid along! I'd *zee* if a boy o' mine should be so pickin'!" And if mother mentioned my love of reading, Esther's scorn would ring through the little cottage. "Ge' at! Taake 'is books away from un—rewinin' 'is 'ealth wi' all this 'ere steddyin'. Ther'll trouble come of it, maark my words—maark my words, Evlun! If 'twas a chiel o' mine—I'd *zee*——!" —with a flash of her hollow old eyes and a flourish of her skinny fist across the bare flagged floor at me, who would sit, mildly wondering, toying with my food on the bench and brooding out through the window upon the squalid, cobbled courtyard. I knew and guessed nothing then of the half-century of domestic eruption, hardening to scoriæ of vice, that had left this volcanic wreckage of a soul in the shrivelled, restless body. I was not aware that the sharp, almost witchlike face had lost its human tone through the struggle to rear a family under the conditions that John Clemo imposed on her. Before I grew up she had gone to live with Horatio, who had returned from New Zealand and, after a brief career as a singer (he was a born musician, the most talented of Esther's sons) had married and settled near Port Isaac, on the North Cornish coast. There Esther became a well-known and picturesque character during the nineteen-thirties, receiving many tokens of respect when she died there in September 1945, in her ninety-second year.

I was never a favourite grandson of hers, but I have only the happiest recollections of the old home at Trethosa: of gooseberries and blackcurrants furtively stolen during the summer "breaks" from the school a few hundred yards further down the road, of lonely wanderings about the garden, the sand-dump and the railway siding that passed between the house and the drying-sheds. That place, scene of so much tragedy, was the scene, too, of those welcome brief hours at midday when between the two sessions of mechanical school routine I could be alone and feel the undercurrents of destiny vaguely tugging amid the tepid, brittle roots of my formal education.

It was there also, and during these midday intervals, that I touched a side of life which did much to develop my human sympathies and to give my intellectual ones a background of humility. Just across the square from granny's home was a tumbledown, thatch-roofed cottage close against the clay-dump—the abode of Billy Creba and his family. Raw human drama was in that house probably more than in any other in the district, though in such remote spots extreme squalor, illiteracy and inarticulate conflicts were still fairly common. Of this group comprising Billy, his wife Sarah, his mother, his sister Ellen and his son Freddy, the most appealing to my imagination was

Billy himself: a gaunt epileptic fellow, a clay-worker, a man of touching simplicity and innocence. He was a teetotaler and non-smoker, deeply religious, though without the intellect to define his beliefs. His conversion was a raw epic of grace similar to those which Christian journalists have recorded in the London slums. Being completely illiterate, he knew nothing of the Bible except what was read to him from the pulpit or at class-meetings. He frequented Trethosa chapel, and I always felt a thrill of awe when, during the evening services, he would rise, a shaggy, tramplike figure, stretch his trembling arms upward and pour out prayers that held the congregation as by a spell. When domestic conditions became intolerable on week-days he was forced to seek other means of relief—sometimes grotesque. On one occasion when the storm indoors coincided with a storm of wind and rain without, Billy stripped off his coat, took up a chair and carried it out into the garden. He sat down in the pouring rain and announced shrilly to the gaping women that "he could bear no more and would stop there till he'd catched his death." This laudable intention failed, and Billy lived to see happier days. His mother died soon after-wards, Ellen was removed to Bodmin Lunatic Asylum, Freddy to a similar place for deranged adolescents, and Billy and Sarah had to quit their home before the claywork company de-molished it. They were provided with another house near Roche and found, I trust, some light at eventide.

The behaviour of that household caused much amusement among the neighbours at Trethosa; but the pathos of such a state moved me deeply, even as a child. I would cry as I thought of downtrodden people like Billy and Sarah—Billy with his anguished prayers at chapel, rudimentary Christian faith upholding him where nothing else could even mitigate the horror of his submerged life. My feeling may have been sentimental but I know that it was good for me, far more good than the cold, heartless influence of the school. It was this attitude of intense sympathy with the stupid, the socially outcast, that, from early childhood, marked me out from the intellectuals and made me derisive of cultural systems which claimed to supplant crude Christianity as a redemptive influence on the lower classes. What could any form of education do for such families as the Crebas? The clever children only made fun of Billy and Sarah, never speaking to them except in taunting, jeering tones. But I could never feel contempt for them; not even pity. The bond was closer, inseparable from those religious and hereditary instincts which cut me off not only from the bourgeoisie—it wasn't really a class issue—but from the progressive elements of the working class.

With such an outlook it was impossible that I should be popular among my schoolfellows. Even my teachers were occasionally sarcastic: the headmaster nicknamed me "Jean" because of my supposed effeminacy—a nickname that stuck to me throughout my later schooldays, though I was not humiliated by it as an ordinary boy would have been. In the playground I was always alone, usually standing by the coal-shed at the top of the sloping yard, watching the boys racing about after balls, playing leap-frog, scuffling and fighting. I would shrink if any of them came near to me. It was not merely that the spiritual atmosphere of the place was uncongenial: I was physically repelled by the presence of boys and could not bear them to touch me. I would stay huddled there in the corner, looking down over that noisy throng, over the open heathland outside and across at the clay-dumps of Meledor on the opposite slope, a mile distant. My mind received something of the beauty of that scene as a compensation for the rowdy, fretting life of the playground.

The rougher boys naturally derided me as a milksop; but the studious found a gap equally wide between my interests and theirs. I loathed the gregarious qualities that went to the making of a Boy Scout, but I loathed even more the aloof, fastidious qualities that characterized the student. I could not become one of a team for any purpose. My hunger for solitude expressed itself even in the two deepest veins of my personality —those of violence and romanticism. On the only occasion that I became so angry with a boy that I had to fight him I insisted that we should "have it out" privately in a secluded field among the clayworks: I could not have struck a blow in the playground or elsewhere with a crowd of boys yelling round us. And on the romantic side, I found it increasingly difficult as I grew older to interest myself in girls whom I saw to be happy in company with other children. The two sweethearts who captured my imagination intermittently from the time I was ten until I left school were girls whom I only met when they were as lonely as I was. One of them lived near Bodmin, the other at St. Austell, and I saw them only at rare intervals when they visited relatives at Goonamarris.

Every time I tried to catch the popular spirit the result was disastrous. I made two appearances as a public entertainer during my childhood—once when I sang a solo at Trethosa chapel anniversary, and once at a concert given at the day-school when I took part in a negro sketch. I failed to impress anyone but mother on either occasion, and was never asked to sing or act in any subsequent performance. At the school concert people complained that I had not put enough soot on my face: my extreme pallor showed through the black streaks, contrasting unfavourably with the appearance of other boys who were naturally robust and also more wholehearted in their application of soot. I remember being vaguely unhappy, oppressed by a sense of pettiness and futility amid the general noise and horseplay in the infants' room before the concert began. I wished I could get away from it all, go out and brood on the things that mattered to me. In such moments of crisis I realized with a sharper bewilderment and pain what a misfit I must always be in the everyday world.

CHAPTER FOUR

Home and Village Life

THE circumstances of my home life on those bare Cornish
uplands were, to all appearances, as far as anything could
well be from the ideal training-ground of a modern writer.
The monotony of setting was unbroken from year to year
except for occasional shopping excursions to St. Austell, six
miles away, and a few day-trips to the beaches in the summer
holidays.   I recall only one such outing which had any
significance for me—a visit to Harlyn Bay, on the north Cornish
coast, where I was fascinated by the macabre exhibits in the
museum, the skulls, skeletons and other relics of the Bronze
Age that had been dug up from Harlyn sands. These gruesome
remains appealed to my love of the ultimate, elemental things,
the things I could brood upon deep within myself, and the
occasion was thus marked off sharply from the usual trivialities
of seaside jaunts. I took part in the Trethosa Sunday School
trips to Porth and Porthtowan, near Newquay, but never
enjoyed them. The other boys knew I would not play with
them on the beaches, and they ignored me. I would sit with
mother on the rocks, staring out over the sea, miserable and
fretful as the day wore on. longing to be back among the clay-
dumps, at home.   Among those dumps I seemed to settle
drowsily down, immersing my consciousness in deep grey
waters that pulsed upon me or flowed unheeded, a dreamy
current of sensation and prayer. I had no ambitions; nothing
could make me alert, resolved to fight and achieve a definite
purpose. I was the child who had survived a nightmare of
blindness, and as the schools could not break the spell there
seemed no possibility of my ever emerging from the strange
stupor of individuality to face and interpret the problems of
the modern world. Even the crude stimulation of village life
was denied me, our home being one of the most remote in a

44

district particularly wild and inhospitable, where houses actually near each other are isolated and barred off by the wedges of the clay-range and the twisted tunnelling of the pits. The social and recreational functions of the four neighbouring villages—St. Stephen's, St. Dennis, Foxhole and Nanpean— were, with very rare exceptions, as unknown to me as if they had been happening a hundred miles away.

During my early childhood there were three other children at Goonamarris, all girls and playmates of mine—for I did like playing with girls, especially one of these three, whom I remember kissing behind gorse bushes on the Slip. But when I was about seven these children went to live elsewhere, and throughout the rest of my childhood there was not a single boy or girl down in the hamlet, the occupants of the half-dozen cottages being middle-aged or elderly folk. I was thus, out of school hours, growing up in an adult world, touched only by adult influences. I had no real chum during my schooldays, and only one boy became more than a mere acquaintance—one of my fellow-actors in the negro sketch, a boy called Brian, who lived in a detached house at the foot of Goonvean hill, a picturesque place backed by the towering woods and white sinuous clay-banks of Tregargus. Brian was delicate in health, like me, and much cleverer than I was in the ordinary scholastic sense: he continued his education at St. Austell County School, an institution which I never entered. His home life was very different from mine, his father, a claywork captain, being a rough, hard-drinking fellow, and his mother a recluse of a sceptical type who sent him regularly to Sunday School. He shared my adventures when I returned home from school around the southern end of Goonvean sand-dump instead of taking the northern route past the clay-pit and the farm. We used to scramble along the slopes of Trethosa quarry, tug and push at any empty waggons we could find until we got them off the rails, slide on the sidewalk of the drying-kilns at Lower Goonvean and over the settling-pools when they froze in winter. I had a healthy love of physical risks despite my spiritual preoccupations. I remember that on one occasion we descended a disused mine-shaft by the wooden ladder still affixed to its wall, nearly rotted through and with several of its rungs missing. A dozen feet of water had flooded the bottom of the shaft, and it seems a miracle that both of us were not drowned.

My association with Brian was not continued in the evenings or at week-ends. He was not allowed to come up and play with me, and I never felt sufficiently in need of his company to arrange meetings elsewhere. My leisure hours were solitary, humanized only by my mother and my aunt Bertha—a fat, dogged, rather vociferous little soul who had accepted with surprising tolerance, if no comprehension, the strange developments in the cottage. The beauty of my home atmosphere during these years played a great part in my true education. It was free, spontaneous, largely an outdoor life in summer, as for hours mother and I roamed about the downs and woods, gathering berries. When in the copse below Barrakellis I would sometimes paddle in the clay-stream, and spent many happy hours riding up and down on the ballast box of the water-wheel that rose and fell among the trees on the bank of the stream. There was also much gardening to be done during the spring and summer, though I was never strong enough to do any of the heavy work. Most of the planting and lifting fell to my mother: male relatives seldom offered to help, and she could handle garden tools as skilfully as a man. Her health had gradually improved since my blindness, and except for occasional palpitation of the heart she had become robust, only the refined, sensitive features of her sallow face marking her off from the typical farmer's daughter. She loved gardening, and besides attending to the vegetables she cultivated a flower bed at the top of the path, a colourful plot of lilies, asters, wall-flowers, sweet williams and chrysanthemums which I, with my queer dislike of flowers, scarcely bothered to look at. I was often on the roads in the evenings, sometimes carrying a pitcher, for we had to fetch water from the pump at Goonamarris, and in summer this frequently ran dry, compelling us to go to the claywork spring in the valley nearly a quarter of a mile below our home. I was in my teens before the Council water supply was brought to a tap outside our garden wall. There were also the provisions to be brought in from Captain Grigg's grocery store on the corner, and the milk to be fetched daily from Morcom's farm, a smallholding opposite the pump with fields that sloped up to the foot of Bloomdale burrow.

I sometimes ventured into the fields during haymaking, but seldom went near the workmen. They were sure to ask me to fetch something, and such requests always made me act like an imbecile. I never seemed to know what was wanted or where it could be found. I would wander distractedly about the field, halting and asking myself endless questions until I became an object of derision to the onlookers. This lack of practical gumption was another of those factors which induced me to be a passive observer and not a participant in the healthy country activities with which I sympathized.

My most vivid memories of farm life are of visits to my uncle's farm, Penrose Veor, just north of St. Dennis, three miles from my home. It was a lonely agricultural outpost on the fringe of Goss Moor, and yielded me many moments of vision and enjoyment: recollections of standing amid the long grass of the orchard, shaking the apple-tree boughs until the ripe fruit dropped; of sitting on a field gate watching my uncle, Dick Grigg, at plough, a white-haired, hearty figure (though it was a stony farm, from which the family drew a bare living), the vast black sweep of the heath stretching away mile after mile in the background, primitive, terrifying; of going out on the moor with Uncle Dick and his half-brother, Tom Bullock, to see the Fowey huntsmen and hounds pass, as they were accustomed to do, on the Tuesday after St. Dennis Feast, the red-coated riders moving cautiously amid the bogland in the pale autumn sunlight; and (less pleasurable) of once attending the parish church just above the farm on the Feast Sunday— the only Anglican church service I have ever attended, and one from which I emerged feeling that I had been in a dim musty vault where every religious instinct I possessed had been stifled.

These memories of Penrose are bound up with a sense of destiny as no other scenes of my childhood ever were. Had we not been so intimate with the Grigg family it is impossible to say how I should have become a writer. The urge to write, the necessity for writing, were to be awakened in me at Penrose on a day when the moorland beyond it and the church on Carne Hill above were darkened, the grimly elemental and dogmatic worlds obscured by a wayward drift of blasphemy that led to many sorrows. I was being prepared for that hour by all the trivial details of my life back at Goonamarris, the raw poetry of an existence lived always on the verge of poverty but never embittered by actual privation.

What do I remember of that poverty? I remember that on winter evenings I used to go out, trundling a wheelbarrow, to pick "smutties"—burned furze twigs—on the Slip: this helped to cut down expenditure on fuel. I remember that frequently mother and I went to the dump for "cherks" as we called them—i.e. cinders—to help save coal. The side of Bloomdale burrow a hundred yards from our house was black with cinders tossed out from the engine-house on the ridge above, and on many evenings mother and I went up with a zinc bath and pails, standing on the slope of the dump in the bitter wind until darkness fell, filling our pails with the cinders. I would sometimes climb fifty feet up to reach the newest layers, crouching ankle-deep in the black ash, glancing down at mother as she waited beside the bath among the shadowy bushes, the stacks of Goonvean growing dim across the fields behind her, the clay-pit remote and melancholy. The beauty of the scene was an enrichment that prevented me from ever feeling humiliated or degraded while thus grubbing amid the dirt.

Winter evenings indoors were spent quietly, mother and I occasionally playing draughts, ludo and other games bought at Woolworth's. I was a bad loser, and would become very sulky if I lost a game. There were no lack of toys in the house: games alternated with meccano construction and magic lantern shows. And often, of course, there would be the school library books to read, opened under the hanging oil lamp in the kitchen

—this being then the living room, the larger of the two down-stair rooms.

One treat which I liked better than games or reading in the early years—though it seldom came—was to be invited next door by old Mr. Treverton and to sit on the bench while he played his gramophone to me. It was an old-fashioned gramophone with an enormous blue horn, and this horn used to fascinate me. I would edge round the table towards it until I almost yielded to the urge to push my face inside the huge, glittering brass circle and stare down the dark crinkly neck through which sounds squealed up from scratched, musty records. Mr. Treverton's records were chiefly music-hall ditties, and sometimes when he had got a record almost to the turntable he would glance at the title and thrust it hastily back into its dust cover, muttering into his moustache: "Edd'n fit fer Jeggy to 'ear, that one edd'n." I would look quizzically into his stern, blotchy face, wondering what the record could be about to be withheld from my hearing. This sensitiveness in a rough, hard-bitten man—for Mr. Treverton had been a sailor and became a dour, silent fellow in his later years, brooding on a life of raw experience that had not been too happy—is typical of the curious delicacy of these simple folk —so different from the cynical unconcern of many modern villagers with their cheap Hollywood and B.B.C. standards. Even when these old people were not religious themselves they preserved a stoic dignity and a sense of responsibility towards the young that was often touching in its naïve, furtive expressions.

The second Mrs. Treverton was of a similar type, primitive and superstitious, obsessed for years by a hatred of the black cat that had belonged to the first Mrs. Treverton. She seemed to think the ghost of this lady was somehow connected with the cat, especially after being awakened one night by the animal's scratching at the springs under the bed. She told us next morning with evident terror: "I thought 'twas John's first wife come back for me!" At all hours of the day we would see or hear her chasing the cat around the house and garden, flourishing a broom. She was a sturdy little woman with a broad, fresh-coloured face, and had followed the crude rhythm of village life. Yet now and then there would return upon her a mood of wistful yearning for spiritual support; remembrance of the old days of revivalist meetings would flick her into serious concern. We would hear her in the back bedroom playing Sankey hymns on Mr. Treverton's gramophone, a lonely old woman of nearly seventy, trying at times to sing in accompaniment, her voice as tuneless as the damp, worn-out records. It was pathetic, and I was just the sort of child to draw from it inferences which a clever boy never would have drawn. The acrid realist is incapable of portraying the whole personality of such people. He is so afraid of becoming sentimental that he misses the facts. The facts were that even these rough, bawdy villagers possessed souls which, like everyone else's, could find fulfilment and satisfaction only in religious faith. They recognized such faith where it was genuine, as in the Moody and Sankey revival, and now that the spiritual flame had passed and was no longer in the churches they drifted like blank stars, groping and often struggling to be kindled by stray relics of the old liberating fire. I knew many such characters, and their cumulative influence made my early collision with the shallow materialism of my age a very sharp one.

There was Tom Bullock, of Penrose Veor farm—"Uncle Tom" I called him, though he was no relation—a frequent visitor to our home during the winter evenings of my boyhood. He was generally regarded as a rough, irreligious fellow, warped by domestic unhappiness. Yet he had only two objects in coming to our home, both very laudable—to beat my mother at a game of draughts and to hear Sankey hymns played on the organ. He sometimes unburdened his mind to mother, and spoke of spiritual struggles which the superficial cynic would dismiss as humbug. When I sat at the organ to entertain him with some playing—I had taken only a few music lessons and could not read notation, but I spent hours playing the organ by ear, often improvising tunes of my own which listeners declared to have "lovely strains in 'em"—Tom would say to me, not jokingly but with solemn emphasis: "Play the old Sankey's, Jack." As I played I would watch his face—a big, raw-boned face with a clumsy nose and a short grey moustache. I noted signs of wistful desire similar to those we sometimes saw in Mrs. Treverton: the coarse features mellower, the sunken eyes somehow cleansed, probing out beyond the world of gross appetite. Mother would often sing the hymns, and there was always a deep religious hush when they closed occasionally broken by Tom asking me in subdued tones what I believed about a future life. This was education indeed for a nature like mine, the Browning type to which "incidents in the development of a soul" are the only things worth study.

Even when no visitors called, this spiritual quality was often a dominant influence at home during the winter evenings. When I think of those evenings of my childhood the picture that remains most compellingly in my mind is that of mother seated at the organ, absorbed and remote in the pale light of the oil lamp, playing and singing hymns out of a tattered, red-backed copy of Sankey's *Sacred Songs and Solos*. She would sing these hymns hour after hour, her full alto voice echoing through the cottage, while my aunt Bertha knitted, a hunched, gnome-like figure in the shadowed corner, and I sat huddled over the fire, trying in vain to interest myself in some book I had brought home from school. Adventure stuff about Indians seemed trivial and meaningless in the presence of mother's voice rendering those simple melodies of the Evangelical faith. I knew nothing then of her tragic marriage, her natural fears for my future that struggled with her belief in a higher destiny, but I felt vaguely that in mother there was a religious force quite different from the formal affirmations of the Sunday-School—an institution which, because of its secular associations meant no more to me than day-school. (The most distasteful of these associations was the annual treat, or "tea-fight" as it was called—a bustling, noisy affair that was a torture to me, all the more incomprehensible because it was inflicted in the name of religion. How reluctantly on those June afternoons

I crept across the marsh, clutching my cup for the free tea!
How I shrank from turning the last corner by the old smithy
and coming in full view of the colourful, hateful scene. The
bright uniforms of the bandsmen and their glittering instru-
ments, the crowds in the field sloping down to the foot of
Meledor hill, the ice-cream and hot chip vans and the
confectioners' stalls ranged along the gutter of the lane winding
up from Trethosa village—all broke upon me in sharp nagging
discords, so that after nibbling at my huge saffron bun on a
bench in the school yard, I spent most of the evening—while
other children were obviously enjoying themselves—moving
glumly about with mother and making myself ridiculous by
frequent, panicky requests to be taken home.)

My mother's dealing with me in religious matters was very
different from that of many Nonconformist parents. Never
did she try to scold me into goodness; nor did she confuse me
with talk about the Christian ethic. She lived that ethic as
no one else I had known ever lived it; it unfolded in her
actions as spontaneously as a flower unfolds in the sunshine.
Her purity and unselfishness impressed me as they impressed
others in their daily contacts with her. Tradesmen were often
moved to heartfelt comment by her scrupulous honesty. The
fruits of Christian discipleship had ripened early in my mother,
and they were there because she had never in her life given an
hour's thought to the mere moral code of Christianity. Whenever she sought to communicate the rare charm of her
character it was in terms of the Pauline Epistles, the uncompromising dogma. And it was the naturalness of it all,
the absence of any artificial pressure of bigotry or fanaticism,
that made this theological approach so real and vivid and
incomparably beautiful. Poetry, intellectual depth, sensitiveness—all were nourished in me by this intense personal
religion in my mother.

It will be obvious from these remarks that I have failed to
develop the contempt which a modern novelist should presumably feel towards early influences of an extremely pious type.
I cannot even join in the disgruntled outbursts so common

among novelists who have been reared amid the "gloom" of the Puritan Sunday. The Sabbath was never a dull day to me, though all toys, secular books and secular gramophone records were put away, and the sand-dump across the road and even the garden become forbidden ground which must not be stepped on to pick a berry or a pod of peas. My passive acceptance of these restrictions may have been another sign of that lack of civilizing "intelligence" which I have already noted in speaking of my school life. But it did at least give me the assurance I needed most—the assurance that there was no "sweet reasonableness" at the heart of Reality, but a perfect integration of wilful moodiness. The Sunday mood was in harmony with my primitive dislike of common sense. The revelation of the home was so complete that I used to welcome rainy Sundays that preserved the flame of worship steadily within the cottage. At chapel the preacher might deny the infallibility of the Bible; at Sunday-School the teacher might talk of sport and scouting: only at home was there security. When illness or the weather kept us indoors we would sometimes hold a service in the evening with Bible-readings, hymns and the *Christian Herald* sermon—usually a reprint of a sermon by Spurgeon, the last of the great English Calvinists, or Spurgeon's American rival and contemporary, T. de Witt Talmage, the flamboyant genius of the Brooklyn Tabernacle. (It is characteristic and fitting that, outside the Bible, my first sense of literary style, of the beauty and power of words when arranged in striking antithesis and vivid imagery, should come not through the sonorous blank verse of Milton and Shakespeare but from the pulpit oratory of Talmage.) Occasionally these services would close in a prayer meeting as neighbours who had attended chapel dropped in to report their impressions of the preacher.

In the early years mother would often read to me on Sundays the books John Polmounter had left behind him—chiefly volumes of sermons and biographies of minor evangelists, Methodist pioneers and missionaries—and also her own Sunday-School rewards and those of my aunt Bertha. These fictional works were of a sort which is now generally regarded as exceedingly harmful to the child mind, full of a piety so intense and uncompromising that the defensive modern substitutes the adjectives "morbid" and "nauseating." These books were of much greater value in my education than the secular "classics" I was compelled to read at day-school.

Chesterton declared in his *Autobiography* that as a boy he had not only liked stories with morals, but had preferred the morals to the stories. This seems to be a sign of the religious temperament, for my own preference was similar. But to interest me a moral had to be deeply spiritual, not merely ethical. I should have been bored by stories of the modern "up-lift" type— tales of healthy open-air life which aim to build up the qualities of a "good sport," strict observance of a code of honour, mere mechanical usefulness. I could never feel easy when I had deliberately done a good deed or anything for which I deserved congratulation. I had a vague, troubled sense of having disturbed the true balance of things in which man took his place as a sinful, dependent creature. Few twentieth-century parents would have been able to deal—or even sympathize— with a boy in whom such traits were dominant. Only an exceptional woman could have surrounded me with an atmosphere in which this obstinate self-depreciation could develop without being warped to fanaticism or misanthropy. My mother succeeded chiefly because she had undergone a deep religious experience herself, but also because she did not try to limit the intellectual side of my quest. She was always eager to open fresh fields of knowledge which could be coloured by the mystic light; and she provided me with plenty of comic papers, so that I had no chance to get stuck in an inhuman rut of solemnity. I must confess that I found a normal boy's delight in these comic papers: every week I cut out my favourite strips and pasted them in a scrap-book.

When I was about ten my mother bought for me a set of Arthur Mee's *Children's Encyclopædia*, which was certainly one of the formative influences of my later boyhood. I was aware, in a desultory sort of way, that from these books I could educate myself, with no supervision, no compulsion: I could turn to whatever subject I liked, ignoring those that did not interest me. Before I was twelve I had gained through this private reading a sketchy knowledge of the literature and art of all countries and ages, and a store of the simpler treasures of English poetry. The historical and scientific sections I left alone: not until I was in my teens did I read most of these, and by that time I was sufficiently independent to disagree violently with many of their conclusions. And later still I came to feel how little even of what I had enjoyed in these volumes had remained with me and been of permanent value. It was "book-learning" like the school studies, and soon grew tame and colourless against the portentous human background.

Now and then a grim epic of village life would break in and throw into relief the pettiness of the student world. One of these I remember vividly, as our home was directly concerned in it. A family called Solomon had been turned out of their house at Foxhole because they had not paid the rent—the wife being a careless, slovenly creature. They came across to Goonamarris with several young children, and in a corner of the Slip close to the field hedge of Goonvean the man built a hut of stone and turf clods, roofing it with corrugated iron. In this hovel, without furniture or even a covering for the earth floor, they tried to set up housekeeping. But the season was winter and the rain fell day after day on that squalid fringe of the downs, dripping from the roof, soaking through the mud walls, blowing in through the rude doorway that was partly screened with sacks. Mrs. Solomon could not get a fire to burn in the mornings and the children were crying for food and hot drink. As soon as my mother learnt of their plight— for ours was the nearest cottage—she gave all the practical help she could. She handed some buns and a jug of hot cocoa to one of the children at breakfast time nearly every day, and often cooked the dinners which Mrs. Solomon would bring to our home. This continued for several weeks, but the conditions became intolerable; the local Council intervened, and the Solomon's were removed to St. Austell workhouse. Their improvised shelter began to fall to pieces soon after they left, and often in the evenings I would go there and brood alone, crouching among the brambles that sprouted in the earthy walls, vaguely troubled, yet also queerly exalted by the sense of raw human drama. It appealed irresistibly to the Clemo side of my nature, and worked through that to the imaginative and poetic qualities. How savagely, squatting there amid the mud where those wretches had loved each other (though I didn't think of that) I hated the neatness of the classroom, the polished politeness, the unreality of it! The school world was a dainty Greuze-like trifle compared with the smouldering Rembrandtesque intensity that fashioned my private life—the intensity, on the one hand, of the prayer meetings in our little front room, and on the other, of such spots as "Solomons' Corner" (as we called it), the primitive sense of people living and breeding under hedges because they had no homes.

Thus my home life and surroundings, so remote from and hostile to the temper of the age that they seemed like handicaps to a modern writer, were actually teeming with the most sympathetic and stimulating influences. They might have cramped a clever boy, and would have embittered an ambitious one, but they were just right for me, who was neither clever nor ambitious but just drifting with lazy insight from mood to mood. Contemporary ideas and movements scarcely touched me at all. We took in no daily newspapers—and, of course, no Sunday ones; I knew practically nothing of what was happening in the world. The only piece of news of a literary nature that reached me during childhood came in January 1928 when, in a news-sheet which had wrapped some article delivered at our home I found an illustrated account of Thomas Hardy's funeral in Westminster Abbey. The event impressed me deeply, though at that time I knew nothing of Hardy's work except the brief note, and the few poems, given in *The Children's Encyclopædia*. I was awed by the sense of death striking down the great ones of the earth as pitilessly as the most obscure, and felt for awhile a childish counterpart of Hardy's own outlook, a sense of futility and waste in the labours and triumphs which superficial minds thought so important. This incident of Hardy's death probably stood out in my mind chiefly because it was an isolated impact. We never possessed a radio, and only once did I visit a cinema—in 1928, when my mother took me to see a film at St. Austell. She wished to judge for herself whether this new invention would be likely to help me or not—and the film happened to be an extremely glamorous affair which so shocked her that we had to leave the building before the film was half shown.

But the spell of sophistication would have been soon broken had it begun to grip me at this period. I was then twelve years old, and before my thirteenth birthday there was a return of the ominous symptoms I had known at the age of five: the inflammation and pain in my eyes, the need to stay in the dark, away from books, strained and defensive in manner. Preventive measures were taken, but it was obvious that another attack of blindness was imminent, of a more ugly and prolonged type than the early one. My schooling was at an end. I was about to be thrust afresh, with ripening apprehension, into the struggle with primeval darkness.

CHAPTER FIVE

Blindness and a Vision

THROUGHOUT the early weeks of 1929 I remained blind.
Darkness brooded sluggishly all round. I knew that my
childhood was over—a childhood which fortunately had never
developed any driving force of ambition that would have set
me fretting and fuming at the insuperable barrier. I accepted
it with passive fatalism, with a turn of mind rather analytical
than imaginative. What lay ahead none of us in that house
could guess; mother scarcely dared to inquire, so completely
did morbidities seem to be overwhelming the tide of spiritual
health which she believed was destined to flow through me.
The cottage became strangely quiet, tense, unnatural. Some
of my old school mates visited me—several girls and one or two
boys; but they soon dropped off. My churlish attitude
confused and puzzled them: the fresh blow had taken me
entirely out of their world, snapping the last bonds of sympathy
and understanding. Their talk of school events, sports and
scholarships, was now not only an intolerable bore but a
positive irritation to a mind craving only to be left alone, to
hear nothing and know nothing but the voice and language
of its own individuality. I seldom spoke to these callers; they
could only stand and stare at me and carry on uneasy conversation with mother, telling her how clever I had been at English
and what a shame it was that I should become blind when
I might have gone onward to such a brilliant career: a vague
prophecy which had no practical basis. I had already taken
the preliminary examination to discover my prospects of
getting to the secondary school, and had failed dismally in it,
finding the whole atmosphere deadening to the imagination,
repressive, bewildering. I had made a mess of the English
paper through being set an uncongenial subject—Quiller-
Couch's *The Splendid Spur*, a book which I found unreadable.

BLINDNESS AND A VISION

Symptomatic of the inept mass-production methods of the schools that a mystical child should be expected to show his qualities when grappling with dry historical romance! My blindness gave me time to ponder over such anomalies and to see that I had escaped none too soon from the purely intellectual stimulus that is so damaging to more complex talent. From Quiller-Couch we had been led on to Shakespeare, the headmaster introducing *Hamlet* as a special treat to the more intelligent scholars. My reaction was again a baffling disappointment to the teacher. A thoughtful, sensitive child might have been expected to enjoy the sonorous lines of that carefully expurgated play, but its cold, worldly wisdom repelled and depressed me. Blindness was a welcome relief from the tedium of learning the soliloquies of Hamlet, the cynical lines of Polonius: "Give thy thoughts no tongue..."

This brooding on my deliverance from the school world had at first occupied my days while I sat in the downstairs rooms, in the darkest corners, my eyes covered with several bandages, thick green cloth between the folds of white linen. But as the weeks passed these bandages grew irksome, and at last they bred in me a sort of horror. I did not seem to mind the darkness so much, but the feel of cloth tied tightly round my face all day long became intolerable. After some discussion an alternative method was found, freeing my eyes from bandages while ensuring that no light reached them. We had an old square board which was pushed out above the stairway when mother papered the inner walls of the landing. This was placed in the recess about ten feet above the bottom of the stairs and became my perch from nine o'clock in the morning until bedtime. There was I, a boy of thirteen, spending twelve hours a day on a little shelf between the ridges of the landing, like some captive bird, in almost total darkness, as the bedroom doors were kept shut. Beside me on the board was a small cup containing boracic lotion and the wad of cotton wool with which I occasionally bathed my eyes to ease their smarting. When I looked over the edge of the board I could see a faint blur of light on the stairs below. But I seldom glanced down:

for hours on end I sat huddled in the corner, motionless, in a sort of dream. At meal-times mother would come part way up the stairs and drop the cup and plate on to the board. I ate little and hardly ever spoke; mother could only guess what were my thoughts, though she knew from my general manner that I felt nothing of bitterness or resentment. At intervals I would hear the sound of voices in the room below, a subdued murmur, sometimes the voices of neighbours—old Mrs. Treverton next door, or Mrs. Angilley, the claywork captain's wife from Goonamarris, mother's closest friend during those years—expressing sympathy and saying what a tragedy it was that I should be denied every normal chance of developing my talent.

It did indeed seem hard; yet it was obvious that I could go no further along the common scholastic road. Some extraordinary intervention was required to take my faculties in hand for a peculiar training if I was ever to achieve a fulfilment of personality. I know now that those few weeks of inhuman isolation at the dawn of my adolescence were an essential part of that training. They restored me to the immediate touch of the world I had vaguely apprehended during my first attack of blindness, and now that I was older and more conscious of God its terrors were changed to a cloudy apocalypse. There was a hint of creative purpose in this second dark wave that broke over me and washed off the dusty accretions of my schooldays. I was clean again, bared to the elements of life: now I could begin really to learn.

My life became entirely one of meditation; I could not even read to interrupt the flow of my consciousness. It is true mother read to me at times, but only books that were already my favourites—the Bible, *Children's Encyclopædia*, a few novels: *Westward Ho!*, Rider Haggard's *King Solomon's Mines*, *Allan Quatermain* and *Cleopatra*, and—my latest discovery before blindness came, the book that gave me my first emotional perception of adult values—Hall Caine's *The Bondman*. The rise and fall of mother's voice did not distract me; it was something outside my world, a pleasant accompaniment to my brooding, not a disturbance of it. The tremendous concentration of my whole intellectual power into self-analysis, in passionate search for the solution of the problem of my loneliness and separation—this prepared me for the prolonged solitary testing that was to come. Now that manhood was approaching I had to face the hard fact that the natural mystic is no nearer to Heaven than the natural materialist; that my individual thinking was as sure to lead to disaster as the mass thinking of the majority; and that my spiritual preoccupations in so far as they derived from my own temperament, were not Christian at all and were thus incapable of changing anything outside my own ego. There was no way of bringing these truths home to me except by letting me wander for awhile in an alien world where my natural faith could be tested against the pressure of commonplace life and character.

Before the blindness passed I had entered this new world; my stoicism was replaced by a complex and fantastic emotional turmoil that would have led hasty observers to declare me a doomed tragedian of the Rossetti-Van Gogh type. It was then, in short, that there came into my life the girl who was to be the human embodiment of the adolescent phase of my vision, the particular point of the external norm that was to shatter the paradise which my mysticism created for itself. As the relation never developed into anything remotely resembling a love affair I can write of it freely without fear of giving pain to anyone. It would be impossible to set the later emergence in true perspective if I left out all reference to the girl who, unknown to herself, first fired me with the desire for literary self-expression. The relationship began under conditions that made my reaction completely abnormal. It was not a story of calf-love, but part of the story of a nature fenced off from common promptings, behaving in a way incomprehensible to the average mind. A very slight romantic influence was sufficient to tap the spring of my creative imagination; this touch was to release over half a million words of confused, tortured writing during the next six years.

Early in April I learnt that a cousin of mine, one of the Griggs, of Penrose Veor farm, was to be married to Harry

Phillips, a young Nanpean fellow, son of a local preacher, then employed as a driver of clay-waggons. When he began courting my cousin he was in charge of the old horse-drawn delivery van of the Nanpean Co-operative Society, and during the summer holidays of 1926-7 he often took me with him on his rounds. Some of my happiest recollections of childhood are of those long rides with Harry in the creaking van, around St. Stephen, Coombe and Trelyon, past the uranium mine at Terras, then being worked by a French company for radium: the steady clicking of the horse's hoofs on the dusty road, the sweet smell of the goods in the shadows behind us, the breeze ruffling the curtains at the back, which were drawn aside when we stopped at some cottage to deliver a parcel. Harry was a welcome visitor to our home—a cheerful-looking young man with frizzy brown hair and a very prominent Adam's apple, whose buffoonery, mimicry and practical jokes were much appreciated. It was natural that mother and I should be invited to attend the wedding, and also natural that I should shrink from the humiliation of appearing before strangers as a blind, helpless youth who must be fed and guided around like a baby. But I was growing tired of my monotonous existence, literally "on the shelf," and yielded to the impulse, the craving for change.

On Saturday, April 27th, the wedding took place. I was conveyed early to Penrose by car, my eyes heavily bandaged. Spring sunshine poured down, warming me through the car windows, cuckoos were calling as we passed over Carne Hill, and at Penrose the air was drowsy with the scent of flowers, intoxicating after the close musty atmosphere of the landing which I had breathed for so many weeks. In mid-morning the bridal party went off to St. Austell, and those who remained at the farm were too busy preparing for the reception to take much notice of me. All except one—Harry's sister Evelyn, a girl a year younger than I, who seemed to take quite a possessive interest in me, hanging round my chair in front of the kitchen dresser, stroking my hair and arms, telling me I should get better soon, taking my hand and leading me to the table at meal times and into the cosy parlour in the evening. Apart from the peculiar mental state which blindness had produced, Evelyn's attentions would have meant nothing to me. They certainly meant nothing to her, though it took me six years to realize the fact. But as an impingement of the feminine quality I needed to complete the inner life I was nourishing in my isolation, they had an effect almost hypnotic. I was hypersensitive and felt the vivid, romanticized thrill of my situation— a blind boy at a wedding, caressed by a strange girl, hearing her assurance that the darkness would pass. My mind, growing dull and stolid through lack of external prompting, was challenged to express new and magical possibilities, all the more persuasive because their sensuous impact was only through sound and touch, a voice penetrating the wall of blackness that hid the speaker and left me free to idealize the mental image of her, changing it with the moods of my imagination.

It is a simple matter of fact that from that day my sight began to improve. I did not go back to the board above the stairs. I came down, and was soon able to face the light with my left eye, though everything looked blurred and fantastic. That I had a new interest in life, a new purpose, was obvious to all. The old sluggish resignation, which had seemed like stupor to onlookers who could not guess my thoughts, was gone. And before the spring had passed there came a day that I remembered vividly for years afterwards. I went to the bookcase standing then beside the kitchen stove and took out a volume at random—my sixpenny edition of *Westward Ho!* My heart was fluttering with a wild hope, my hands trembled on the leaves. I was alone in the room. Swiftly I opened the book at the last page, glanced down—then called to mother excitedly, and while she stared in amazement I read aloud the closing paragraph.

The first brief phase of my adolescent struggle was over, resulting indeterminately. I had returned to a normal world, but with a vision that was to make me increasingly an alien therein, a rebel against normal standards.

The summer of 1929 was an important one in my development, but I have no clear memory of its details. Outwardly
my life was again monotonous; I went nowhere, saw only
casual visitors, heard nothing of Evelyn. Days passed in a
dreamy rhythm of transition, vague in slow-moving beauty,
very remote from common experience. As gradually my sight
strengthened I grew familiar with an earth that seemed to
reflect and solidify the strange colours which had flamed upon
me at Penrose. I was entering spiritually into the sort of
world Browning described in *Pauline*, and as far as possible I
let Nature co-operate in adjusting my habits and valuations
to the new atmosphere. I was not yet allowed to read for more
than a few minutes a day. I spent most of the time outdoors,
lounging about the back garden hedge, lying sometimes for
hours with my face amid the long hot grass, chewing dandelions
and the acrid "greensauce" leaves, watching drowsily the white
hawthorn spray rock gently against the blue heavens or become
smudged upon cloud, the birds and butterflies fluttering over
the garden, passing beyond it until my faint sight could not
distinguish them amid the gorse, bramble and glittering sand
of the clay dump. My only companion outdoors during these
idle days was the black pomeranian dog, Gyp, and I used to
fondle him as he lay close to me or watch him dash up and
down the hedge, barking frantically at the clay-laden lorries
that rumbled by. His presence helped to assure me that the
poetic flowering at Penrose had been rooted in actual life, not
imaginary, He had been given to me two years earlier by
Evelyn's brother Harry, and by an odd coincidence he had
not only been born at Evelyn's home but had also arrived on
her ninth birthday in July 1926. Even the dog I regarded as a
symbol, a pledge of destiny.

The first practical sign of my break with the old order was
my refusal to resume attendance at Sunday-School or chapel.
I not only became a non-churchgoer but expressed open
hostility towards all forms of organized religion, sometimes in
the presence of neighbours. Rumour spread about the district
that I was spending my Sundays in aimless walks around the

Slip and Goonvean, scrambling along clay-ridges and throwing stones into the pools. Mother had to put up with a good deal of criticism from the Methodists at Trethosa. They regarded the restoration of my sight as a miracle, and it struck them as strange indeed that I, who had been so religious, should apparently feel no gratitude for my recovery but rather cease altogether to care about God.

Looking back now with fuller knowledge I can see that this first step towards a mature individual faith had landed me in a kind of pantheism. It was not that I felt any Shelleyan or Wordsworthian rapture in Nature—that was still beyond my temperamental range; but I could not recognize the chapel God in the Power that had restored my sight. God had become to me more cloudy, diffused, a vague Spirit of the universe, mystical and, of course, non-moral. This Spirit, I thought, had led me to Penrose and there drawn my darkened consciousness into the unity of its moods. The balance between intellect and emotion, dogma and poetry, that had been preserved during my childhood was rudely broken; the two elements were thrown into conflict. Adolescence had aroused and strengthened the more natural qualities, the emotional and poetic ones; the world of dogma was overwhelmed. Even the old claywork symbols were softened, richly coloured, pressed into the service of the heretical pagan tide. It was a very quiet change, owing nothing to external influences—except Evelyn, who, as a regular chapel-goer, had certainly not meant to unsettle my faith. The revolution was spontaneous; I had not been guided or prompted by books or friendships with "emancipated" young men. There was no one I could look to for advice or sympathy or enlightenment. I could only drift or grope my way through as the tide swept on or was turned aside or dissolved over rapids by an external Providence.

My mother had probably guessed that the Methodist routine at Trethosa would fail to hold me in my teen years. With my growing aversion to Sunday-School I had shown an equal distaste for the ordinary chapel services. They had begun to bore me when revivalist fervour was replaced by the cold rationality of an ethic. The old preachers were the only ones I could bear to listen to; they so obviously had what I wanted, the peculiar combination of dogma and joy which none of the younger, more educated men possessed. The victory of the old over the young was therefore the only thing that could have kept me in touch with the chapel. The young people may have been honest and sincere enough in their aims, but these aims were not theological and they were certainly not joyful in their attainments. It was obvious that the Church was not their true element. In an atmosphere of pure worship they were miserable and restless, and as soon as they gained a measure of control they hastened to bring in a little colour and modernity from the world in which they were really at home. Their flight from God, their fear of the direct contemplation of Him when all the trappings of art, Nature and cultural media had been stripped away, was to me a pathetic and alienating portent. Only the old believers who were not afraid to be drawn into God and filled by Him could save the situation; and when I saw that their defeat was inevitable I began to look elsewhere than to the churches for the continuation of Christianity.

Cold-blooded people who interpret religion in terms of common sense will no doubt find this confession insufferable. They will attribute my taste to a morbid craving for emotionalism. But such persons are scarcely competent to judge at what level of religious experience emotion becomes morbid. The true vision of love, when at last it came to me, was not at all morbid, but it was religious in the profoundest sense—in the sense that the human attachment through which it developed would have been silly or monstrous had I not seen in it a new altar for the flame of dogma that had been quenched in the churches.

With this personal background it is inevitable that I should be somewhat irritated by the assertion, made on every hand, that youth during this period turned away from the churches because of their indifference to social reform, their failure to adapt their teaching to the advance of scientific thought and throw off the shackles of outworn theology. So far as I am concerned the facts were entirely the other way. To my basic mystical needs the whole temper and policy of the "progressive" churches was irrelevant. They were concerned solely with the ideals of comradeship and friendliness—qualitities which are the first to be blunted by a genuine religious experience, though they are renewed at a deeper level as the spiritual life matures. I knew there was no room for me in a church that made no provision for this initial anti-social phase of Christian experience, a church which, though founded to be the channel of that mystical disruptive power, was actually embarrassed when the power broke through its superficial routine and isolated a soul in naked spiritual vision. The fact that my vision became perverse and blasphemous was due mainly to original sin in myself—I could not be a Calvinist and deny that; but I may perhaps, without uncharitableness, imply that my teen years might have been less wayward had there been fewer Modernists and worldlings in control of Cornish Methodism.

My mother, though troubled by my early break with religious convention, felt that God must answer her prayers in His own way; and during these months when actually I was floundering towards chaos I would sometimes make a remark that reassured her, hardly knowing myself what I meant by it. I remember telling her how clearly I had come to see that the Bible and the modern Church taught two different religions. and that I preferred the religion of the Bible, a religion of supernaturalism and miracle. I would let the Church go its own way to its own heaven, a social Utopia which contained nothing I wanted. Mother thought my decision merely a rash expression of her own point of view. She was beginning to have grave doubts about the tendency of the churches. It was not John Polmounter's faith that she found at Trethosa chapel now. She continued to pray earnestly for me—little guessing that every night just before supper-time I went with Gyp across Bloomdale fields, climbed the clay-dump and from its summit looked out eastward to Nanpean, Evelyn's home. A religion that could scarcely be called Biblical then welled within me, aching with the flare of sunset on the village, the cool evening breeze raking out scents from the gorse clumps on the dune, the flowers around the clay-pit and the cornfields of Goonamarris ripening below. I was alone on the ridge, far up against the sky, childhood behind me, the mysterious goal in view, there in the gathering twilight—Nanpean. A strange romantic exaltation possessed me, like that which D. H. Lawrence often described—the sense of being at the back of creation, waiting for the god to stoop and touch into concrete fact the world I saw as nebulæ among those shapes and hues. This romantic excess was absurd enough in a boy of thirteen, but essential to the pattern, for it pinned me down to that inhuman vision until my creative power had strengthened and could get to work upon it. There was no other possible opening to my literary life, and meanwhile I could not have expressed my feelings in writing even had the state of my eyes allowed me to do so.

There were practical discussions at home that balanced these dreamy moods. My future in a financial sense was now to mother a grave problem. It was useless for me to think any longer of becoming a sky-tip worker, though, during those evening vigils on Bloomdale tip, I yearned for it more than ever, drawn by the æsthetic thrill of working up there among the clouds and the free winds, aloof from the tiny human figures moving on the roads and fields. Mother had latterly hoped that I might get a soft job at Treviscoe Co-operative stores, but this also was ruled out as my sight was still defective and the journey to Treviscoe in winter through the morning darkness, past the clay-pit and the unfenced tanks of Goonvean, would be hazardous. Apart from the physical risk, I knew that I should find such work uncongenial. I did not feel that measuring paraffin in a village store was beneath my dignity—my ideal of dignity being that of a tramp or a savage; but indoor work seemed effeminate, and the thought of being cooped up with other youths was a nightmare to me.

So the year passed, and my fourteenth birthday found the

position not materially changed. My sight was by that time almost normal in the left eye, though the right one was permanently impaired, incapable of correct focusing. The verdict of all the doctors who had examined me was dead against any studious pursuits. For the next few years I must practically live in the open air and, as one of them emphatically phrased it, "must not even look at a book." With characteristic indifference to the advice of experts I had spent most of the winter indoors, reading voraciously everything I could lay hands on, from Edgar Wallace thrillers to Jehovah's Witness tracts. Many of the sixpenny reprints of classics and popular novels had found their way into my home, loaned by neighbours and relatives or bought by mother at Woolworth's or local newsagents. I was rapidly gaining a realistic, adult knowledge of the world. Tolstoy's *Resurrection* and *Anna Karenina*, Hugo's *Les Miserables* and Daudet's *Sapho* brought close and palpitating the tragic undertones of life. I felt no morbid fascination and very little shock as I grew aware of sexual horror, organized vice, the crude appetite of physical love. I realized later, when mother told me of the Clemo's, of my father's emotional disharmony, the real nature of Hetty's madness, why I accepted this side of human behaviour without fastidious recoil or prurient curiosity. Knowledge of sexual perversion could not unsettle me because in a sense—though I had never committed or imagined the practices I read about —it was already a part of my nature.

This mental stimulus quickened the growth of my own literary power, and in the spring of 1930 the break came. One day when mother and I were discussing afresh the few occupations that were open to me I remarked hesitatingly, on an impulse: "What about if I was to write stories like—like they 'Ockings?" Mother was bewildered by the idea and regarded it as quixotic, a passing whim. I do not remember much of our early talks on the subject, but they must have been very strained, for I could not bring myself to mention the prompting motive, the impact of destiny I had felt at Penrose, which was becoming more and more dreamlike and idealized as months passed with no further development. But whatever mother's attitude may have been, I soon found the writing urge to be independent of encouragement from without. I had produced my first real story, a crude, sentimental love tale. Mother read it and was so impressed that she wrote out a fair copy on a dozen sheets of an exercise book and sent the manuscript to one of the religious weeklies. We prayed very earnestly that it would be accepted—but within a few days it was returned, accompanied by the first of the two hundred rejection slips I was to receive during my apprenticeship. Mother shared my depression at this set-back. "If God meant 'ee to write stories, 'E would take what you wrote," she said. This acute theological problem—the idea of God inspiring a man to write yet refusing everything he produced—was to burden mother for many years to come, though my dogged persistence assured her at last that there must be a Divine purpose in this artistic struggle. She knew nothing of literary technique and could not help me at all in the mechanical side of my work. But there seemed no other way in which I could earn my living; and if I always aimed at preaching in my stories it would not be exactly sinful. . . .

Reminder of the Hockings gave mother an idea for our next move. Hearing that Joseph Hocking lived at Hayle, thirty miles off, she ventured to write him a letter, telling him of my predicament and mentioning the probable derivation of my talent from his family through Esther. Whether he was irked at the recollection of Esther's marriage I do not know, but a few days later we received a rather curt little note from him, regretting that owing to ill-health he could not help us, and adding: "As to the lad of whom you spoke, he, if he has the real stuff in him, will make his way. . . . He must persist in *doing his best* and then sending his work to what seems the most likely quarters until he succeeds." This advice was vague and left us where we were before, except that it caused a good deal of self-analysis on my part to try and discover whether my talent was the "real stuff" or not.

We were not left long in doubt: recovering from the double

disappointment my creative faculty broke out in a new and unexpected direction. In rummaging among the pile of old papers and magazines on top of our dresser I had come upon several copies of *Netherton's Almanack*, a Cornish annual that had been published at Truro since 1847. It contained humorous sketches written in broad Cornish dialect. The comic atmosphere was infectious, a welcome corrective of my own morbid drift, and soon I had surprised myself by writing a story of the same type—a piece of sheer buffoonery that brightened our home and brought more laughter into it than anything had done since my blindness. I sent the yarn to Netherton's office at Truro and a few weeks later received a letter from the editor, accepting the tale and offering half a guinea for it.

This stroke of good fortune changed the whole outlook; my gratitude brought for awhile a more healthy tone into my religion. The release of humour had checked my lawless mysticism, and in this respect that first published effort of mine is of some psychological interest. I had found the element so much needed to balance the weight of spiritual vision which was to be so oppressive and tormenting in my heterodox moods. After writing the first comic story I knew the trick and practised it instinctively whenever mysticism reached the danger point. Often during the next few years when I was under the pressure of religious perversion a ludicrous phrase or incident would flash across my mind, and within five minutes I would be throwing off the stagnant gloom by writing something hilariously funny. Most of the stories so written were sold, and few who laughed over them could have guessed that they were such desperately defensive products. There were many grotesque reflections from my own childhood in them, scarcely recognized as memories until the tales were perused in tranquility. One of them contained a dialect description of the linhay we had before our zinc wash-house was built, and a comic account of the sort of accident which I daresay had happened to me when as a boy I possessed a wheelbarrow:

"The linney was a lil freck of a place out beside the house—lil old shanty wi' a roof full o' holes an' a broke winda, Charlie went across to un and flinged open the door. Inside 'twas gettin' dum already and he could hardly see proper what was there. He catched sight o' the barra handles sticked up over a lime bucket, and stanked fore to grab 'em. 'Twas some job to git the thing out, for the floor was in some pickle. There was wood boxes an' jam-pots an' pails all strewed around, anyhow, an' the wheel o' the barra was catched in behind a saucepan with a cabbage in un and two turnips. Charlie haled to they handles some force, and all of a sudden the contraption gived away. Over went a box full of earth, right on top of a jam-pot, scattin' of'n to sherds; over went the saucepan and cabbage an' turnips come rollin' across the linney, bunk agin Charlie's feet. He'd been pulling so hard he couldn' save hisself, and back he went too, wallop on the floor, wi' the barra on top of un...."

Charlie was going to the downs for a load of "smutties"— another recollection of my childhood's practice; but finding the barrow broken he has to fetch the sticks in his arms. Before he begins to pick them his sweetheart, Susie, comes along, wheeling a neighbour's baby in a pram. Susie is very distressed:

' "I dunno wot to do by un. He want his dummy. An' I left un behind. 'Tis wished goin' on like this here."
' "Awful," ses Charlie, wagging his head down at the mite in the pram. In some tantrums the chiel was, yowlin' 'pon top of his voice. "Ought to do zummin', Susie, why, people will think you be tearin' the beggar up...." '

Susie persuades him to mind the baby while she runs back to the village for the dummy-teat. She is so long fetching it that Charlie uses the pram as a wheelbarrow, loading it with the charred furze twigs:

"He hadn't got a yard afore the wheels bunked up agin a stone and the sticks falled fore, right in on top o' the baby. Charlie reached over and grabbed 'em and pulled 'em back, but he couldn't undo what was done. The chiel's face and eyes was plastered with smut, and his lil woolly 'at was spotted up shockin', and so was his bed-cloas.

" 'I've done it now,' ses Charlie to hisself, and he glaazed around, trying to hide in behind the pram. He didn' dare go no further, the chiel would be smothered in smut; as 'twas he was coughin' it up as if 'twas chokin' of'n.

Another ten minutes and he'd catched sight o' Susie coming—good way off, right over other end the downs. But by that time he was worked up to such pitch he couldn't stay to face her. Leavin' pram an' baby an' smutties he scoot back to the road and down the hill to his home...."*

I do not know what a psycho-analyst would read into this, considering it as a sudden explosive release from religious obsession. For all I know the dummy teat may be a Freudian symbol illuminating my emotional disharmonies. At any rate, this is the only kind of fiction I got into print before I was thirty, and it was certainly ironic that during the most painful years of my mystical development, years in which I experienced no personal happiness or gaiety of heart, I should appear before the Cornish public chiefly as a purveyor of slapstick.

It was more than a year after the Penrose wedding before I met Evelyn Phillips again. The thrill of my success with Netherton was still fresh when Evelyn's parents invited mother and me to take tea at their home one Sunday, the occasion of an anniversary service at Nanpean chapel. In great agitation of mind I went with mother to the strange, fateful house—one of a long block of modern houses at the top of the village—and the mysterious Vision of Penrose became in an instant something more solid. The impact of form and colour made the vision complete, but it also disturbed a conception so exclusively ideal. Evelyn was there—a plump, dark-eyed girl of thirteen with a mass of brown curls, sharply contrasting with her younger sister Ada, who was then thin and straight-haired. Evelyn was glad my sight had returned, and stared at me with a new fascination when she learnt that I meant to be

* "Charlie, the Smutties and the Baby": *Netherton's Almanack*, Christmas 1935.

an author and that my first story had already been taken; but she obviously guessed nothing of the part she had played.

Before breakfast next day I had written my first "poem," a melancholy lyric called "The Dreams of Yesterday." That too, though in itself a trifle, marked a turning-point in my adolescent career. It led to my disclosure of the secret impulse that was impelling me in my writing, and it also brought us into financial straits. Mother read it and looked serious, as if it confirmed suspicions she had harboured for some time. She commented deliberately at once: "I believe seein' Evelyn yesterday 'ad somethin' to do wi' this." I flushed and stammered a denial, but had soon unburdened my mind and begun to talk vaguely and defensively about "inspiration." Mother was perplexed; she had never before heard of such a thing. I showed her the account of Dante and Beatrice in the *Children's Encyclopædia* and told her my experience was like that. She remarked that "it do seem very strange," and later added in a tone of foreboding: "Dant' didn' marry 'er." I assented with glum irritation. No, of course, it had nothing to do with marriage. . . .

Soon afterwards we saw an advertisement of one of the fee-snatching music publishers, inviting lyrics. I sent along my effort and received a flattering report upon it. Undoubtedly the lyric would achieve great popularity if it were set to music and published, and their fee for these offices was only £15. Mother's little nest-egg had dwindled to £20 by this time, but thinking that success all along the line would follow my advance at Truro she paid the fee. The song duly appeared in 1931, and less than a score of copies were sold. Mother lost £13 on the venture and was more than ever convinced that my attachment to some Ideal Beauty incarnate in Miss Phillips was to bring me no good.

Meanwhile I had turned to the rejected short story, and the lengthening of that occupied me during the remaining months of 1930. Stimulated by half-a-dozen other visits to Evelyn's home—always in mother's company—ideas and incidents flooded upon my mind, sometimes keeping me downstairs till after midnight, crouched over the kitchen table, the oil lamp standing just in front of me, so near that its heat made my face sweat as I scribbled, filling page after page of an exercise book. I made the hero of the tale flee to America and got away from the Cornish setting in the more romantic background of the Rocky Mountains. The story ended with a girl confessing to the hero that she was going to have a baby—an astonishing climax to a novel written by a boy of fourteen. Mother read it and was probably pained, but she had decided that the whole thing was beyond her judgment or control, and never tried to interfere with my self-expression even when it wounded and shocked her. She did not keep my activities a secret and soon the whole district knew that I had adopted writing as a full-time career. At first there was a good deal of scepticism— so much, indeed, that I paused in the writing of my novel to throw off a few subsidiary efforts which appeared in print during the autumn and winter to confound the doubters. In October I contributed my first Press letter, on "Books for Boys" —in which I pleaded that boys of fourteen should read love stories instead of thrillers—to the *Cornish Guardian*; in November a poem of mine was printed in *The Christian Herald*; at Christmas the *Netherton's Almanack* yarn appeared; and in January 1931 a letter about Gyp, with his photograph, was published in *The Tail-Wagger Magazine*. This barrage compelled local people to see that I possessed a little talent, and on the whole they did not extend the sympathy one might have expected them to show towards a boy so severely handicapped. Mother received anonymous letters denouncing her as a hypocrite for letting me write such twaddle. My old headmaster was at first very interested in these developments, and when my novel was finished he read it and praised it in Trethosa school. But when, soon afterwards, I began to make a local uproar through Press letters about sex and salvationism, his attitude changed to something less than a polite tolerance.

The educationists—pledged to encourage and assist youthful ability in its struggle for recognition—were eager to wash their hands of me; my own generation, to which I would

naturally turn for fellowship, met me with a blank stare; while
ordinary villagers remarked pointedly to mother: "I dunno
'ow Jack can write—'e dunt *look* clever": which was true
enough. Snapshots taken at this period show me glowering
and dishevelled, more like an illiterate "dead-end kid" than
an intelligent youth.

The only outsiders who sympathized and believed in my
future were the old, uneducated Methodists, one in particular
—Colly Bullock of Barrakellis farm, the most primitive
Christian among our immediate neighbours. A small sinewy
man, rather grim-looking with his shaggy moustache and
eyebrows, he stopped at our home almost every Sunday on his
way back from chapel, and usually delivered a sermon of his
own in the road outside before going on down the hill to
Barrakellis. His religion had a rude energy that appealed to
me as much as it disgusted the refined young moderns at the
chapel. Having known him throughout my childhood I had
first-hand proof that Victorian prudery was confined to the
educated and less Christian classes: the crudity of his speech
on delicate subjects was often embarrassing to the polite.
Some of the most vivid memories of my childhood are of
return journeys from Trethosa chapel on winter evenings when
Colly and his wife accompanied my mother, my aunt and
myself—Colly pouring streams of religious eloquence into the
cold night air, frequently stopping in the moonlit road and
keeping us all grouped round him for several minutes while he
whirled his walking-stick around at the shadowy bushes to
emphasise his comments. On weekday evenings he would
sometimes come up to our cottage, bringing his concertina,
and would hold me spellbound as he sang and played the old
Cornish songs and Sankey hymns. The barbaric fervour of
Colly's cracked voice and swinging limbs gave me a glimpse
of the dark pulsing heart of a Christian past of such rich vitality
that it made paganism, whether ancient or modern, seem an
anæmic counterfeit. His spiritual realism enabled him to
sympathize with my aims, and one day while mother was
explaining to him as best she could the strange "vision" that

had come to me at Penrose and the subsequent urge to develop it in writing, Colly broke in vehemently: "Dunt you worry about that boy, Mrs. Clema. I'll never doubt 'e's a Christian. God's leadin' of 'n where 'E dunt lead very many." I was touched by this assurance, and felt afresh my kinship with these old people, naïve illiterates who traced all unusual experiences to the direct working of God.

It was fitting, therefore, that the next practical step should come through a man of this simple, robust type. There was one person at Trethosa who had heard of my predicament and had some idea of the humiliations that awaited me as a working-class boy with hardly any schooling to help me forward; and his old warrior soul blazed up in a resolve to do something about it. This man was Sam Jacobs, the pioneer of the Labour Party in the district. Some account of him is given by A. L. Rowse in *A Cornish Childhood*; but I knew Sam Jacobs rather better than Rowse did. Sam was one of the most emphatic Nonconformists in mid-Cornwall, a leader at Trethosa chapel, for several years my Sunday-School superintendent there. We children were a little awed by his gaunt figure: he looked stern and seemed to be always agitated about something, eyes fiery under the bushy white brows, voice harsh, gestures aggressive: a born fighter. After he joined the Labour Party he became involved in the class-war that politics brought into many village chapels during the period, and at length he withdrew his support from Trethosa Methodism as the Modernist Tory element gained the whip-hand. But piety inspired him to the end in his crusade for social righteousness.

Sam had been deeply moved by the calamity of my blindness, and when he heard that I meant to be a writer in spite of all obstacles he sought out mother and asked what help she thought I most needed. Mother confessed that I was making no headway financially and that she had no idea how I was ever to earn a living by my pen. Special training was no doubt required: we had heard there were schools that gave tuition by correspondence, but we could not afford the fees. (The money

that would have paid them had been thrown away on that
ridiculous song, but we didn't tell Sam that.) He determined
that such a course of instruction should be provided for me,
and set about his task with characteristic vigour. He badgered
the British Legion, the Ministry of Pensions and other societies
which he thought were under an obligation to help me in my
plight, left fatherless by the War. The rebuffs he received
from the guardians of snobbery and red tape sent the iron into
his soul—far more than they did into mine. I was not, indeed,
particularly anxious to obtain help, the financial side of the
business did not interest me. Sam knew nothing of my temperament; he saw me only as a struggling proletarian. I remember
that when he reported the British Legion's curt dismissal of
my case he spoke of the financial aid granted by the Legion
to other young fellows who did not need it, sons of local gentry
who had lost some relative in the War. His indignation was so
great that he exclaimed: "Mrs. Clema, if I wasn't a Christian
'twould make me swear!" But at length the temptation to
swear was not so acute: Sam came over to Goonamarris with
a letter from the Ministry of Pensions office at Plymouth
requesting him to submit a specimen of my work. The only
story I had then got into print was the *Netherton's Almanack*
yarn, and Sam looked at this rather doubtfully, as if he
wondered whether the Ministry officials would be able to
make head or tail of it, written as it was in broad Cornish
dialect. However, he went off with the almanack in his pocket,
and a few weeks later came again, obviously proud of his
triumph. A grant had been made so that I could take a course
of tuition in short story writing with one of the best-known
London Schools of Journalism.

In the summer of 1931 I was enrolled as a pupil of this
correspondence school. But it was soon apparent that Sam's
fiery crusading on my behalf had been, from a financial standpoint, a pitiful waste. Gordon Meggy never had a more
exasperating pupil. He was plainly disappointed and perplexed.
I had plenty of ability, yet, somehow, it refused to shape under
his hands into any profitable mould. He continually changed

his tactics. He advised me to write light love stories to counter
my tendency to gloom, then remarked that I seemed to do
better with more serious and dramatic material. He sent me
bundles of popular weeklies and told me to model my fiction
on the tales they contained, and when he read my attempts
he counselled me to concentrate on my novel, "in which you
seem to be really interested." I sent him the novel—by that
time a wholly Cornish story again: I soon outgrew my Wild
West sympathies—and he declared it to be hopeless. (It was,
of course: forty thousand words in childish imitation of Hall
Caine melodrama.) He then forwarded, free of cost, the
complete article-writing course, explaining that it was easier
to begin with articles than with fiction. But my articles were
even worse than my stories: I told him that I must re-write the
novel, and he agreed that this appeared to be my true medium
"as you do not seem to take kindly to the popular type of
contribution."

The fact was that the whole process jarred on my temperament, exerting the same repressive influence as the last examination at school in which I had failed so dismally. I loathed the
set exercises, the deliberate copying of published work, the
preparing of synopses. I was irked and paralysed by the mechanical atmosphere, repelled by the sneers at "inspiration,"
the polite hints to avoid religious subjects, and outraged by the
idea that writing should be a lucrative hobby. The cheap
superficiality of popular fiction—all about sport, office and
hotel life, glamour—was antipathetic to me, and I made a
dreadful hash of conversations when told they must be "crisp
and snappy." I was coming at that time deeply under the
influence of Victor Hugo, and I wished my characters to have
the grandeur and dignity of those in *Les Miserables* and *Notre
Dame de Paris*. It was a torture to be diverted from this to the
slick sophistication of the modern social scene, to gay little
friendships and trivial matings in which neither God nor sex
seemed to be involved. I was living in a remote country area
where modern slang had not yet penetrated, and was naturally
irritated by the sharp, staccato, cinematographic style of the

contemporary writing to which Meggy introduced me. I felt instinctively that the chief thing that mattered in literature, if it was to be a profound and moving revelation, was *intensity*, and I felt that, as Hardy says in *The Return of the Native*, "intensity was more usually reached by way of the solemn than by way of the brilliant." And my first glimpse of current literary movements showed me that they were working on the opposite principle: a contemptuous repudiation of solemnity, an emphasis on brilliance without soul or depth. Once again I found myself in the wrong world, a misfit.

The course of tuition should have lasted only six months, but it was extended by various means to nearly two years. Meggy would not drop me until he had done his utmost to set me working with the efficient regularity of an automaton. My contact with him ended in the autumn of 1933 with his report on my first full-length novel, which I had written in my own way, guided by only a few technical hints from him. His main criticism of it was that my characters were "unnatural": they quoted the Bible while making love—though not, of course, the dogmatic parts of the Bible. The hero was obsessed with the idea that the spiritual presence of his young sister, who had died, was sanctifying his relation with his girl, which would otherwise have been "carnal." The book showed clearly my morbid fear of the physical side of life, and that I was trying to escape into a negatively spiritual world which I regarded as a poetic and purified form of Christianity. I had to create characters in my own image, even if it meant that nothing I wrote was ever published. And Meggy seemed confident that I should ultimately succeed, despite this wild unworldliness and lack of practical sense.

He failed with me, as any tutor must have failed; but he was a true friend, and I was grateful for his kindly interest and the genuine enthusiasm of his encouragement. When I showed moods of depression he would write vigorously: "Don't be too humble; work away. You can do it. It's because you have so much grit in your character that I am taking such trouble with you." It was he—in association with the local rector—who badgered the Ministry of Pensions into giving me a typewriter—the machine on which all my subsequent work has been typed; and he did his best—a vain battle with red tape, alas!—to get my pension extended beyond the age of sixteen on the grounds that I was not able to earn my own living while a pupil of his correspondence school.

CHAPTER SIX

Pursuit of the Ideal

OTHER and more important happenings than my beginning
a course of journalistic training marked for me the year
1931. One of the most vital of them was unrecognized at the
time as having any connection with my own life. At the end
of April a daughter was born to a young couple named Rowse,
who had just become our next-door neighbours, the Trevertons
having shifted to Nanpean the previous year. Early in May I
saw the girl, learnt that she had been called Barbara, and felt
only the vague uneasiness which youths are wont to exhibit
in the presence of very young babies. I little guessed that before
that girl was ten years old she would have set my feet on the
road that led to spiritual stability, clear vision and even
material success. At fifteen, I was not conscious of wanting
any of those things. I wanted only to explore my new world
of the Ideal: and destiny seemed eager to gratify my wishes.
Events began to move me inexorably towards Evelyn.

When Barbara was a few months old my mother came in one
day with a copy of Hall Caine's *The Manxman*, which she had
bought at a local newsagent's. As she handed it to me I
observed something strained and shocked in her manner, and
in reply to my question she revealed the news which she had
just heard in the village.

Mr. Phillips, Evelyn's father, had been blinded in a claywork accident.

It may be imagined how a temperament like mine, with its
almost superstitious regard for signs and omens, received this
announcement. I recall the hushed, remote mood in which I
spent the days immediately following, reading *The Manxman*—
a book that fitted the hour: the story of an intellectual young
man fascinated by the daughter of a local preacher. That
Evelyn's father, whom I had heard preach at Trethosa chapel

during my childhood, should lose his sight just as I had recovered mine, was surely proof of a fated attachment between us. I was awed, preparing myself for the possibilities; and within a few weeks the way to Nanpean opened as if by magic.

Evelyn's brother Harry, now living at Penrose Veor Farm, was thrown out of work as horse-drawn waggons became obsolete for clay transport. He soon found a job as driver of a milk van for a farmer near Grampound who was extending his round to the St. Austell district. Harry offered to give me rides in the car as he had done in the old Co-op. waggon before his marriage, and from the summer of 1931 until the spring of 1932, I walked on several mornings a week to Foxhole to meet the milk van as it came out from St. Austell. I rode to Nanpean and thence back around Rostowrack to Goonamarris. Harry usually stopped at his parents' home for a cup of tea, and I too would be invited indoors. Thus I was seeing Evelyn nearly every day, though only for five or ten minutes at a time. But the brief contact was enough to keep me bursting with inspiration: always after returning from Nanpean I sat at the kitchen table pouring out thousands of words for the rest of the day, sometimes late into the night, in a mood of ecstatic detachment from mundane affairs.

The Phillips's, of course, guessed nothing of the motive that had made me accept Harry's offer so eagerly. Evelyn was still in her fifteenth year, too young to begin a courtship even had I wished for such a development; and I certainly had no thought of it. Neither then not later was I "in love" with her in the ordinary sense. I felt for her that entirely unholy reverence, that "desire of the moth for the star," which Christianity so roughly handles in its doctrine of original sin. I wanted only to live in the mingled bliss and agony of this creative fire, conscious of her, of fate lengthening the pattern towards some vague permanence untouched by the grossness of practical life. My stubborn resistance against Meggy's efforts to make my work saleable is proof that I did not want a common love affair. I reached my sixteenth birthday in this fashion, quite content to be earning about £1 a year.

CONFESSION OF A REBEL

After a few months of such smooth progress there came another sudden break; I was driven to adopt a more conventional approach and somewhat to unmask my purpose. The frequent exposure to cold and rain as I waited in the mornings for Harry's van had impaired my health, and various persons objected to my presence among the milk bottles. They told Harry that I was obviously consumptive and that my coughing would infect the milk. (A false charge: though I had been delicate I had no trace of tuberculosis: fortunately for me, neither the Clemos nor the Polmounters had ever been tainted with it.) At first Harry tried to laugh these complaints aside, but as irate housewives threatened to withdraw their custom he was forced reluctantly to drop me. When the news reached the Phillips's they made it clear that I could still call on them any evening if I thought it worth while to stroll up for a chat. I was grateful for this, though humiliated by the ignominious end of what I had considered an intervention of Providence.

My visits to Nanpean thereafter were not so frequent, but I stayed several hours each time. The atmosphere became more homely and I disclosed my general literary aims to the whole family; never especially to Evelyn. She sat knitting or sewing and listened to the talk, or played the gramophone: all very static. She was never more than friendly and was often rather cold, ill at ease, as she began to realize that I was oddly different from other village youths. Sometimes I would bring a short story I had written and read the manuscript aloud. The family listened politely as a rule, but occasionally there would be an interruption, some squabble developing between Evelyn and her sister Ada or her brother Fred, so that I had to stop reading until someone's hair had been pulled and a chair or two upset. Being an only child I was distressed at these family manners; they did not fit into my ideal world at all.

My company was, I think, more welcome to Mr. Phillips than to Evelyn herself. I could discuss with him theological bookish questions in which his wife and children were not interested. He was a pathetic figure slumped at the table, sometimes fumbling with a Braille manual—a very thin, sharp-faced, nervous man, then in the middle fifties. A rigid Evangelical, studious by nature, Phillips had been warped by an uncongenial atmosphere both at home and in the Church. He had also suffered a fate similar to Sam Jacobs' through the encroachment of politics on the religious life of the district. And the warping process was completed by something like a monomania on the subject of smoking. He would not admit any man to be a Christian unless he gave up tobacco, and his bitterness towards the churches became almost fanatical when his own sons justified their smoking by pointing to the example of local ministers who indulged in the habit.

Phillips was a life-long champion of lost causes, and by the time I met him the strain had grown intolerable. Blindness had struck him; he was also becoming deaf; he had few friends and towards these his attitude was moody, erratic. I admired and pitied him; there was a curious bond of sympathy between us. We were both rebels against the shallow geniality of modern Methodism; for both of us blindness had made a final separation from the church. In our religious outlook we seemed to have much in common, for I was always careful not to offend his susceptibilities and as far as possible expressed my primitivism in Biblical terms at the Phillips's, keeping my perversions and heresies to shock mother with at home. I was not aware of any inconsistency or hypocrisy in the practice; it was an instinctive form of self-defence. And I certainly did regard myself as a Christian—of a peculiar sort— throughout this period. It was agreeable and stimulating to find that for Phillips also Christianity meant that elemental, ultimate faith which sees in reason the subtle anti-Christ and cries with Tertullian: "I believe because it is absurd."

He little dreamed in what way my faith was absurd, and that when I returned to Goonamarris a world of fantastic illusion fused again and flamed out like a blasphemous star. Pure belief that abases intellectual pride was to come and triumph in me, but not before the Phillips's home had witnessed ugly scenes that probably made Phillips doubt whether I could be a Christian at all.

The most important of my literary developments during the year 1931 was my emergence as a Press controversialist. The only public evidence of my spiritual growth until I entered my thirties is to be found in the files of the *Cornish Guardian*, in the chaotic, inflammatory letters, and a few immature poems, which I contributed to that paper. The phase is therefore more noteworthy than such things usually are in the life of a novelist. I was not writing in order to "succeed" in a worldly sense, but to communicate a vision. As long as my ideas reached the public I didn't care whether they appeared in a novel or a newspaper controversy. I owe a great deal to the publicity which the editor of the *Cornish Guardian*, A. Browning Lyne, gave me during the years of my struggle.

My first two duels were with men over seventy—a fact which revealed from yet another angle that my sympathies and contacts were never likely to be normal. All the men who helped to develop me during my teens were elderly. For the young people, especially the educated ones, the County School tribe, I did not exist: in my scores of controversies I never had a youthful opponent. The young simply were not interested in the subjects that engrossed me—the non-social or anti-social visions of the mystical-moral borderline. From the outset I was forced to realize how shallow is the common assumption that the essential conflict is between "crabbed age and youth." The deadliest hostility is not between age-groups but between types of character. The gulf between the mystical teen-ager and the mystical septuagenarian is less broad than that between the adolescent mystic and the adolescent materialist. Always, even during my childhood, I had been aware that I did not fit into my own generation: it was the old folk who understood, whose eyes still looked upon the world I yearned to enter, the crude pulsating world of faith and emotion stripped and glowing with the elemental obstinacy of the child-consciousness.

It was a debate on "Youth and immoral novels" that provided the first stimulating exchange of ideas. My friendly antagonist was A. J. G. Hawken, commonly known as the Sage of Fraddon—a queer character, a scholar who, after taking his M.A. degree at Oxford, had returned to Cornwall and spent the rest of his life in writing letters to the Press, chiefly on religious questions. He countered my defence of realism in fiction by asserting the supremacy of the ideal, and as I was then bogged in the sickliest idealism I felt the self-contradiction of my attitude and partly agreed with him.

At Christmas 1931 a letter of mine on sex and religion was challenged by a man whose influence on me was to be more intimate than Hawken's and with whom I kept up a private correspondence until his death in 1939. This was S. E. Burrow, a Cornishman who had settled at Bournemouth after a long and adventurous life spent mainly in evangelistic work among the Forces abroad. Burrow had also been an editor and was the author of several story books of a pious, Victorian type. He had contributed since 1926 a weekly column of dialect material to the *Cornish Guardian*, humorous but edged with biting sarcasm when he touched on controversial aspects of modern life. He approached me from the start with the prejudices of an antipathetic temperament. He was one of those hard-headed Evangelicals who haven't a scrap of poetic or æsthetic appreciation in their natures, yet manage to translate the mysticism of the Gospels into living reality—which natural mystics often fail to do. His concern for me was genuinely Christian: recognizing "unusual promise" in my talent, he wished to claim it for God. While castigating me in the Press he assured me in private letters that he had great hopes of my future but felt that if these were to be realized he must "write somewhat sharply sometimes." In his earliest Press attack he referred to my "curious mentality," dismissed me as "a priggish, self-inflated dogmatist who has tried to look clever by putting on grandmother's horn-rimmed spectacles," and when I had replied to this, very seriously, repeating my claim that children were missing the real significance of Christmas through the prudery of parents who kept sex knowledge from them, he filled a column with doggerel verse intended as a lampoon, and ended with a few words in prose, calling me sarcastically "a patriarch of fifteen who can hold forth like a professor on the mysteries of parturition." Comment of this sort exhilarated me more than the printing of my stories, which after the first had appeared in *Netherton's Almanack*, was a tame business, leading nowhere, as cheques meant nothing to me. The budding egoist preferred personal remarks, however rude, a recognition of my individuality. The permanent good of this verbal trouncing lay in its toughening of my mind and broadening of my outlook, and the more objective view of myself which it forced me to take in self-defence.

I do not know whether it was my dialect tales or my Press letters that led to the next development, but considering my temperamental bias it was an inevitable if very regrettable lapse. Leaders of the Cornish Celtic Movement also recognized the promise in my effusions and made their bid for the use of my talent. They wrote to me explaining the aims of the movement and inviting my support. The novelty of the challenge fired my imagination, and for awhile I laboured to enter heart and soul into the distinctive Celtic spirit. I cultivated a proper disdain of everything English and persuaded myself that pure Celtic ancestry was the probable explanation of my "difference" from all other youths in the district. That the phase was a brief side-tracking of my romantic enthusiasm is evident from a controversy I had with the Grand Bard of Cornwall, Morton Nance, in 1935, in which I denounced the Cornish "national" movement as a misguided, futile and wasteful effort—a view which I still hold. There were too many people in Cornwall at that time who did not seem to be interested in anything that had happened since 1777, when Dolly Pentreath died—the last person known to have used Cornish as a natural language. The groups of students all over Cornwall who were giving time and energy to the revival of that local and spent dialect would have been better employed in learning German so that they might read *Mein Kampf* in the original. My own life, however, was then as remote from current politics as it would have been had I been confined to some moorland cell built by an early Cornish saint. The sudden glow from the past, with its hint of mystery, was an extension of my dream world. I read everything I could find about ancient Cornwall, and wrote poems about its legends, customs and prehistoric atmosphere. Some of these were published, and with the few shillings I received for them I bought a Cornish grammar. I sprinkled my stories with Cornish phrases copied from the text-book, learnt the Cornish equivalent of many simple English phrases, and amused the Phillips's by repeating them at Nanpean. Evelyn listened with growing irritation. All this took me further from the practical, everyday world she inhabited. I must have bored her with my talk of the Gorsedd, the *Tyr ha Tavas* (Land and Language) cult, the Old Cornwall Societies; and when I prophesied that I would one day become a bard, standing amid some hut circle in my ceremonial robes, recognized by the crowd at last as a remote and mystic personage—well, she was sensible and refused to be interested.

These visions were too glorious to endure long, considering my handicaps. I never gained a real mastery of the language. The jargon about tenses, genders and conjunctions was Greek to me. I had learnt only the rudiments of grammar at school, and wrote by instinct with a minimum of technical knowledge. When I had written a correct sentence I knew only that it *sounded* right; I could not have parsed it. And when I made a flaw in construction, as I often did, I knew instinctively that something was wrong. I would try alternative phrasings until I found one that satisfied some inner sense of rhythm and harmony: this was always grammatically correct. There is more fun in learning grammar in this way than through dry text-books; but there is also a disadvantage. When one only recognizes correct English by a sort of intuition one can never learn a foreign language. And Cornish was a foreign language to me, as it is to all modern Cornish people. The impelling sense that it was the language used by my ancestors was at length blunted by my realization of the infinite remoteness of both it and them from the world in which my vision must be manifested. The entire absence in me of a pure historical sense also hastened the collapse of my Celtic sympathies. My mysticism, veering between Christianity and pantheism, could find no stimulation in a museum atmosphere. It demanded warmth, light, passion, a stream of living consciousness pouring newly through the flowers of a present season, breaking in from the universe but not from the past. When my true faith was freed it made short work of any lingering antiquarian kinks. In none of my mature writings is there any description of the merely picturesque side of Cornish life enshrined in local customs and superstitions. By the time I achieved technical proficiency in writing I had become a Calvinist, and could no more trouble to record the traditional peculiarities of Cornwall than Bunyan could bother himself with the folk lore of Bedford.

The pathetic attempt to explain my idiosyncrasies by the magic word "Celtic" received its death-blow from a very personal source, an impact that not only quenched my glamorous Celtic twilight but also helped to plunge my whole life for a while into dark chaos.

In my seventeenth year my mother began revealing to me the squalid story of the Clemos and my father's tragic disharmonies. She did not disclose it all at once, but gradually, hint by hint, during our many discussions of marriage and morals. My views on these subjects were already becoming heterodox—I championed free love and would argue for hours about what I was pleased to call "sanctified smut"—and it was partly as a warning to me that my mother forced herself to tell the ugly secrets which she had kept for nearly twenty years.

Until then my father had been scarcely more than a name to me. Mother rarely spoke of him, except to explain, when I was old enough to understand, that he had been drowned in the War. She took me, then a small boy, to St. Stephen's cemetery and showed me his name carved on the War

Memorial. This had aroused in me a vague wondering, but it soon passed; no one added the details that would have gripped my imagination. I was never curious to know what sort of man my father had been. Even at the Clemos' old home during those midday broodings in the garden I did not associate the place with my father or think that he had once lived there, played around the railway siding and the clay-dump. My mother filled my life, satisfied me.

Her disclosures were to have a far-reaching effect for good upon my spiritual and literary growth; but their immediate result caused her to regret bitterly that she had burdened me with such knowledge while I was under the stress of the Nanpean affair. The most unwholesome part of my reaction was the entire absence of any consciousness of shock. One would expect a sensitive youth, living in a dream world of ideal beauty, to recoil in horror from the brutality of such revelations. But though the roots of my character were shaken I was aware only of the awakening of something malicious and cynical, a destructive force that had been biding its time. It seemed already familiar to me; and with passive, sardonic detachment I now felt its workings and welcomed them.

This anti-social bias had been a part of my nature since childhood. At no period of my life would it have been any use appealing to my self-respect. If I was told that any particular habit was beneath my dignity I would be all the more inclined to practise it. I realized that "dignity" was a masquerade of pride, and I was never happier than when consciously barring it out of my conduct. At school I had loathed drill even more than arithmetic: it seemed to me a particularly detestable form of tyranny, making me submit, even in my physical movements, to those popular standards of efficiency and smartness which were so hostile to me. I liked to slouch about with my head down and my hands in my pockets, careless of the opinions of society. In my thirteenth year I had visited St. Austell alone for the first time, and bought a pasty in a restaurant there. Instead of eating it at the table I carried it out into the street and munched at it as I walked along the pavement, utterly indifferent to the amused glances of the crowd. I could not understand why anyone should think it strange, or why people were so stupid as to fetter themselves with codes of social etiquette that destroyed all individuality. When I told mother quite casually that I had enjoyed my pasty outdoors, she was staggered: though my upbringing had not been so strict as that of most other village youths, mother was not then entirely free from the notion that "nice" manners were a part of true religion.

But my individualistic kinks now swept away my last scruples about conventional behaviour. A general disintegration of character was soon apparent. No one who knew me could any longer doubt that as long as I lived I should be an original and a rebel, or that by nature I was the nastiest sort of rebel—the sensual, cunning, malicious sort. The idea of such material producing Christian work or experiencing Christian love was so absurd that a "commonsense" faith would never have believed it possible. Often for days on end I wouldn't wash my face or comb my hair; I refused to bother about shaving, and the stubby growth continued until mother, both pained and exasperated by my unsightly appearance, insisted on shaving me herself. I seldom laced my shoes until the afternoon, never troubled to fit my neck with a collar and tie, and when mother fitted these on so that I might be "presentable" to pay some visit, I would keep them on until the end of the week, wearing them in bed, too lazy to remove them before sleeping. I protested when rents in my clothes were darned: if I preferred to look like a tramp, why shouldn't I? For the first time in my life I began to hate Sundays—not for any religious reason, but because on Sundays I had to wear my best clothes. I had come to feel utterly wretched when respectably dressed, aware of an acute, gnawing disharmony. Only rags fitted my role, my personality. I knew now that I had sprung from a family that had produced more than its share of moral degenerates, and only when my habits and appearance conformed to this degradation did I feel at ease, self-contained, not divided. Burdened with the sense of my separation from normal, decent young men, I felt a hypocrite when compelled to dress like them.

I remained even then fiercely true to my role; character persisted under the disguise and my stubborn gaucheries made my visits a matter of dread to friends and neighbours . I could scarcely take a meal without upsetting my tea or dropping my knife and fork on the floor. I could not lift a piece of cake or bread-and butter from a plate without grasping it in such a way that it fell to pieces on the table-cloth or into a fruit dish; and when removing or putting on my overcoat I usually managed to knock some articles off the table or sideboard with my elbow. I committed these blunders with stolid unconcern, never apologizing. I moved in a world of my own, and gave myself up to it the more passionately because I was obviously such a misfit and nuisance in the external practical world.

My talk showed the same degenerate tendencies. As I entered my middle teens my dialect broadened until it was far more slipshod and grotesque than my mother's speech. I delighted perversely in using odd words and pronunciations: the phase was in this sense a part of my literary education, an experimenting with the sound and colour of words. But my lack of the restraint of personal dignity allowed the habit to reach extremes that were well-nigh idiotic. My capacity for imitating any unusual form of speech which I read was an added complication. Scraps of various dialects were mixed up with the prevailing Cornish and the whole delivered as a disjointed, ungrammatic hotch-potch, so that the general quality of my conversation was rather below the level expected of a village idiot. But the idiot talked ridiculously because he did not know any better: I used this slovenly lingo from choice, acting on an instinct that probably had very deep psychological roots.

It is the fashion among certain intellectuals to make much of their eccentricities in the hope that they will be mistaken for geniuses. That is not my motive: such of these traits as have survived were preserved and transformed by Christianity, and the matter would be scarcely worth mentioning now except that it proves that I was not at all the "clever" sort of fellow many people thought me. Clever young men do not go about trying to give the impression that they cannot even talk sensibly. They do not make asses of themselves in their friends' houses in order to have the malicious satisfaction of imagining the amused titters and contemptuous remarks that will follow their exit. I deliberately *wished* to make the worst possible impression on everyone I met—Evelyn included. I seemed to be swallowed up in a perverse egoism that rejoiced only in humiliations and indignities. My interpretation of the motive varied with my moods. When under strong religious emotion I would attribute it to a mystic craving for martyrdom, while in lighter moments I saw it merely as a joke intended to perplex and embarrass people who expected me to speak and behave like a young prig. I recognized something of the process later when I read Dostœvsky's *Crime and Punishment*, thrilling responsively to the confession of the wretched Marmeledoff: "Crucify me—nail me to the cross! I thirst not for pleasures but for sufferings and tears." Later still, in John Cowper Powys' *Autobiography*, I found what seemed to me the same excessive grovelling—a quality which certainly existed in me in my teens, though in my case it was not associated with the sadistic imaginations and infantile eroticism which he records. But the attitude of a "zany-saint" is so entirely un-English that I could not retain the sympathy even of Christian friends. S. E. Burrow, knowing little of my private life but judging me mainly by the explosive outbursts I flung into the *Cornish Guardian*, tried again and again to check what he regarded as the extravagant swagger of a conceited adolescent. He pointed out that "decent people are ashamed of you, and most laugh at you. Is that what you desire?" I replied that it was; that I would not dare to call myself a Christian unless I deliberately invited such a crucifixion as Christ endured at the hands of the smug, superficial guardians of conventionality. I told him I wasn't going to "throw God's gift of experience back into His face" by seeking the aid of any other education—that of schools, churches or social contacts. To which he answered: "This is all wild and senseless talk. What sort of life are you going to fashion for yourself out of the experience you can get at St. Stephen's?" A complete extrovert, he interpreted "experience" in terms of bustling activity, travel, variety of interests and social relationships, and he thought that my solitude was making me sentimental about life, and especially about girls. In one of his letters to me on moral questions he wrote: "Girls are not the innocent infants you imagine them to be. They are *not* ignorant—they *know*—but they are reckless and just run the risk." I knew that already, though placing Evelyn divinely apart from such grossness; but Burrow's realism was another proof that the Victorian puritans were not the blind and prudish ostriches many people thought them. They judged human nature and conduct by the doctrine of original sin and thus realized the magnitude of the moral problem and that nothing but the conversion of the individuals could deal with it. The puerility and squeamishness were in the Modernists who traced the moral collapse to Victorian taboos, pathetically confident that stability and dignity could be restored by more education, more sex knowledge, more "guidance." I treated these elegant optimists with derision; I had some inside knowledge of the problem, and it proved them wrong. But my profound respect for the old Evangelicals was constant throughout my life; it never wavered even during this period when I had least in common with them.

My mother had reason to know that my oddities were symptoms of something more dangerous than the mere "audacity of youth" which Burrow saw in them, and she tried to instil normal virtues by more relevant arguments. She told me repeatedly that I should "never get a girl unless I pulled myself together." It was a sign of my morbid psychological state that even such warnings as this were meaningless to me. I had no wish to "get a girl" in the ordinary sense. I loathed the idea of courtship as generally understood and practised: the herd instinct, gangs of youths and girls together, laughing and joking. Courtship of the usual kind involved gaiety, and even the Bohemian in me shrank from that, demanding something less innocent, as the mystic demanded something more spiritual. At the Phillips's I had expressed myself strongly against dancing, and the family were pleased, thinking this an indication of the true Puritan temper. But I knew that it was not quite so simple, because I found that, while I detested the life of ballrooms, I did not object at all to the life of brothels, but often felt a thrilling sympathy with it. My hatred of the frivolous pleasures of youth was a symptom of gravitation towards a dark, primitive lust of the blood, similar to D. H. Lawrence's. And the fusion of this with a perverse religiosity had made me a hybrid who could find no fellowship either in the Church or in the world. Compared with the loneliness to which I was doomed a merely *intellectual* disharmony with one's surroundings is a trifling matter. In the very nature of things I could have no friends among my own generation. I avoided all social contacts with girls—not, as many people supposed, because I was shy, but because I was too primitive to meet them on the superficial levels where respectable friendships were conducted. I was so entirely a creature of instinct that I could not master the rudiments of worldly convention, and it seemed a cruel irony that I should be generally regarded as a cold fastidious bookworm.

My reception at the Phillips's became decidedly cooler as months passed and I ended my seventeenth year with hardly any financial return for the continuous stream of literary production. The storms of controversy I provoked in the *Cornish Guardian* had given me a certain amount of local prestige, tinged with a scandalous element in 1933 when I not only denounced the immorality of Cornish villages, but started also a long controversy about Epstein's "Genesis." S. E. Burrow was again my chief opponent, and stung by his remarks about my immaturity I claimed with vehemence that no one could judge me aright who did not apply to me the words Rossetti applied to Chatterton: "Surely a boy up to eighteen may be pardoned for exercising his faculty if he happens to be one among millions who can use grown men as his tools. Certainly some of his passages read startlingly. What is the answer to this enigmatical aspect? Why, that he *meant* it, and that all would mean it at his age who had his power, his daring and his hunger." I also made the rash admission that my first full-length novel had been submitted to a publisher, thus giving critics a useful card to play against me in future duels. Sarcastic references to this "fust novel" were frequent in Burrow's causerie for some years afterwards. The Phillips's had naturally been impressed by all this, and treated me as a sort of show-piece. Neighbours would drop in to have a good look at me and make flattering prophecies about my future. "'Aw, e'll maake 'is vartune all right," Mrs. Phillips would bawl, pushing me to my feet in her rough, vigorous way. "Woan't 'ee, Jack? Maake yer vartune all right." As soon as I had convinced them that this was not my aim at all—and it was hard to convince them, for why should a man write if he didn't want to make money?—Evelyn was allowed to show her feelings with more freedom. Her rebuffs became quite pointed. I would arrive to find her donning hat and coat, and her mother would make some lame excuse for her going out just then. Evelyn would depart without even saying "Good-bye" to me, and though I usually stayed until supper-time I seldom saw her return. I learnt later that when she left the house in this fashion it was often to mix with other young men—while I remained at home with her father, discussing the decadence of the Church and the finer points of Pauline theology. The situation was comic enough to an objective view, but many years were to pass before I was really detached from it, so crushing was the dual stress of degradation from the past, bafflement in the present.

The road between Nanpean and Goonamarris became my Via Dolorosa. On one or two evenings a week I went out along it without hope, and a few hours later returned, sometimes in tears, often in dull despair; passers-by glancing curiously at the untidy youth stumbling along in the gutter, muttering prayers to God or wild denials of His existence. Now and then the cloud of depression would settle on me soon after I arrived at the Phillips's: I would get up and leave without a word of explanation. When I reached home I did not tell mother why I was back so early, though she guessed the reason. Usually I went straight to the organ and played Sankey hymns for an hour or two before going to bed, groping blindly towards the faith of my childhood. But the blasphemy was deeply rooted in my creative powers, and when they got to work I was enclosed afresh in my heretical vision. Next day I would be turning out more poems or scraps of stories, consoling myself, passionately escaping back into the dream world; and because the written word was so real to me I would again regard Evelyn's repulse as a momentary shadow veiling the Fulfilment, the end that was so sure because my artistic consciousness, the one true thing, believed in it.

I had no other interests or contacts, no hobbies or recreations. My old school mates had become dead to me since my blindness: I never went around Trethosa or Treviscoe where I might encounter any of them. I met all the usual challenges from girls of my own age with the glowering, sullen hostility of a young moron. For three years my life revolved in this vicious circle, vain traversing of the multi-coloured rays from that inhuman heart I had glimpsed at Penrose Veor: the situation of Browning's *Numpholeptos*.

Of this period I can write in the words of St. Augustine: "I wandered more and more into fruitless seed-plots of sorrows, with a proud dejectedness and a restless weariness. And Thou heldest Thy peace...."

CHAPTER SEVEN

The Collapse of Heresy

ONE of the tasks which Meggy had undertaken, besides trying to teach me to write stories, was the moulding of my taste in reading. He knew that I was an uneducated country boy, reading indiscriminately and becoming enthusiastic about books that could hardly be helpful to me from an artistic point of view. But as he was ignorant of the Nanpean affair his advice seemed wide of the mark, and I scarcely heeded it at all. My circumstances forced me to assess books not as works of art but as lifebelts. During this period of strain—and, indeed, right on into my twenties—I never read a book for pleasure or cool, deliberate study. I challenged every author I read with the desperate demand that he would interpret my experience. If he could throw no light upon it I had no use for him, however great a genius he might be. Had Meggy known this he would not have been surprised that I was gripped by Marie Corelli and indifferent to Arnold Bennett. It was Marie Corelli, not the delicate and sophisticated "artists," who had expressed a view of love as a "romance of two worlds," and that was the sort of thing in which I had become entangled. I was dismayed and bewildered to find that the world's literature had done so little to sift and clarify the truths and errors to which one was exposed on this spiritual borderline. Meggy might have told me that it was not legitimate to apply such a narrow personal test to books, but it was inevitable that I should do so. The tendency, deepened by my strange adolescence, had been at work even in my childhood. I have never had to discard any of my old literary antipathies: they were instinctive. Writers whom I disliked at school—Stevenson, Scott, Dickens, Quiller-Couch—have remained practically unread by me ever since. (My aversion to Dickens was modified somewhat in my later twenties when

I read *David Copperfield*, but I still do not find any of his other works readable.) It will be observed that these writers have one characteristic in common—a superficially "healthy" atmosphere which implies a denial of the doctrine of original sin and makes them treat love exactly as they treat Christ, with a politeness that skims the surface and dare not go deeper for fear of what might be discovered there. My essentially dogmatic nature was repelled by their broad humanism and, in Stevenson and Quiller-Couch, by the Pelagianism implicit even in their style, the cold grace and elegance that could never co-exist with an urgent, disquieting belief in the Fall. For the same reason I found most dramatic poetry unreadable —especially Shakespeare's. It was at this teen-age crisis, in 1933, that I obtained a cheap copy of Shakespeare's Complete Works. My early distaste for him was confirmed, and has, I fear, only strengthened with later experience. Neither in his plays not his sonnets did he present anything that I could recognize as love. So far from interpreting universal moods and passions, he seemed to me to be bogged in a trivial worldly rut, ignoring every phase of the mystical and religious consciousness. I could not find a single Christian in his portrait gallery, and thus he failed me at every point when I turned to him for guidance in my dilemma. The sense of the futility of worldly genius when faced with ultimate spiritual problems, made me increasingly contemptuous of it. My attitude was, indeed, similar to that which Tolstoy defended in *What is Art?* His thesis has been condemned on the ground that it "would set a lively tract above the greatest plays and novels ever written."[*] I quite agreed that the tract was more important.

These remarks make it clear enough that I entered upon my career without a trace of that passionate devotion to literature, that reverence for art, which are usually shown by the serious student. My motive was not literary at all, but religious, and my private vision had distorted but not destroyed my old credal sympathies. Theology, even in its crudest forms, could engross and quicken my whole personality, while literature,

[*] Frank Swinnerton: *The Georgian Literary Scene.*

except as a presentation of the raw material through which the theology worked, was a bore. Those who knew my bias often remarked in those days that my true place was in the Church, carrying on the tradition that was established on both sides of my family, by the Hockings and my great-uncle George Bullen. But I never once thought of the Christian ministry as a possible vocation. I knew my own nature too well. Like Francis Thompson, I was "girt with a thirsty solitude of soul" that made my approach to Christianity abnormal, and I should have been equally a misfit in any denomination. I could give, as in later years I did give, a simple doctrinal exposition to a group in a Methodist school-room; but such witness left vast tracts on my nature unused—those queer tracts of the borderland where so much of my mental energy was generated. Only the scope and freedom of a novel could employ my most individual gifts: the aware-ness of beauty and symbolism in the clay landscape, the rude country humour, the realism that demanded a mystic trans-formation of that which is for materialists obscenity. The churches offered no platform for such poetic and imaginative qualities. I knew, too, that I could never hope to pass the examinations set for entrance into the ministry. Study in the usual sense of the word was impossible to a temperament like mine. My brain worked by fits and starts, and became para-lysed under supervision. I possessed insight only at the point where sex and religion were fused; everything else was unilluminated, shadowy. And with all this there was the inexorable drive towards artistry in words which forced me to spend much time grubbing among the shadows, trying to find some treasure that I could draw back into the circle of light: some æsthetic tone, some rhythm, that would help me towards fulfilment and balance, harmony. In all these things I could glimpse the irony of God—the fact that, though I often detested literature, He meant me to be a writer; and an artistic one, though I hated art.

The only author whom I read with more sympathetic interest through Meggy's advice was Galsworthy. I had just discovered *The Forsyte Saga*—picked up in sixpenny instalments at Woolworth's—and while I was not sufficiently developed to appreciate the satire and subtlety of his characterization, I was aware of a nostalgic beauty that affected me in the emotional scenes; the spiritualised landscape with its aching poignancy struck a thrill of genuine response in my nature. Galsworthy's work was to help much in moulding my æsthetic taste, though its influence soon waned when I discovered my true affinities in Hardy and T. F. Powys. The germs of my kinship with Hardy were present even in my earliest writings. Meggy had noted the bias towards rural tragedy in the novel I had sent him, and he counselled me to model my future books on *Tess of the d'Urbervilles*. With my usual obstinacy I did not even bother to get the book; I was nearly thirty before I read any of Hardy's mature works. Those reviewers who thought I was deliberately imitating Hardy in *Wilding Graft* did not know that I had been writing in that vein for ten years before I felt the stimulus of Hardy's influence. Considering all the circumstances—the romantic narrative talent I had derived from the Hockings, the sombre tragedy of the Clemo family, my own childhood steeped in a remote rural atmosphere and the dignified language of the Bible—it was inevitable that my work should resemble Hardy's and that I should be allergic to the essentially urban technique of my contemporaries.

The book that did most to satisfy my craving for light, and prepared me for the coming blow at Nanpean, was Carlyle's *Sartor Resartus*. It seemed personal and prophetic, and had an almost morbid fascination for me. The experience of Teufelsdrockh was oddly similar to mine: the simple piety of childhood, the mystical excess of the adolescent conception of love, the idea of the girl as an "appearance" of the Infinite. Evelyn was a little like Blumine, and I could not escape the fear that the story of hopeless idolatry and betrayal presented in that book was to be repeated in a remote Cornish village where no one would understand its significance. I went about reciting mentally the agonized appeals of Teufelsdrockh, his protests against the "Everlasting No" and the grey "Centre of Indifference" that stretched beyond. I lived almost entirely on the plane of spiritual melodrama, and but for the relief that came in writing comic tales in advance for *Netherton's Almanack* the strain might have produced a serious breakdown.

Carlyle's work naturally affected my style also, and in 1934 I wrote a book of religious essays called *Christ or Eros?* which was no doubt very funny, being written in imitation of the grandiose, burlesque and contorted language of *Sartor Resartus*. After the manuscript had been refused by a couple of publishers I lost heart and burnt it—one of several productions in prose and verse which I wrote at intervals when my inspiration would not flow freely into fiction.

It was at this period that my creative urge sometimes demanded an entirely new medium, and I tried to express myself in drawings. I had never shown much aptitude for drawing at school, but that may have been because I wasn't interested in the objects set to copy—mainly flowers and household utensils. The controversy about Epstein's "Genesis," and my reading of his recorded conversations in *The Sculptor Speaks*, made me for awhile passionately curious about the plastic arts, and I scandalised the neighbours by drawing pictures of naked women and pinning them up on the kitchen walls. Mother did not object; there was nothing obscene about them. They usually showed the nude figure standing or kneeling before the Cross, and were thus clearly a release of my mystical vision.

So my education was continued, while the personal drama moved quietly and inexorably towards its denouement. It was a queer life, and tuition, even in the purely intellectual sense, often came in queer ways. Sometimes a chance gesture would bring me into contact with a fresh world of ideas which I required at that particular stage of my emergence. Again and again, after choosing a book or periodical on what seemed a whimsical impulse, I would be forced, like Browning after he bought the "old yellow book," to

"Mark the predestination, when a Hand,
Always above my shoulder, pushed me...."

CONFESSION OF A REBEL

The Biblical promise which had so comforted mother in her darkest hour—that "thy children shall be taught of the Lord" —was being fulfilled in a very real sense, and often in a dangerous sense, for God uses strange tools to perfect a man's orthodoxy.

One move which came at about this time might have changed my whole philosophy of life had not original sin provided me with an antidote. In a writer's magazine I had noticed a paper called *The Literary Guide* recommended as a market for serious articles, and thinking this would be more in my line than the "popular" journals I wrote to the publishers for a copy. I was surprised to find that the contents were almost entirely atheistic, and at once abandoned all desire to write for it. But The Rationalist Press Association, having got my name and address, made a commendable—even, it seemed to me, a frantic—attempt to gain my support. Month after month I was deluged with catalogues, leaflets, etc. containing notices of, and extracts from, the works of Victorian and modern secularists. In this way, quite free of cost (for I didn't buy any of the books advertised), I grew familiar with the writings of Bradlaugh, McCabe, H. G. Wells, and the rest of the voluble and acrid tribe. This contact with free throught broadened my intellectual background, but I cannot say that it had any marked effect on my beliefs. I was temperamentally incapable of materialism, and only in a limited degree could I experience doubts of anything that was not materialistic. I adhered instinctively to the cult of the irrational and thought the scientific approach the silliest and most boring form of heterodoxy. The teaching of such iconclasts as Wells could neither disturb nor inspire me; I remained completely indifferent to it, mysticism being one of the rocks on which neat little plans for a decent world inevitably get smashed. I felt a malicious pleasure in being apart from the mass of gullible students, a primitive heretic who would fill the rationalist pundits with bewildered exasperation. I would not let my mind be disciplined, tidied or informed by them. I preferred at that stage to be passive and see what sparks of truth would fly from the unhindered friction of my own moods, fancies, intuitions. It had already produced some exciting flashes of romantic revolt, enabling me to sit on an individualist fence from which I could mock both science and organised religion. This is a common weakness of the mystical temperament—the fantastic desire for the originality of pure egoism. In rejecting the teachings of science I could feel that I was on the side of the angels, and it was an added satisfaction to assume that the angels were not on the side of the theologians. Throughout these years I accepted the Christian doctrines not as a theological system but merely as statements that happened to fit in with my own contempt for common sense. I loathed the evolutionists and the higher critics, not as assailants of Divine truth but as assailants of my personal insight. Their jargon intruded on my private idiom, even the idiom of my blasphemies; I was not interested in their kind of rebellion. Nor was there anything congenial to my mood in the avowedly pagan fields. I read Swinburne, Shelley and other idolaters of the old Greek ideal, but always with the sense that their landscape was alien, that its lush sensuous joy was unreal, meaningless to me. Neither the chilly light of scientific materialism nor the heat of pagan revolt against it could nourish me at all. Had I discovered the works of Francis Thompson or G. K. Chesterton during my teens I might have found in them some clue that would have drawn me towards Roman Catholicism, which offers more scope to the religious decadent than Calvin would have allowed. My theological outlook was nearer to the Roman Catholic spirit than to that of current Protestantism. I had no patience with the liberal movement of religious inquiry that sought to trace every Biblical idea to some remote source in Babylonian legend or Egyptian cult. The scholastic approach with its avowed aim of "purging" Christianity of its supernatural sanctions and evolving a "reasonable" faith, found me implacably hostile and tended to deepen my perverse craving for the elements of magic, miracle and primitive superstition. I did not know at the time that here was the raw material of a good Catholic, and before I realized the fact I

had found peace in a different fellowship, one that enabled me
to balance these traits with the Puritan hatred of worldliness.

Developments at Nanpean showed me, more vividly than
books could have done, the ultimate tendencies of my nature—
especially one incident that occurred at this period. Calling
at the Phillips's one Sunday morning I learnt that Evelyn
was going to sing in the choir that evening at Old Pound
chapel, away up on the moors towards Karslake. I resolved
to go and hear her, though I had no idea what I intended to
do afterwards. I had never been to Old Pound before, and
felt rather self-conscious as I turned from the familiar scene
at Goverseth hill up the strange, twisting lane. The few
villagers stared at me when at length I reached the chapel,
but once inside I felt more at home than I should have done
at Trethosa. It was a small, barn-like place with none of the
modernizations that had crept into the big village chapels. The
building was gloomy despite the clear sunshine without, and
my sight being still defective I could not distinguish Evelyn
among the members of the choir. I wondered at first whether
she was there or not, and gradually, unaccountably as it
seemed, there came over me a feeling that it did not matter
anyhow. What mattered was the service itself, the handful
of moorland folk who had gathered to worship.

The congregation was similar to that which Browning
describes in *Christmas Eve*—old women who twiddled their
thumbs and old men who rocked themselves and squeezed their
eyes shut as they sang. They were all working people, uneducated. Their clothes were old-fashioned for the most part;
none of the girls had make-up on her face. All was fresh, clean,
pure beauty: the sort of beauty of which I had been starved
and for which my whole nature was crying out.

The service was evangelistic; most of the hymns were
Sankey's, hymns that had been the favourites of my childhood,
that mother had sung so often at the organ in the winter
evenings. There was one in particular which I had not heard
in a place of worship for ten years: it had been expelled from
the Methodist hymn-book as Conference realized the need

of being "progressive." Instinctively I found myself assenting to its confession:

> " 'Tis the old-time religion, and it's good enough for me ;
> It was good for our mothers and it's good enough for me—
> 'Tis the old-time religion, and it's good enough for me".

This was sung to a weird drawling tune, like a negro spiritual, each line being repeated three times. The effect was profoundly moving, and being in a very emotional state through Evelyn's presence I received the full impact of its crude barbaric power. Sentimental I may have been, but I could have wept there in that moorland Bethel that evening—wept for joy in the sense of release and illumination. I seemed to glimpse my whole spiritual development from a new angle. Had I perhaps, all along, been searching for the secret of Nonconformist Puritanism, aware that it might contain a revelation sufficient for my life and destiny if only I could view it by a sudden oblique light, as no one had ever viewed it before? Were even my moral heresies and perversions of Christian belief attempts to throw this individual light upon the old orthodox values and get at the deeper truths which conventionality had encrusted and overlaid? I felt the thrilling possibility—could not help feeling it: everything around me was so *real*. These people honestly meant what they professed: they were not like sophisticated Anglicans repeating the Creed and mentally commenting at every clause: "This is merely symbolic; this is only pictorial."

I had come to that building ostensibly to court a girl; I left it filled with a great love for primitive Christianity, for these sturdy believers. I was so much stirred by this fresh contact with the revivalist atmosphere that I almost forgot Evelyn, and went home without even waiting to speak to her.

It is clear from this incident that the struggle between the ascetic and the sensualist, though very far from being won, was moving in the right direction; and though the world of the ideal usually held me it was beginning to show cracks through which a grey wave of dogma now and then washed in, bringing the tang of reality, a foretaste and an assurance now that I was approaching the total break-up of my natural faith.

The Old Pound episode headed things to a crisis. When next I visited Nanpean Mr. Phillips informed me very gravely that Evelyn had complained about my presence at Old Pound, that she resented my following her about in this fashion, as she was still too young to begin a courtship. I was not surprised at the news; I had known for months that Evelyn was growing increasingly annoyed at the gossip that had linked her name with mine. But I hung on and decided that I must see her alone and put the facts before her in the exalted manner of a Teufelsdröckh. I began badgering her to come across to Goonamarris and have her photo taken with me. Oddly enough, her parents offered no objection, and one day in August 1933 she came, bringing with her the Phillips's dog, a terrier which she had trained to sit up with a pipe in its mouth: a rather cruel trick—not to the dog but to her father, who could not see how even the dog was made to mock at his anti-smoking mania.

We went to the woods below Barrakellis, and after I had snapped the terrier and its pipe my mother took a few snapshots of Evelyn and myself, though not in a pose that suggested much warmth on either side. When we got indoors again we found that the pipe had been left behind in the coppice: a ruse which any girl would have thought of if she wished to be alone with a fellow. But when I offered to fetch it Evelyn merely remarked coldly that she wasn't going to tire herself by returning to the wood, whatever I did. This rebuff confirmed mother's suspicion that there was no possibility of normal love developing for me at Nanpean. She must have wondered at my blindness as I raced jubilantly down to the copse and gazed at the tree under which Evelyn and I had stood as at a shrine where a miracle had occurred. I found the pipe and Evelyn went home with hardly a word of thanks, leaving mother very subdued, knowing that collapse was inevitable.

The winter of 1933–34 began gloomily enough. Just before Christmas I suffered another attack of eye trouble which, though it did not produce total blindness, was much more painful than the earlier attacks, and borne in less amiable mood. Evelyn and her mother visited me when I had recovered a little, but I was very weak and unsightly and Evelyn was extremely cold. It was the last time she entered my home, and the contrast between this visit and our meeting at Harry's wedding was the bitterest irony I had yet endured. There was nothing in her now of that tender pity she had shown at Pentose; my infirmities merely irritated her. She was sixteen and becoming realistic. She had seen me grow from a gentle, intelligent boy into a wayward and repellent youth who was somehow obsessed with her, yet not in love with her. She could not comprehend or deal with the situation. Hints and gestures that would have sufficed with average young men had no effect on me—at least, not the one she desired. The effects were seen at home in black moods of despair, hysterical outbursts of blasphemy, violent tempers and diary entries in which phrases like "bloody hell" were frequently employed. The world of Ideal Beauty was fast breaking up.

To this emotional deadlock and physical affliction was added the crushing sense of material failure. I was still earning less than £3 a year and now felt the financial humiliation more keenly. My second full-length novel—my fifth book if one counts the short novels and essays—had been completed and was making unsuccessful journeys to London. Short stories and articles were being returned to me almost every week by editors in various parts of the country. I was beginning to realize that it was not chiefly faults of technique that barred my advance. It was partly the fact that my individual tempera-ment and vision meant nothing to editors and publishers. They demanded of me the very qualities I detested most. For four years I had been pouring out a stream of work attacking subtlety and sophistication, which I saw as the arch-enemies of sincerity and stability in religion, morals and all human relationships; and my work was refused because it was not subtle and sophisticated. Here too I faced deadlock, and was to face it for the next ten years. My creative powers were almost worn out in this vicious circle before success at last came to me.

The sense of my inferiority to Evelyn on a wage-earning level made me feel ashamed and frustrated. She had been employed in domestic service at Nanpean, but early in 1934 she was sent to another household at St. Austell, and for several weeks I did not see her at all. She soon tired, however, of the strict conditions in town and returned home—a move which I regarded as a Providential sign that there was still a chance for me. I resumed my pursuit, becoming more and more earnest and desperate. The Phillips's were now openly hostile, apparently at a loss to know how to get rid of me without slamming the door in my face. Nerves were frayed on both sides; there were poundings of the table, angry outbursts. Sometimes the family would work off their chagrin by squabbling among themselves, Mr. Phillips shouting impotent counsel, his eyes groping behind the dark glasses, unable to see what was going on. Evelyn began to taunt me about my flirting with a Foxhole schoolgirl called Violet who dropped in now and then at our next-door neighbours, the Rowse's, to wheel Barbara out in the pram. Violet had indeed inspired some of my light love stories and poems, and I think I really was in love with her for awhile, though the affair did not get beyond a playful squeeze or two and a few jokes, as I met her only about half a dozen times and did not see her at all after she left school. Evelyn's sneering suggestion that I "go wi' Violet" led me for the first time to use some bad language, to the shocked surprise of the Phillips's. Mrs. Phillips confessed that both she and Evelyn had spent sleepless nights because of the frantic ravings against Violet which I inflicted on them. They thought I must be going mad—and I thought so too at times. The tragic irony of it all was becoming too much for me, and the intolerable situation headed swiftly to the last ugly scene.

Mrs. Phillips had picked up in the village a rumour connected with the Clemos, and one Thursday evening in March 1934—just after my eighteenth birthday—she flung this piece of scandal at me across the supper table. I rose, pale and trembling, declared vehemently that it was "a damn lie," and a little later made an undignified exit from the house.

I never entered it again. Two days afterwards we received a package from Mrs. Phillips containing all the presents I had given Evelyn—a handkerchief and a few photos—and a letter to my mother informing her that my eccentric manners had so upset the family that no further visits would be allowed. Evelyn had decided to find another situation at St. Austell and would never again see me or communicate with me.

The sense of finality was paralysing for several weeks; but provision was already made for the next stage of my emergence and when I again responded to the human rhythm it was through Barbara Rowse, then three years old—some warm, innocent caress that roused me to consciousness of a world in which happy laughter remained, a world untouched by the lightnings of that nebulous cloud that had brooded over Penrose and Nanpean.

My first instinctive reaction, however, was a more reckless assertion of belief in the gods who had failed me. I was driven to protect myself by the same sort of irrational fanaticism as D. H. Lawrence exhibited. Like Lawrence, I seemed to be "crucified into sex," though for me the "dark gods" were implicit in Christ so that instead of rejecting the Gospel I had turned it into something sensual and blasphemous. This attitude had inevitably given me occasional glimpses of the real truths, and for the most part it was these flashes that lit my published work, the brutalities and perversions being confined to my diaries and to manuscripts which no paper would print.

The only immediate literary consequence of this spiritual upheaval was a poem or two and a series of long, incoherent letters in the *Cornish Guardian*. During the spring and summer of 1934 a controversy on "Christ and Sex" raged in that paper, and few who followed it with shocked interest could have guessed that it was originated by a young man flung so desperately back on a mystical vision from which practical proof, and even the hope of it, had been stripped away. I began by announcing defiantly—knowing that Evelyn and her mother would read my words—that "my own pathway to the stars was along the despised, twilit trail of sex," and ended my letter with some lines from a poem I had just written, a prophecy that I would

> "Arise to let men know
> That Christ's own face can glow
> In love's embrace, and kisses be as prayers."

I wrote in the feverish conviction that never before had anyone regarded love as I regarded it. Not until ten years later did I find that Francis Thompson had expressed the same creed in his *Orient Ode:*

> "Even the kisses of the just
> Go down not unresurgent to the dust;
> Yea, not a kiss that I have given
> But shall triumph upon my lips in Heaven "

It was, indeed, no more than a statement of the mystical implications of orthodox Christianity, warped and defensive because of my own starved condition. But the hard-headed Evangelicals were scandalized. S. E. Burrow came out with a two thousand word long rejoinder, declaring that "only a sex-poisoned imagination could have pictured such a gross and revolting caricature." He was horrified that I should put Christ "on the fleshly level of a sex-mastered lover who is asking for more kisses." This brought in A. J. G. Hawken, championing my position with the avowal that "Jack has on his side all the learned Fathers of the Christian Church." My own reply contained the pathetic boast that I had had "a bit of experience" to back up my argument. A Watford clergyman then came into the fray, lamenting my "want of balance" and advising me to consult the Greek originals of certain texts which, he claimed, I had misunderstood. Week after week the battle raged, becoming a lively topic of discussion in many Cornish homes. Personalities were freely exchanged, and the correspondence closed in a manner none of us had expected, proving that it had been followed in distinguished and unlikely quarters. A letter appeared from Miss Daphne du Maurier, pointing out that the controversy had "lowered the tone" of the paper. She declared acidly in reference to myself: "We are not interested in his views, religious, political or sexual, and if he wishes to express them let him do so in private correspondence and not before our eyes in print." She added also the curious comment that my writings—and I think she included Burrow's in the criticism—were "ugly to the eye," which suggests that even fashionable lady novelists can lose their sense of humour when trying to suppress something they do not happen to like. But her derisive remarks caused the controversy to end in black gloom for me. It was bad enough to be publicly sneered at by people whose names carried no more weight with the general reader than my own, but to be snubbed by a famous novelist—one of the class who should have recognised my talent and encouraged me—was beyond endurance. In my first rush of resentment I burnt her letter, and have had to quote the above extracts from memory. I have often regretted destroying that specimen of Miss du Maurier's writing: not that I would class it with *Rebecca* in literary value, but having kept everything else that was printed about me it seems just another irony that the most amusing outburst should escape my collection.

A very helpful distraction which was granted me at this crucial time was the friendship of Frank Baron, well-known in Cornwall as a writer of dialect tales, something of an anti-quarian, who had spent many years collecting material for a history of his birthplace, Mevagissey, and was made a bard of the Gorsedd. He was a bachelor, middle-aged, and at that period Anglican lay reader at Indian Queens, a village nearly five miles north-west of my home. He had first written to me during Christmas, 1933, to congratulate me on my current *Netherton's Almanack* tale, and his discriminating criticism of my Press letters and poems was an agreeable change from the rubbish, abusive or otherwise, which I had previously received from unknown readers of my work. Baron's was a more cultured mind than S. E. Burrow's, broader in sympathies, Anglo-Catholic in its religious tone. A lively correspondence developed between us, and before the Nanpean affair ended I had visited him in his lodgings at Indian Queens, bringing back with me his gift of several books on sex and psychoanalysis, which revealed to me something of the material factors inherent in my experience. He must have found me very shy and uncommunicative; I was burdened by the Nanpean crisis, no agreeable company just then. On Easter Monday of 1934 his tall, burly figure passed along the lanes leading to Goonamarris, where he spent an enjoyable afternoon, looking through my manuscripts and carrying away a few of them to read quietly at home. Through the spring and early summer he was laid aside with illness, but in August he wrote me from Mevagissey, where he was recuperating, and gave me the welcome news that he had sold two of my humorous tales to Saundry, of Penzance, for whose *Almanack* he had written regularly for thirty years. Later he introduced me to a Camborne firm which also accepted some of my dialect sketches, and submitted half a dozen of my longer stories to Jordan, the Truro bookseller and publisher. Jordan paid a trifle for the manuscripts and intended to issue them in book form, but was deterred by his experience with other local authors and informed me that he was "tired of issuing books for Cornish people who do not buy them." These tales have never been published.

More gratifying to me than this practical aid was the unfailing sympathy Baron showed in the spiritual and artistic qualities of my work. He noted my obsession with sex, but did not deplore it. "Your letters and poems are full of allusions gynæcean, hymeneal, and sometimes almost obstetric," he wrote, adding that "many people who read your work might get a wrong impression through their own carelessness. A depraved mind runs away with a faulty grasp of what is intended in this field of metaphor." He was particularly pleased by a poem called "Winter Scene in Cornwall," printed in the *Cornish Guardian*: "That Winter thing was exceptionally well done. Reminded me of Keats. It had the very atmosphere of frost and dreariness, the murk that comes with frost only in certain places, and the clay area is one.... I had never read a more true or more poetic portrayal of a scene which the lines brought quite startlingly clear to me." Of another poem he recorded an anecdote: "I cut it out of the paper and took it in my wallet on to the beach to read to some visitor whom I thought would be interested. To my joy he had also read it and was able nearly to repeat it from memory, showing that it had clearly impressed itself upon his mind.... I think it gave me a clearer understanding of you than I have hitherto gained." Such tributes as this, no mere empty praise but the considered judgment of a keen, fastidious mind, meant much to me. They were almost the only crumbs of encouragement I received on the literary plane, though the blow of rejection was sometimes softened by the enclosure of an appreciative letter instead of a formal slip. One London firm in returning a collection of my verse remarked that "there is ample evidence that you have had a big experience as a poet," and a little later my second novel came back from a leading publisher accompanied by a note from Richard Church, who expressed his interest and "would like to see further developments of your handling of the novel form."

One or two surprises of a different nature helped at intervals to deaden the desperate hunger of this year. An extract from a Press letter of mine was included in the book, *Vital Sayings of the Year, 1933*, though the recognition had little significance, as the views of hundreds of other nonentities were displayed in the volume. I also won first prize in a *Methodist Recorder* essay competition. The award was a collection of Bernard Shaw's minor pieces, including *The Adventures of a Black Girl in her Search for God*. With charcteristic audacity I wrote and told the editor that while I was pleased that he had given my essay first place I did not approve of religious papers giving atheistic books as prizes. This shows that my spirit was not entirely crushed; but such vigorous moods alternated with times of prostration both physical and mental, and the morbid periods were, I think, the more frequent.

It will be obvious that during these years my life was appallingly self-centred. I read no national newspapers and seldom listened to the radio. The movements of the contemporary world were still almost as remote from me as they had been during my childhood. By this time I had heard that a man called Hitler was making a commotion in Germany, that the Reichstag building had been burnt down, and that there had been a "purge" of something or other. But to me all this was vague, distant and irrelevant. I was less of a patriot even than my father had been. I was never aware of myself as a citizen, a member of the working class, a representative of the New Generation. I did not consciously exist on these planes; I accepted none of their responsibilities and demanded none of their rights. When in 1934 I was invited to join the local debating society I wrote back to the secretary: "I reckon your blooming debating society can get enough gas without trying to deflate me. Sorry!" This cheeky repudiation of kinship with all groups and classes had apparently brought me to disaster, but the Nanpean collapse served to drive me even more in upon myself. Some traces of social revolt had indeed begun to disturb me; I had imbibed certain Christian Socialist theories from my reading, particularly from Tolstoy and from Hall Caine's political novels. But this was a confused protest and had really nothing to do with politics; it was part of a general sense of frustration and injustice. I could not but feel that there was something terribly wrong with a social system that was forcing me, at eighteen, to live on the charity of my mother, who had to maintain us both on her pension of 26s. 8d. a week. But I never looked to the politicians for relief. I accepted the grind of poverty as just another manifestation of the anarchic law that had ensnared me at Penrose. Red tape or Red revolution were not likely to remedy the material hardships of a mystical writer. Socialists would probably say that a working-class man had no right to be a mystic; that mysticism was a capitalist vice and its presence in a proletarian proved him to be a traitor, a liability to the State. As far as I was concerned the whole problem went beyond men and was rooted in the mysterious workings of the universe.

It was inevitable, therefore, that a certain weariness and apathy should become my dominant mood when the first fever of disillusion had spent itself. As the winter of 1934–35 approached I grew less and less responsive to the major stimuli within my reach; not wishing to talk much, even with mother, not caring to go into the villages. My diary entries at Christmas show that the reminder of religion irritated me: "All that sterile bathos, cliché-phrases—I'm sick of it." Nothing about the season was worth recording except that "Barbara has a new pram for her doll, and blocks and a dear toy piano." This protective retreat from adult values was fortunate; it prevented me from making those fresh stirrings towards active normality that would have involved me in a more humiliating, and almost immediate, collapse.

No doubt there were plenty of experts in the district who knew, and advocated volubly, the correct means that were needed to restore me to something like useful citizenship. A variety of friends and interests, probably membership of a Youth Club, recreation, and such discipline as would develop a healthy, balanced character. But their efforts would have been frustrated by the next stroke of affliction that fell upon me.

It was observed that I was often replying in a more than usually idiotic way to questions addressed to me, and at length we realized that I was answering stupidly because I had mis-heard what was said. I was, indeed, becoming deaf, and the condition worsened with alarming rapidity. Before my nineteenth birthday I was too deaf to take part in any conversation and experienced the relief of being ignored instead of shouted at when visitors called at my home. The local doctor was consulted—a man new to the district, as Manson had died a year or two earlier. He was obviously perturbed and despatched me with all haste to specialists at Plymouth hospital. Their verdict was one of the heaviest blows my mother had ever received—so staggering, in fact, that she dared not tell me at the time what they had reported. X-ray examination revealed that the trouble was extremely grave, and there was little prospect of my ever being able to hear again.

The world of darkness lay behind me, in which a Vision had been granted; now I had entered the world of silence wherein some new language might separate me still further from the common tones of experience.

All hope of my living down the Nanpean mess by a normal affair in one of the villages was now dashed; all chance of cultivating wholesome interests through contact with society. I was shut in where no girl but Barbara could begin to build me up in reality and dogma now that my old life of illusion and poetry had crumbled.

CHAPTER EIGHT

Silence and Transition

I HAVE now come to one of the most difficult parts of my story. The situation was so complex that the impression made on the reader will depend entirely upon which points I choose to emphasize. If I stressed the morbidities, revealing what a fundamentally sensual nature is like when stripped of its protective illusions, the result would be a mere pathological document. If I ignored the morbidities and wrote only of the happy hours I spent playing with Barbara it would appear a simple instance of the way God brought "compensation" into the life of a strangely afflicted youth. And if I left out the darkest and brightest aspects and confined myself to the fact that I went on writing in spite of all discouragements and produced another novel during the first year of deafness, I should prompt more tributes to the unconquerable spirit of man—which is the last thing I wish to do. Indeed, I shall take some delight in showing that there were times when the spirit of man in me was conquered; and that it was for this reason that I became a Calvinist.

My sense of dismayed frustration sprang from so many causes that it is impossible to tell how much of it was due to deafness alone. Richard Jefferies' description of the effect of unrelieved solitude is an accurate picture of the condition that threatened me: "A species of thick clothing slowly grows about the mind, the pores are choked, little habits become a part of existence, and by degrees the mind is enclosed in a husk."* My conscious life had a remote, ghostly character. Slips of paper were often handed to me as I sat at my desk in the front room—questions or items of news written down in mother's big round handwriting. I would look sometimes at the dog Gyp barking at the postman, see the jaws move but hear

* *The Story of my Heart.*

nothing; and as the postman was usually bringing some manuscript the dog became a fantastic symbol of myself, aware of danger, making protest, but powerless to prevent the blows falling. This fancy, however, did not long persist, for one evening, in the spring of 1935, Gyp went out for a walk alone and never returned. We heard that he had been run over and had gone away to die on the downs above Goonamarris, within sight of Nanpean, where he had been born. I spent many hours searching there for his body, but could find no trace of it.

The strain on me was far worse than that of blindness had been. I was exhausted by the long Nanpean struggle, and had relief not come speedily I should probably have collapsed.

But relief did come. Within three months of the time I had first gone to Plymouth hospital, so deaf that even if anyone shouted into my ear I could catch only a faint, unrecognizable sound, the specialists confessed to mother that they were surprised. My hearing had begun to improve; I could even distinguish voices on the right ear, and though still unable to talk with anyone but mother I was freed from the horror of stone-deafness. I have no doubt that this partial restoration was an answer to mother's prayers; and the incompleteness of the recovery was an answer to her chief prayer that God's purpose for my life would be fulfilled. I realize now that the world of childhood to which my deafness so largely confined me was the only one in which my spiritual life could be purged and freshened for its new approach to orthodoxy.

As in former crises, a diversion was provided which kept my mind from settling into the stupor of introspection. This time the balance was retained through a long correspondence, on purely literary matters, with John Rowland. He, too, was a Cornish writer, though no longer living in the county, and being of the younger generation he did much to stimulate my interest in the contemporary world of ideas and literary experiments. When he first wrote to me at the end of 1934 he was awaiting the publisher's verdict on his first thriller. The verdict was favourable, and before we ceased corresponding two years later he had published half a dozen books, while I was still trying in vain to get even a short story into print, except in local papers. This contrast might have increased my bitterness, but somehow it didn't. I had already faced that sort of question and realized that the commercial valuation of writing could hardly be expected to favour the mystic. Oddly enough, although Rowland was a rationalist and I was an irrational Christian, we agreed in our judgment of many personalities and trends of twentieth-century culture: in our dislike of the cynically arrogant intellectuals, the pathetic pretentiousness of Cornish "Nationalists," leaders of the Gorsedd and *Tyr ha Tavas* movements, and the apostles of even less reputable gibberish—James Joyce for instance. (I had read extracts from Joyce's work in *John o' London's Weekly*. Most of my knowledge of modern literature was derived from that paper: authors who had been mere names to me became gradually solid and significant as biographical and biblio-graphical details accrued.) Nothing of my private circum-stances was reflected in my letters to Rowland; they were apparently the products of an alert, healthy mind, well satisfied with life and responding eagerly to every challenge. This, I think, was due to a habit of concentrating my energies fiercely upon the task of the moment. Deafness, poverty, the Nanpean débâcle—all were forgotten when my brain received the order to be "literary" for half an hour.

One notable result of my deafness was a marked change in the attitude of my old Bournemouth friend, S. E. Burrow. He had become exasperated by his failure to turn me into an average Christian, and had no sympathy with my literary aims. He told me repeatedly that it seemed I had thought I could start at the top, and that it would have been better had I begun as a junior clerk in a newspaper office. He counselled me to model my fiction on that of the Hockings, and when he saw that, instead of doing this, I was cultivating a style which he regarded as obscure and "highbrow," he was naturally dis-pleased. He thought I was being deliberately perverse, and publicly accused me of "the sheer cussedness of wanting to be different from everybody else." But when I wrote and told

him of the sudden blow of deafness, I received from him a
letter in which he expressed regret for his harsh criticism of a
lad "so severely handicapped," and added: "Life is full of
mystery and the Father's discipline often difficult to understand.
But it is always parental, and there is always a 'Nevertheless
afterward——'. You will get yours in God's good time, so
press on and look up!" Such messages as this were as welcome
to me as the more cultured appreciation of Baron or the literary
gossip of Rowland. From then onward I realized Burrow's
friendship as a deeper and closer bond; scarcely a day passed
in which I did not think of him and feel the help of his prayers.

It is true that, even after this reconciliation, my reckless
outbursts drew forth one or two sharp rebukes from Burrow.
But I had no doubt of his good intentions; and I remembered
that he was now an old man of eighty whom one could hardly
expect to be always consistent. His last protest of any importance came in May 1935, when I filled a column of the *Cornish
Guardian* with a violently Socialistic attack on the Jubilee
celebrations. Burrow, ever a fervent patriot, was indignant,
called me another Jimmy Maxton, and ended his diatribe with
a biting pen-picture: "It is sad to think that while the nation
as a whole will abandon itself to thanksgiving, worship mingling
with hilarity, friend vieing with friend and thinking less of
self than of others all the time...it is sad, I repeat, to picture
Jack R. Clemo on Jubilee Day meandering gloomily and
solitarily among the clay-dumps of St. Stephen's, absorbed in
the pitiful task of nursing his own bad attacks of the dumps!"
Had I told him of the Nanpean affair he would have known
that I had cause enough to wander gloomily among the clay-
dumps. Every day for weeks before that feverish Monday I
had looked across the valley and seen the faggots, tar barrels
and other combustibles being piled on Foxhole Beacon, the
Union Jack fluttering at length above the huge mass of fuel,
I knew that on Jubilee Day Evelyn would be there, and the
thought of her being free to enjoy herself so near to my prison-
house over a year after the break at Nanpean—this moved me
to an ugly mood of rebellion which I projected and dramatized

as a social protest on behalf of those who would be mocked by the "orgy of commemoration." Referring to the "sad, brave tragedy" of the unemployed I wrote: "These people do not want to look back. They do not want to remember what happened in 1910. They know well enough that 1914 followed it, that 1935, with its stagnation and misery, has followed it. They look forward to the years which are coming, and they see no hope." This reflects my own spiritual condition, and local Socialists were misguided when they sent me appreciative letters and invited me to take part in the General Election capaign of 1935 in support of the Labour candidate, A. L. Rowse. I had no interest in politics and was merely protesting against a national mood of gaiety in which Evelyn shared and from which I was excluded. I spent Jubilee Day in glum silence at home, though after sunset I climbed Bloomdale clay-dump to get a view of the bonfire and illuminations over on the Beacon: perhaps also to indulge in a romantically maso-chistic mood, wishing to be hurt by the contrast between this lonely baffled brooding and those evening vigils on the same ridge five years earlier when I had felt my destiny drawing me towards Nanpean. I remained seated on the peak until nearly midnight, watching the Beacon fire die down, the last rockets flare up over Foxhole, burst into showers of coloured stars—green, blue, red—and fade slowly like spent comets into the darkness. Only the dull glow of the fire and the nosing headlights of innumerable cars lit up the landscape as I scrambled down the dump and came in—my diary senti-mentally affirms—"thinking, longing for Evelyn, with the void still in my heart."

The Nanpean obsession lingered in me yet, though the spiritual world it had produced was destroyed. Evelyn still inspired my writing at two levels—that of truculent bitterness and that of frivolous cynicism. An instance of the latter kind was a lyric I wrote about this time called "Heaven Number Eight," in which I lampooned the spiritual conception of Heaven and declared—as wretched and maladjusted people are wont to declare—that the gratification of sensual desire was the only paradise I wished for. The lyric was set to a foxtrot tune and so impressed a London music publishing firm that they issued it at their own expense in December, 1935. To their bewilderment, and my own intense relief, not a single copy of the song was sold. Providence was trying in every possible way to show me that the Nanpean inspiration was false and could never lead to success; but though my reason accepted the fact my imagination continued to weave fanciful hopes. Throughout 1935 and even into 1936 my diary entries frequently expressed the belief that my dismissal from Evelyn's home marked the beginning of an interval, and that as she had come in 1929 to restore my sight, so after necessary preparation she would come again to restore my hearing. This nonsensical idea shows that at heart I feared the shock of a new movement which must eventually break the monotony upon which I had entered. I was in the state that Francis Thompson so well understood: "Though romance may return on you in cycles and crises, you are ever dreading its next manifestation. Nor need you be 'romantic' to others: the most terrible romances are inward, and the intolerableness of them is that they pass in silence."*

The only external incidents of my life for the next two years were my journeys to Plymouth, where my ears were examined and tested at frequent intervals. Mother could not, of course, afford the fares, and these were paid, through the local rector, by one of the war charities. I went alone after the first few visits, and the trips provided some diversion, though they also increased my emotional disharmony: the contact with city life was torturing in the sense of bewilderment and isolation it brought me. I realized more than ever that I could never hope to understand or interpret the modern world—particularly modern girls. I moved among the polished, elegant figures like a caveman, baffled and inarticulate, sullenly withdrawn into myself, deaf to the surrounding idiom of civilization, subtlety, social grace. I was repudiated and impotent here, I and my uncouth sincerity which hardened

* *Life of Francis Thompson* (E Meynell).

under the sting of these masked personalities. The oppression of the fashionable centres was often so great that I slunk away to the poorer quarters, roaming about the slum alleys, trying to ease myself, to receive an intimation I could recognize. There was a sympathy, a sense of being at home among the grimy gutters and tenements. The Clemo strain fitted in with this squalor; I was among the misfits and outcasts here, and sometimes found a thrill of joy, so deep that it brought tears, in the furtive smile of some ragged little girl playing amid the garbage.

I sought more respectable forms of relief in the Public Library in Tavistock Road, though the bookish explorations yielded disillusion rather than solace as I discovered how far some of my literary idols—Tolstoy for instance—had strayed from the Christian ideal, I had previously felt Tolstoy a kindred spirit, especially in *The Kreutzer Sonata* with its savage indictment of worldliness in sex matters. But to me such an attitude was invalid unless it was the product of belief in a Divine revelation. I regarded the Puritanical unbeliever as a mere egoist accepting the sanctions of his own personality as ultimate and sufficient. My stubborn Biblical loyalties could destroy for me the appeal of any author, overwhelming the literary sympathy as completely as my obsession with Evelyn was overwhelmed at Old Pound chapel.

I acquired several bargains at the second-hand bookstalls in Plymouth, which I came to know very well. Chief of these purchases was a set of Garnett's *International Library of Famous Literature*—nineteen big volumes picked up at sixpence each. These were brought home in the autumn of 1935 when Evelyn's brother Harry—who now owned a car and with whom we remained on the most cordial terms despite the Nanpean estrangement—drove mother and myself to Plymouth to fetch the books. For the next few weeks they were piled on the floor in our front room, the bookcase being already full and all the drawers of my desk packed with manuscripts. Day after day I did practically nothing but browse among them, often taking Barbara on my knee to look at the pictures. A few of the contents of these volumes had some slight, temporary influence in drawing my thoughts towards Calvinism—the extracts from Calvin's *Institutes*, Jonathan Edwards' *Freedom of the Will*, and Carlyle's *Cromwell*. I was especially moved by the latter with its vivid portrayal of the conflict between the "deep believing man" and the "vulpine intellect." But I did not derive from this treasury of literature the permanent help and enjoyment which a normal student would have done. My mind was not the sort that could benefit from a mass of reading matter, but only from concentrating upon those few writers who were sympathetic to my own angle of vision. Dozens of great writers whose outlook had nothing in common with mine—the scientists, philosophers, historians, essayists—were dipped into and promptly dismissed from all further interest. The novelists I studied more carefully, but made no fresh discoveries that affected my own work. Even the mystics represented in these books, such as Blake and Swedenborg, meant little to me. My mysticism had never been of the type that is attracted by the occult; nothing merely psychic or supernatural could fascinate me for long. Nor was I much interested in vague agnostic mysticism like Emily Bronte's. I had once, in a Press controversy, endorsed her declaration:

> "Vain are the thousand creeds
> That move men's hearts—unutterably vain."

True, I had accepted the Christian doctrines, but in such a perverse, romantic way that I had no kinship with any section of the Church which adhered formally to these tenets. Gradually, as the Nanpean drama unfolded, I had been dislodged from this lonely and superior position. I had noted in my reading of biography that writers who adopted it usually met with disaster in their personal lives. They became "riddles of genius"; and after the Nanpean downfall I was so afraid of becoming a nasty sort of riddle myself that I would submit to any dogma, however hide-bound, narrow or superstitious, if it would enable me to escape that fate. I almost feared to write anything original lest it should commit me to a tragic life. It seemed that if one began to be really "literary" one couldn't go on unless one committed adultery, like Shelley, or had an illegitimate baby, like Wordsworth, or kept a mistress, like Dickens. I remarked in my diary that "Genius is the devil's substitute for the Holy Spirit"—a rash generalization, but one that is supported by facts, for these rebel geniuses seemed to strike from the very excess of their depravity an illumination akin to that which a Christian receives through prayer and Bible-study. I had become sadly disillusioned about the literary life, and no longer wondered that Puritanism tended to suppress all writings except tracts and hymns.

This reaction was no doubt due partly to my mother. She had made no attempt to keep pace with my intellectual development, though in later years she was to become the most well-read working-class woman in the district. Occasionally she would dip into some book that was influencing me, but seldom got beyond the first page or two. She preferred the *Christian Herald*, which helped her in preparing the addresses she gave now and then at local missionary meetings. But she had allowed me the most complete freedom of inquiry, never protesting that I was wasting my time in reading bad books. I had told her that in order to equip myself for my own type of work I should have to read books that were atheistic or immoral. She did not object, but would sometimes reply with earnest conviction: "I've put 'ee in God's hands an' prayed that 'twon't harm 'ee." One has only to contrast this spirit with the scolding, peevish attitude which the average uneducated mother tends to adopt towards an incomprehensible son to realize the value of Christianity in a working-class home. It was my mother's confidence in the Will of God that enabled her to grant me this liberty of mind. She was not extending to my fads a self-conscious toleration; still less was she indifferent, merely resigned to my going my own way. Her attitude was positive, surrounding me with a living power of insight and discrimination. Her naïve comments on literary matters kept me face to face with ultimate standards. When I praised the artistic qualities of some sceptical or pagan author, she would answer simply: "What do that matter if 'e lost 'is soul?" I had tried to dismiss this question as irrelevant and archaic, but the biographies of these men supported mother's viewpoint. There was ample proof of the fatality that overtook those who regarded their art as a religion. The appalling history of the æsthetes of the 'nineties—of whom I had begun to pick up scraps of knowledge—deepened my sense of being at the cross-roads, facing the alternatives that must confront every young man who, with a wayward creative temperament, has been reared in a Christian home. There was never any doubt as to which course I should choose. I had learnt to my cost where a heretical individual vision and an integrity of *natural* faith was likely to lead. The external religious sanctions of my childhood were becoming supreme once more; whatever could not be reconciled with them must be abandoned. There were times when I saw no hope of reconciling these Puritan sanctions with any personal vision that could inspire my writing, and felt that the writing would have to be dropped and that I would concentrate my energies into prayer for those Christian causes that were still loyal to the super-naturalism of the Bible.

It was, I think, an act of Providence which brought me at this crucial stage in touch with the poems and biography of Browning, for he alone had set the example that solved my problem. I had read some selections from his work in 1935, and soon afterwards *The Barretts of Wimpole Street* was serialized in *John o' London's Weekly*. I was profoundly moved by it. I had known before, of course, that Browning had made a spectacular marriage with an invalid woman, but had regarded it only as an episode in the life of a writer who had died a long time ago. The fresh study of his poems in the light of Besier's play, however, was startling and fascinating. With the prophecies of *Paracelsus* and *Sordello* so literally fulfilled in the Wimpole Street affair, and the great utterances of *Men and Women* interpreting it as experience, the whole story became vivid, challenging. I at once read several ·biographies of Browning, including Chesterton's, and was thrilled by the proof they afforded that the sort of faith towards which I had been groping, and which Browning had so perfectly expressed was sane and practical when rightly focused and integrated. It had made Browning, as I wished it to make me, "not at all like a damned literary man." He alone among writers, as far as I could judge, had emerged from adolescent morbidities to enjoy a love-life in which Christian mysticism and normal human feeling were ideally balanced; and he had done it through realizing that the consummation of earthly joy, deadened by formal Puritanism, is nevertheless

> "reached
> By no help of lake or mountain, but the texts
> whence Calvin preached."*

This was the exact and peculiar blend of truth which I had been seeking, and trying to manufacture out of my perversities, for five years. It assured me that sensuous vision could be reconciled with the most rigid orthodoxy, and encouraged me to deepen my own experiences along the borderline. My feeling of intense gratitude to Browning, and my acceptance of the Wimpole Street miracle as an omen for my own future, were expressed impulsively towards the end of 1935. We obtained a new pomeranian dog, a little black puppy, and I called him Flush.

These glimpses of my ultimate goal were stimulating, but many sloughs of despond had yet to be waded through before my feet were firmly set on the upward path. As my teen years drew to a close, leaving me still deaf and practically penniless, it was natural that I should feel my crushing handicaps more keenly. My manuscripts were being regularly declined, often coming back crumpled from editors and publishers who probably thought I was earning good money at another job and could afford to get them re-typed. I remember that sometimes mother used to iron the rejected manuscripts to take out the creases so that the same papers could be submitted elsewhere, and when my typewriter ribbon became worn out I would pass it under a damp brush which temporarily restored the colour and postponed fresh expenditure as long as possible. During these years mother often helped with the housework at Morcom's farm at Goonamarris—Mrs. Morcom being bed-

* *La Saisiaz.*

ridden—to earn a few extra shillings and maintain for us the usual working-class standard of homely comfort to which I had been reared. Only the extraordinarily low rent of our home— £6 per annum—enabled even this to be kept up. My aunt Bertha was still living with us, receiving parish relief and now almost incapacitated by diabetes. We were regarded as a pathetic household by the villagers; and certainly few homes could have known darker shadows. My own black moods were the chief cause of unhappiness to all in the cottage, and since everyone agreed that I had reason enough for complaint, there was little heart in their efforts to make me more cheerful. The very day after my twentieth birthday, March 12, 1936, I seem to have been pretty well smothered in hopelessness, for my diary entry begins with the despairing confession; "Oh! Barbara, if it weren't for you I would be out of it all, in the rest of the grave...."

My deafness had destroyed the last trace of manliness in my behaviour: though not in my writings. It is a curious paradox that my published output at this time—humorous stories, Press letters, etc.—was extremely bold and vigorous. In my personal life I was absurdly childish, querulous and irritable, crying for hours over trifling set-backs, resenting all adult sympathy, even mother's, and turning only to Barbara for refreshment and guidance.

The psychological state which produced this bias is very difficult to describe—because it is so rare. I had strayed so far from normal feeling that I could not reach it by any common means. I had become so perverse that contact with adult values could only increase the perversity. I had to go back to the beginning and start afresh, to apprehend everything with the spontaneity and innocence of a child. For this strange education I had to be barred off as much as possible from the influence of adults, shut up where the medium of childhood was the only one through which experience touched me. And considering my ultimate destiny as a Calvinist one can see how right, how essential this procedure was. A path so remote from ordinary life must lead a man either to Christianity—the only system that combines astringent dogma with an exhortation to "become as a little child"—or to sheer idiocy. There was no room for humanist or rationalist solutions. These may be tried in the common dilemmas of everyday life, but they become irrelevant when one is surrounded and engulfed by completely abnormal circumstances. I had always felt that rationalism was absurdly superficial, and now on this borderland I saw more clearly than ever that rationalists consider only the rule, never the exceptional case. The exceptional case is the thin end of the wedge of miracle; it carries for the rationalist a nasty suggestion of the sort of things that "don't happen" in his world. How far, and in what direction, could "reason" have taken me in my predicament? If a man's psychological life has been disintegrated as a result of blindness, if he is then barred off from normality by deafness, and if, in addition, he has a strong creative urge and is trying to write novels in working-class poverty—what, according to rationalists, ought he to do? The reply would probably be that a young fellow in such fantastic conditions should be placed in the care of a psychiatrist. And that would have been the end of the story— a very dull and unexciting end which no one would have enjoyed. God had other ideas. He placed me, during my "convalescent" period, very largely in the care of a girl less than seven years old—and the results were astonishing.

For two years Barbara had been with me nearly every weekday, coming in just after breakfast and sometimes staying until the evening, with only the briefest breaks for meals. There were no other children at Goonamarris at that time, so she had no one but me to play with, her mother being busied with housework and her father at Trethosa clay-dump, where, oddly enough, he was engaged in tipping sand over the shell of my fathers' old home. Barbara was an intelligent child, and I had plenty of books for her to look at and plenty of paper on which she could scribble. I spent hours reading to her— comic papers and nursery rhymes from the *Children's Encyclopædia*. She often sat on my knee while I wrote and typed, and sometimes spoilt a page of typescript by stabbing her forefinger mischievously down on the wrong keys. Most of my early novels were eventually handed over to her, and one by one the records of my Nanpean dream were covered with pencilled scrawlings, Barbara's first attempts at writing, drawing and arithmetic. On fine days she frequently persuaded me to leave my desk and romp with her, or play ball, outdoors. I gave much more time to her than to my literary work: that became a dull, automatic mental process for awhile when I could no longer trace it to Evelyn.

On Sundays, which Barbara usually spent with her grandparents at St. Dennis, I would brood over the Bible, Spurgeon's sermons and Browning's poems, trying to fuse the fresh memories of Barbara with the wider sense of a destiny covering my whole development. The memories were not uniformly bright, for Barbara was quick-tempered though seldom sulky, and recollection of our little tiffs would send me desolately to the Book of Job. But there was always the feeling of movement; quarrels were followed swiftly by caresses; and the moods caught me and changed the tone of my world so rapidly that I needed a deep spiritual anchorage, the steadying influence of a fixed belief. The vivid actuality of Barbara's contacts with me, never stagnant or idealized, made me see her as the omen of my true faith as Evelyn had been the omen of my false one, though I was too exhausted and confused to tell exactly what my true faith was to be. My imaginative reaction as well as my growing interest in Spurgeon's sermons, suggested that it would be solid and realistic; for when Barbara started to attend Foxhole school in 1936 I began plotting a new novel called *Private Snow* which brought me great hopes of success three years later when the finished manuscript was read by Sir Arthur Quiller-Couch. It was the first book I wrote entirely under Barbara's influence, and it was far healthier than anything I had produced through the Nanpean inspiration.

The only person, other than Barbara, who played a stimulating part in my life at this period was William Martin, an ageing Socialist, humanist and poet, then living at Bodmin. My contact with him began through his deliberately seeking me out at Goonamarris in the autumn of 1936. He had been drawn thither by my mystical outpourings in the *Cornish*

Guardian, and he was not the first stranger to call at my home through reading those contributions. But the others had been ageing local preachers and retired ministers who wished to interview me personally about my religious beliefs. Martin's interest was more literary. He fancied me as a fellow poet and propagandist, and after his introductory visit and the disappointing discovery that I was too deaf to converse with him, he began writing me the most extraordinary letters I have ever received. They were more violent than mine and much less grammatical, and so full of contradictions that I was quite unable to tell from them what he really believed. Though he railed against the Church and spoke of God as an impersonal Law, he was liable at any moment to burst into rhapsodies about his "elder Brother," as he called Christ. He would often break into doggerel verse in the middle of a letter, and always signed these effusions "W. Martin, Poet" before resuming the prose part of his message. His printed leaflets, which he peddled throughout mid-Cornwall, bore the inscription "W. Martin, Miners' Poet" at the foot. He had indeed been a miner in Northumberland, where he was born, and his early struggles had warped a nature that was fundamentally religious. He had begun training as a lay preacher at a Wesleyan college, but was cold-shouldered because of his humble origin and broke away in defiance to become a mining engineer and a flaming Socialist. His work as an engineer had taken him abroad, he had seen "the oppressed and persecuted of other lands and the hand of the so-called missionary laid heavily upon the poor." His wartime experience as a fighting man in France had obviously shaken and embittered him, and he could never touch upon the War in his letters to me without being carried away by an ebullition of rage against the "dirty microbes" and "devils" who had caused it, and even against "the parsons' God who has done nothing for 2,000 years, only bloodshed, martyrdom, poverty and oppression." In conversation with my mother he hinted at a domestic tragedy which had been a sombre background to most of his public crusading. He was now a widower.

CONFESSION OF A REBEL

I remember still the short muscular figure with the fresh-coloured, ravaged face and grey moustache sitting in the arm-chair in our front room on New Year's Day, 1937, when he spent almost the whole day at our home, reading my published writings and some of my manuscripts. He had brought in his wallet a poem of mine cut from the current issue of the *Cornish Guardian*, and spoke much of it, especially one verse:

"What if night encompassed oftener than the sunshine ?
Poison entered cup divine ?
Is not all creative process done in darkness ?
Where the miracle if first there be no poison
Needing change to wine ?"

This buoyant faith, so sure of the Redemption that it could greet the Fall with a cheer, was very unlike his own pessimistic humanism. Being a Modernist he refused to believe in the Fall because he feared that Christianity wasn't big enough to deal with anything so drastic. He was puzzled to find a young man who had no such fears, a young man whose testimony to miracles was becoming exasperatingly authentic even in circumstances that seemed to justify cynicism and despair. Martin questioned my mother a good deal about my spiritual experience: he little guessed that a key to it lay in the slim, dark-haired girl who tripped in at intervals during the morning and afternoon and led me out to play hide-and-seek among the shrubs. The romps with Barbara were a great relief to me that day: the strain indoors was considerable, as I could not hear the talk; could only sit in glum silence at my desk, following my own thoughts as I waited impatiently for Martin to go.

That was the last time I saw him; he never entered my home again, though he kept up his correspondence with me until Easter. The reason for the swift collapse of our friendship was that I was no longer the only or the chief object that drew his mind and heart to Goonamarris. It was a somewhat painful episode for us all, and caused much tension and heart-searching in our home before it was settled by Martin's last angry letter to my mother announcing that he was leaving Cornwall and returning to Northumberland.

CHAPTER NINE

Towards Orthodoxy

MARTIN did much to inspire me with confidence in my work, though he warned me that I might have to pay the price for my vision in "tribulation, tears and sacrifice." I felt I had already done that, and that some measure of reward was now almost within my grasp. In October 1936 my eighth novel had been accepted by a well-known firm of literary agents in London. The directors were obviously impressed by its promise and asked me to send them my next book as soon as possible. During the whole period of my correspondence with Martin, therefore, I was busy on this new novel, in high spirits, expecting always to surprise him in my next letter by news of the forthcoming publication of the accepted manuscript. Its successor was finished in April, 1937, but just after the break with Martin I sustained a nasty blow: both manuscripts were returned to me by the agents, with a curt note which informed me that my "second" novel was much less saleable than the earlier one, and that in the circumstances they were reluctantly forced to drop me from their list of clients. Probably they were right, as this book expressed my most extreme Puritan revolt against the mystical excess of earlier work; it was drab and colourless, without a gleam of poetry or humour. But it had one or two good scenes, and these were re-written and fitted into *Private Snow*, with which I was progressing slowly, transmuting Barbara's influence at every step. The task was difficult, and the building up of this book alternated with an attempt to recast the one which had raised such hopes. By the end of 1937 I had moulded it into a novel called *Cuckoospit*, which was as faulty as the original version had been. The tendency to patch and re-write old incidents instead of inventing new ones was increasingly characteristic of my method, and was probably due to my deafness, the inability to get in touch with active life that would supply fresh material. I expended tens of thousands of words in re-fashioning scenes so feeble in themselves that they should have been scrapped at the outset. My writing was always haphazard, undisciplined, without conscious direction. I deliberately avoided the popular manuals and textbooks that offered literary beginners a short cut to success, and found the more reputable guides alien and distasteful. I once borrowed Quiller-Couch's *The Art of Writing* from the local library, glanced at it and returned it unread. I recognized its chilly lecture-hall atmosphere as a threat to the spontaneity of my individual moods and recoiled to the protective solitudes of my inspiration. I wrote as I was moved, sometimes producing three thousand words in one morning and at other times only three hundred words in a month. I could not write to order or maintain a regular output. Creative power came to me in flashes, and during the intervals, which tended to lengthen as I grew older, I was dull and stolid, as indifferent to literary matters as the other village folk, quite content doing nothing but household chores, playing with Barbara, or rummaging in my old clay-smeared clothes around the sand-dumps for scraps of timber to burn, my thoughts those of a simple-minded peasant who seeks communion with God. I wished to work as nearly on the lines of the old religious prophets as a writer could, and it was because I got closest to their fervid exaltation in my Press letters that I "frittered away"—as my critics put it—my best energies in this undignified and unremunerative propaganda. Even now that I was in my twenties I loathed the commercial element as much as ever. There was nothing of the self-conscious integrity of the artist in my attitude. The severe idealist who is willing to starve for his art seemed to me to be a pretentious ass sacrificing essentials to non-essentials, and probably—because of his assumed self-sufficiency—far nearer to Hell than the Philistines he raved against. My motive was evangelical, not æsthetic. I would be "taught of the Lord" and must therefore renounce Mammon.

Occasionally I received some slight token that this eccentric way of mine had its own peculiar rewards. I remember how my conviction was strengthened in the spring of 1937 by an unexpected letter from S. E. Burrow. It was a letter that told a story. A few weeks before, he had preached at Southampton on the mysterious dispensations of Providence, and had illustrated his point by telling the congregation of a young man he knew who possessed literary talent and had dedicated it to God, but could make no headway because of the double handicap of deafness and poverty. When he next visited this church a woman had come to him after the service and reminded him of his reference to this afflicted young man. She had been led to pray very earnestly for him, and as proof of her sincerity she handed Burrow a ten shilling note to confirm my faith in God's ultimate deliverance. Burrow sent the money along with the characteristic, boyish comment that he was "wondering whether this will please or annoy you." Of course I was pleased—not only by the knowledge that I had been preached about at Southampton, but by the proof that it was still the simple, old-fashioned Christians and not the worldly "talent spotters" who understood and encouraged me.

Another influence which helped to confirm me in my remote village life of meditation was my discovery, during this period, of the work of T. F. Powys. I had never heard of him until 1935 when John Rowland in one of his letters advised me to read *Mr. Weston's Good Wine*. A year later I was much impressed by the interview Powys gave to *John o' London's Weekly* when he abandoned writing—the account of his thirty years of mystic isolation at East Chaldon, on the Dorset moors. The grandeur of this renunciation of the bustling activity and worldly ambition which usually attend a literary life, made an instant appeal to me. I stuck the article in a scrapbook and read it repeatedly until its tone of sober contentment had helped to relieve any sense of frustration I might have felt at being deprived of the normal literary and social stimulants. No other incident in modern literary history had so gripped my imagination or come so close to my sympathies. I had sometimes been fascinated to think of the granite cottage neat Zennor, in west Cornwall, where D. H. Lawrence had suffered agonies during my infancy; but Lawrence's complete rejection of Christian values prevented my response from being deep and enduring. Powys was sufficiently Christian—in the deeper, mystical sense—to inspire a feeling of permanent spiritual kinship. The fact that my behaviour perplexed the good folk of Goonamarris as much as Powys had puzzled the East Chaldon cottagers, showed that I was already firmly set on the same path; and with these personal associations emphasizing Rowland's advice, I was ready to receive the full impact of Powys' work when, early in 1937, *Mr. Weston's Good Wine* was published in the sixpenny Penguin series. I bought a copy at once, and was more profoundly moved by it than by any book I had read since I discovered Browning. From my particular point of view there was a fundamental unity in their message, though at first sight no two authors could seem to have less in common. I felt in their work a revelation of Calvinism warped in opposite directions. In *Mr. Weston's Good Wine*, against a background of "everlasting night," was a fusion of religious and sensual realism similar to that which Browning presented against a background of eternal sunshine. Browning's sense of spiritual love turning from pure Nature to "the texts whence Calvin preached" was matched by Powys' conception of God entering upon a world of gross practices and declaring in the words of Isaiah: "I, the Lord, do all these things"; the inference being that "those who live in the presence of the Most High should be the most delightful lovers." This was the angle of vision which Gordon Meggy had noted, and condemned as "unnatural," in my first novel, and I felt less lonely, less of a literary pariah, as I realized that at least one great modern writer had plumbed the depths I had been forced to look into. There had always been truth in those depths, but during my teens I had tried to interpret it by the "inner light" of natural mysticism, not by the light of dogma striking down from beyond Nature. The result was that I had seen the Divine Purity as a beautiful ideal when actually it was a savage fact, at work among the dark roots of life, grappling with original sin. Reading and meditation were now showing me that Christianity

was not a religion of ideals but of realities, not a picture of
what the world would be like if everyone lived a good life, but
the communication of a sense of miracle in the fact that,
whether people lived the good life or not, this earth was still the

> "Stage and scene of Thy transcendent act
> Beside which even the creation fades
> Into a puny excercise of power."*

That was Browning's view; and Powys's had a similar elemental
quality. In his allegory Mr. Weston's good wine was love to
the young and death to the weary, but for those who had lost
faith through the sin and suffering in human life his wine was
the Bible. This idea of the Bible as a gift of God, as elemental
and independent of scholastic criticism as love or death, was
very close to my own conception of it. My belief in its truth
was no longer perverse or unreasoning, but I still found
Modernism as much of a squalid indecency as ever. I was
exasperated by the common plea that the teaching of the Bible
was not invalidated if we had to regard many of its records as
myth rather than history. Critics who talked like that seemed
to me to miss the whole point of the religious significance of
the Scriptures. I did not turn to the Bible for its teachings, but
for its *facts*. My faith was sustained by the conviction that these
marvellous things had actually happened. If God really had
"begotten a Son upon the body of a Jewish woman"—in
Shelley's phrase—and if that Son had done what the Gospels
say He did, then there was a life of triumphant achievement
within the reach of every man, whatever his hereditary handicaps. But if miracles had never occurred, if Christ's teachings
had merely been the religious opinions of a Jewish prophet who
hadn't made even a temporary dent in the machinery of the
Fall, then each individual must go on fulfilling the laws of his
own nature without purpose and without hope. I had done
that during the four years of my obsession at Nanpean, but I
was gradually ceasing to do it. There was thus a very personal
ground for my belief in miracles. Since God had done such

* *The Ring and the Book.*

queer things at Goonamarris, why should I doubt that He had done queerer ones in Palestine? Why should I even doubt that these odd happenings in my life were the result of that historic release of the turbulent and incalculable forces of a "new creation"? My whole outlook was certainly being created anew; it was becoming clear to me that "natural law" reveals the God in whom mere theists believe, but only miracles reveal the God in whom Christians believe. Through His operation I was being helped and guided towards a faith that was not at all a fulfilment of natural laws, for these had made me a misfit and this new faith was going to enable me to fit in. It seemed to be a complex faith, for I found extreme points of it reflected in both Browning and Powys. I was not yet sure of the exact point which I was destined to reflect, and my desperate need of hope and confidence made me gravitate instinctively towards Browning's extreme that was sometimes warped from orthodoxy by a too facile optimism rather than towards Powys's extreme, warped from orthodoxy by an apocalyptic pessimism. But in course of time I was to realize that both extremes were essential to me, as well as the steady, undistorted norm of Calvinism represented by Spurgeon.

My diary entries were increasingly Calvinistic, whether in random generalizations or personal records. At first the notes were crude and tinged with an unpleasant element of malice, as in the comment: "I believe there is an eternal war on between God and man, and I am an optimist because I believe man will lose." But this egotistical detachment soon passed as Barbara's influence soothed and adjusted me for the grafting of the dogma in its true Christian form. My spiritual life was in a state of flux, and its expressions seemed to depend on Barbara's moods more than on anything else. Some Press letters of the period, written in hours when I was unsettled by Barbara's imperfection, showed traces of Modernism. In a letter printed in *John o' London's Weekly* in October, 1936, I declared that a strict orthodoxy was "a fetter and an acknowledgment of weariness" and that "Dogma blunders against the fact that Christianity is indefinable," and in a local paper I stated that "religion has too long been occupied with the intangibilities of a hypothetical future state." It seems very odd that I, and not a bishop, should have penned those fatuous phrases. They certainly did not express my true spiritual movements; they were written only because the harmony which Barbara usually brought was temporarily disturbed—because she "wouldn't sit on my knee" or "got sulky while playing draughts and *would* move two squares at a time." The diary entry for my twenty-first birthday reveals the essential stresses that were developing me. Following a little tiff with Barbara I recorded that "I broke down and cried until we went to bed while God's waves went over my soul, yearning un-utterably to die and be at rest, eternally out of God's reach; cried myself to sleep, remembering the old happy days and being tortured beyond endurance." And the next morning: "B. came in before breakfast, so happy, as if she hadn't given me a night of hell. And thus is the mockery increased a thousand-fold—that because she is so young one can't speak of it to her, explain, reason with her. All is God's doing, beyond my reach. Well, let Him go on: it amuses Him, I daresay—a veritable Setebos with no 'Quiet' to catch and conquer Him. Poor Caliban Jack!" This is the natural human reaction to the Calvinist doctrine of Divine sovereignty; but by the end of 1937 my defiance and revolt had almost entirely vanished; I had surrendered, sure of the Divine mercy behind all the enigmas of Providence.

An important factor in this change was that the dying, fumbling tentacles of the Nanpean horror had been cut from me at last. The end came suddenly. On October 10th, 1937, while my mother and I were discussing my general moral outlook I said enough to convince her that I wasn't likely to be wounded by the news she had kept throughout the period of silent healing and transition. She told me that Evelyn had been married for two years to a St. Austell shop assistant. My deafness had served a useful purpose in preventing me from hearing of it before. I received the information calmly, with no regrets and very little interest. The process of adjustment through

Barbara had been so thoroughly done that I did not dwell upon the bitter irony of those hopes and fancies I had still woven about Evelyn when she was already the wife of another. I felt only a sense of immeasurable relief and freedom, and wrote in my diary: "And now the past is really gone from me, and I can say with praise what I once said in despair—the words of Jean Paul Richter: "Gone is gone, and dead is dead." And on October 24th:

> "Alone here at 2.20 p.m. I tore the snapshots of E. from the album, knelt on the hearth and dropped them into the fire. I held in my hands my New Testament, yesterday's date against the text, "It is the Lord's doing, and marvellous in our eyes." As the last photo turned to ashes I took up Barbara's photo and pressed my lips to it and felt the solemn joy of a fresh dedication. God was very near."

With that gesture I had fully entered the world of childhood; my feet were set upon the path that was to lead me upward through the various stages of childish tenderness to the mature, cleansed vision of the love that is physically sexual.

The process had its perils, but most of them were offset by the objective interpretation or dramatization which I soon found in *The Browning Love Letters*. This volume was my mother's present to me at Christmas, 1937, and immediately became one of the half-dozen books of destiny in my life— books that so deeply influenced me in times of crises that I cannot conceive what might have happened had I never read them. Browning's poetry had been a work of this sort; there was hardly a page of my diary from 1935 onward without quotations from his poems. (It will be noted that even in the tragic little incident on my twenty-first birthday my mind had turned to his *Caliban upon Setebos*.) But the love letters were more direct and personal; they gave me just the imaginative poise I needed, balancing the "childishness" of my actual experience, broadening its significance and rooting it in a sense of spiritual maturity. The Calvinistic phrases so frequently used in the letters of Browning and Elizabeth Barrett—

"predestinated," "ordained," "granted by God," etc.—expressed what I was feeling about my friendship with Barbara. I remember how the tears rushed to my eyes when I first read Browning's triumphant avowal: "So it has always been with me in my life of wonders—absolute wonders, with God's hand over all. And this last and best of all would never have begun so, and gone on so, to break off abruptly even here, in this world, for the little time!" Unlike Browning, I wasn't sure what had begun, or what it was leading to, but I was prepared for "absolute wonders," having had such a foretaste in Barbara.

At this juncture, however, I was reminded pretty forcibly that the barriers around me were more formidable than any Browning had encountered—worse, even, than Elizabeth Barrett's "trailing chain of weakness." Just before Christmas I had suffered an unexpected relapse of my hearing, and for over a week I was stone deaf. It was a bewildering and terrifying setback and reduced me again, temporarily, to frantic despair. Barbara still came in as usual, but all was changed, remote, distorted; I was "dumb, striking daily a mute note in the scale," and at nights I "slept badly, lying awake in the dark, knocking my head against the pillow to see if I could hear a rustle—but no sound." The attack passed without any help from the doctors: by the New Year I could hear Barbara's voice again, and opened my 1938 diary with a poem twenty-three verses long, expressing thanksgiving for deliverance.

A note of wondering gratitude was dominant in my diary entries through the winter of 1937-38. There was a serenity, a sense of ripeness and completeness that often fell like a benediction, moving me to quote passages from the Psalms and Old Testament prophets. The more I nourished this simplicity of belief and emotional response, the more balanced and "tough-minded" I became intellectually. My theological bias is revealed by the fact that I spent nearly a quarter of my income for 1937—half a guinea, to be exact—in obtaining one of Spurgeon's sermon proofs from the trustees of his orphanage at Stockwell. I was more than repaid for the sacrifice by the thrill of joy I felt when I opened the slips of galley proof and found them covered with corrections in Spurgeon's copperplate hand-writing. This personal relic was, and remains, a great treasure to me, for on the purely spiritual side I owe more to Spurgeon than to any other man. I read his sermons and his devotional work, *The Cheque-book of Faith*, almost every day during this period.

Barbara's parents, of course, guessed nothing of what her influence meant to me, and the villagers merely pitied me when they saw us playing together in the road. The fact that I was no longer writing in the papers about sex but only about God, no doubt convinced them that I had given up all thought of love and resigned myself to the "compensations" of religion. Many of them had decided by this time that the reason for my failure as a novelist was pretty clear. Barbara's mother sometimes expressed this view in conversations with my mother in our front room. What was the good, she asked scornfully, of my trying to write love stories? What could I know about love? I had never been out with a girl! In one sense the situation was similar to that in Nanpean: I was still among people who could never comprehend my reactions or guess the depth of experience that came to me in every trifling contact. Francis Thompson had known, through his association with the Meynells' little daughters, that the world of "workaday wisdom" is sure to wonder

"that thy little kiss
Should be to me all this."*

Average persons cannot understand this unusual sensitivity and receptiveness, or sympathize with the moral problems involved in it. Even my mother could not help me here; she was bewildered and uneasy about my friendship with Barbara, and was sometimes less tolerant of it than she had been of my reading of atheistic books. It seemed to her that I was going from bad to worse: I had outgrown the inspiration of a girl of sixteen only to find myself in the more fantastic position of being inspired by a girl of six. That was not at all the kind of develop-

* *A Child's Kiss.*

ment mother had prayed for, and she was oppressed by the fear that things had taken a wrong turn and were bearing me towards another sickening disillusion.

While this spiritual drama was unfolding at Goonamarris a more open drama was already attracting attention on the other side of the valley, at Goonabarn; and though it seemed quite irrelevant to my affairs it was soon to make upon them a fateful and tremendous impact.

The central figure in this drama was Barbara's grandfather, Marshall Rowse, a man chiefly remarkable for his zeal as a leader of the Jehovah's Witness sect. He had been a conscientious objector during the Four Years' War, and while in prison he had met some of the Jehovah's Witnesses, then known as Russellites. He had accepted their theories and had returned home with the burning desire to convert the predominantly Methodist people of mid-Cornwall to the true faith. He went all over the district selling Judge Rutherford's tracts and haranguing housewives on doorsteps. During my childhood he often called at my home and would stand for nearly an hour in the doorway arguing with mother about the end of the world. His home at Goonabarn, under Foxhole Beacon, became the local rallying-point of the Witnesses; meetings were held there weekly, and now and then there would be a big demonstration in the field outside, speakers arriving from various Cornish towns and declaiming shrilly about Armageddon and the Sixth Beast, to the astonishment of Rowse's cow. Apart from this aberration, however, Rowse was a man of fine character and integrity, a claywork mason by trade, simple in his habits and with a quiet beauty in his home life, though he was grim in appearance—a dark thick-set man, a typical Cornish Rowse. His wife, over ten years younger than himself, was home-loving and religious and had borne him three children, of whom Barbara's father was the eldest.

At this period Rowse had become involved in a family feud that arose over some injustices in a Will, and a cousin of his called Angilley, an unbalanced fellow who ended in the lunatic asylum, had threatened to "do him in." One evening, in the autumn of 1937, he had waited at the end of Goonabarn lane, armed with a club, until Rowse returned there from work, and had attempted to carry out his threat. The blow he struck might well have killed Rowse had it caught him unawares, on the head as it was meant to do. But he had expected some such assault and parried the blow, taking it on his upraised arm, which was broken. I remember seeing him several times thereafter, his arm in a sling, his face looking very dour and fear-ridden. He had indeed been much shaken by this attempt on his life, and as Angilley lived only a few hundred yards away he was continually haunted by a sense of danger. His religious scruples would not allow him to take the matter into the police-court, so he consulted the Jehovah's Witness organizers at St. Austell. These people provided him with a home at Trewoon, four miles south of Goonabarn, and to this he and his wife and youngest child removed towards the end of 1937. The matter seemed to be satisfactorily settled, with no possible bearing on the fortunes of his granddaughter and myself.

But a fate as sombre and remorseless as that in a Hardy novel was concerned in the shaping of these events. Weeks and months slipped by while I romped with Barbara at Goonamarris and Rowse preached about the Millenial Dawn at Trewoon. And then came a day of Destiny—February 26th 1938.

It was a dark, wet day, and from the start I felt in it a queer, tense atmosphere of menace. By the morning post my novel *Cuckoospit* was returned for the sixth time, though the publisher admitted that it was "quite well written"—a remark with which I was becoming familiar and rather nauseated. These "rejection days" always put me under a terrible cloud of futility and gloom which only Barbara could lift. And that day—a Saturday—she was ill with influenza; the morning passed over me in numbed, stricken loneliness. But just after dinner her mother brought her in, explaining that she was going to St. Austell shopping and would leave Barbara with us all the afternoon and evening, though she wasn't well enough to romp or play games. We got out the comic papers and had just begun looking at them—Barbara on my knee at the desk—when we were disturbed to see the local policeman open the gate of Barbara's home and move rather hesitatingly up the path. A few minutes later Barbara's mother came in again, much changed, pale and semi-hysterical. Being deaf I knew nothing of what had occurred until my mother touched my arm and told me in an awed tone the news which the constable had brought.

Marshall Rowse had just been killed—while Barbara and I were trying to interest ourselves in the comics. He had been returning on his motor-cycle to Trewoon and had collided with a stationary lorry in the main street of Foxhole. There was much conflict of evidence as to how the accident occurred. Eye-witness accounts printed in the local papers said that the machine had "wobbled towards the lorry," as if it were suddenly out of control. Another theory was that as the wind and rain were beating into Rowse's face he had kept his head down and hadn't seen the lorry at all. Whatever the explanation, the event was swift and tragic, and he died instantly.

It was an ironical end. Rowse had fled from Goonabarn to avoid being murdered by his demented cousin, and now he had been killed while returning to his refuge along a stretch of road that he would not have used had he been living at Goonabarn still. I brooded much upon this fatality; it seemed to be an instance of the way in which the pathetic dodges of human free will are overtaken and mastered by inherent doom.

The rest of that day was a very strange and oppressive one at my home. Barbara's parents had gone to Trewoon, though the body was never brought back there, Mrs. Rowse preferring not to see the terrible injuries her husband had sustained. Barbara had no more use for the comics; she lay on the sofa, not fully understanding what had happened, but petulant, feverish, coughing a lot and pushing me away sometimes when I made to caress her. I sat beside her, hour after hour, looking down at the flushed, pain-smitten face, wondering what in all these calamities God's purpose could be. In my drawer lay the manuscript of *Cuckoospit*, freshly back from London, fragments of nearly a dozen other book-length works rejected in former years, and the half-finished manuscript of *Private Snow*. Eight years of unrewarded struggle behind me, the last three with deafness added to the ills of poverty and a misfit's nature; only the friendship with Barbara enabling me to bear the yoke. And now the black pall of tragedy hung over us both, distorting and sundering, leaving me stripped and helpless.

Within a month the blow had fallen, Barbara and her parents shifting from Goonamarris to live at Trewoon with Rowse's widow.

CHAPTER TEN

The Grafting of Dogma

I SUPPOSE that I am almost the only Englishman (outside the lunatic asylums) who, in March 1938, knew nothing of Hitler's move against Austria. This was due partly to my deafness and the fact that we were still taking in no daily newspapers; but there was a deeper personal reason. During this period of stormy grafting the political world had again passed beyond my horizon. For nearly a year after I heard of Evelyn's marriage my diary contained not a single reference to international affairs. This was my apocalyptic year and I was caught up into a cloud so far as the European drama was concerned. It was only after the grafting had become creative and given my writing a new, individual quality that, with the jolt of the Munich crisis, I began to re-establish contact with those wider issues that had taken on a more or less normal interest for me as I entered my twenties.

The Italo-Abyssinian war, for instance, had moved me deeply, and on hearing of the economic sanctions imposed by Britain against Italy I had noted in my diary that there was "great risk of England playing that d—— fool part of 1914 over again." I wrote to the local papers in violent denunciation of the hypocrisy of the national Press, basing my charge on impressions gained in reading a few papers loaned by neighbours. I declared that if poison gas had existed in former ages "Drake would have singed Spaniards—not only their beards—with it. Our soldiers would have used it against the Indians, the Zulus, the Boers. And we today, in our schools, would still teach our children to honour these men, glorify them, uphold the priceless heritage—save the mark!—of their barbarity. Let us be fair with Italy! Britain has a past, though our national Press ignores what we all, if we are honest, know." This indictment enraged many good patriots and I was at once labelled a "pro-Italian Fascist." I denied the charge, though there was some truth in it. I remember that when I passed the Fascist headquarters in Plymouth in 1936 I felt a curious thrill of sympathy and attraction as I saw the Blackshirts lounging around outside. I will not, indeed, deny that had I not been deaf I might have got into a deal of mischief at that time. I was temperamentally an anarchist and I loathed the moral slackness and complacency that had resulted from the democratic ideal of easy tolerance. I had a vague but deep admiration for Mussolini and Hitler: the qualities in them which the cold English temperament derided as bombastic and theatrical appealed irresistibly to me with my mystical bias towards epic vitalism and fanaticism.

It was impossible for me ever to take the cultured, civilized view of human rights—or of anything else. I demanded Christian gusto and scorned the weary dignity of the classic ideal. Ever since my childhood I had detested the Greek spirit and loved the Gothic. In studying the art sections of the *Children's Encyclopædia* when I was only twelve years old I knew that the smoothness and clarity of Greek sculpture was repellent and false to me; it hurt and outraged something deep in my consciousness, and I turned with relief to Gothic gargoyles, to Rodin and Epstein. This peculiarity had now shown itself in my political and even my religious tastes. In philosophy, for instance, I gravitated instinctively towards Nietzsche and could never read a page of Plato. Every probing of my intellect and heart revealed the same basic laws—the hatred of polished grace and arid refinement, the love of the grotesque, the irrational, the blood-violence of a borderland. I had transferred to mature levels the essence of the strange, rather terrifying joy I had felt as a child at revivalist meetings when the crowd was singing the old hymn:

> "There is power, power, power in the Blood,
> Power in the Blood of the Lamb."

This primitivism had become diverse in a nature like mine that was capable of intellectualizing it. It made me sympathetic, as

I grew older, to oddly assorted kinds of eccentrics—to Hitler, to D. H. Lawrence, to the Aimee McPherson type of American "hot-gospeller." It is significant, however, that while the first two enthusiasms have passed I am still as appreciative as ever of the "vulgar hysteria"—as spiritual paralytics call it—of American revivalism. The religious aspect of an enthusiasm was the only one that could grip me for long. Thus I should have become a political misfit even among the Fascists had I been able to join them. Though I liked much of Nietzsche it was rather in Luther's sense that I accepted the dogma of violence. I believed that the true place for it was inside Christianity and that whenever it was applied outside Christianity it became perverted. The Nietzschean doctrine of the Superman was really a perversion of the Christian dogma of Election. The heroic age of the future was the Christian Millennium in which "the saints shall rule the world." I considered, therefore, that we could get nearest to an heroic age under the dictatorship of a Christian, a Cromwell or Calvin who would see to it that rebellion against God was no longer a paying game. The foundations of democracy were, in my view, undermined by its complete ignoring of theological truth. Its avowed purpose was to make life as agreeable for those who crucified Christ as for those who shared spiritually in His crucifixion, and this I knew must lead to moral apathy, religious impotence and chaos in all human relationships. I wanted, in short, a world run much as Calvin had run Geneva, a government that would not allow the proud and greedy and frivolous to persist in their illusion that they were on the winning side. If the Fascist and Nazi leaders were attempting something on these lines I entirely approved of their policy.

A reluctant but definite sympathy with ruthlessness had been bred in me by my experience of the methods of God. The *idea* of dictatorship was forced upon me from above, and I had to respect it. God was not giving my free will a chance to influence my destiny. By shutting me up where I could not choose my own work, my own pleasures or my own friends, He was forcing me, willy-nilly, to fulfil a pattern alien to my tastes and

desires. I had not submitted without strenuous efforts to escape
and break this tyranny. Some of the diary entries I have quoted
—and they are among the mildest—will prove that. But my
flight was no more successful than Francis Thompson's had
been: the baying of the Hound of Heaven was "round me like
a bursting sea" wherever I turned. It had silenced all the
voices of society that would have taught me the arts of compromise, smothered all the calls of Nature to which I would
have responded, and made the language of my own ego a
weak, meaningless jargon, a tattered sound lost in the wild
beating of its tempestuous mastery. The sentimental idealism
of modern "religion" with its pitying allusions to the barbarous
theology of our forefathers, drew from me a laugh of derision.
I knew from the scars in my own life that the Almighty was
hunting the souls of men as deliberately in the twentieth
century as in any previous age. The elect were still being
compelled that the non-elect might be persuaded. And if God
could only perfect His material by such arbitrary interference
with human free will, how could the creatures hope to succeed
in their limited and finite rule by a policy of freedom, fair
play and mutual help? This harshness was, of course, a
temporary product of the discipline of my youth, and does not
represent the viewpoint of later years. The subsequent history
of the European dictators convinced me that totalitarian
government in the twentieth century must be a very different
thing from that which Cromwell and Calvin sought to establish.
The Christian motive in such men is bound to be corrupted by
the modern educational and political systems through which
alone they could rise to power. This realization cooled my zeal
for all political revolutionaries, and when the General Election
came in 1945 the penniless proletarian and potential Fascist of
Goonamarris went gravely back to Trethosa school and voted
for the Conservative candidate.

The result of Barbara's departure was sudden and startling
to me as a writer; her going forced me to the crisis in which
imagination and dogma, which had hitherto obstructed each
other, were fused and released for the kind of Christian work

I was destined for. After I had recovered from the shock of Rowse's tragic death I turned back to my rejected manuscripts and began planning my next assault upon the London publishers. I persuaded mother to read *Cuckoospit*, and she suggested that the failure of such novels might be due to the claywork setting. She held the usual view of genteel and refined souls in the clay district, who regard the scenery as drab, ugly and without character. The Hockings, born and reared among the sand-dumps and mica-beds, had completely ignored the area in their stories, no doubt sharing the general view that it was quite unsuitable as a romantic background in fiction. Perhaps they were right and the public would not be interested in descriptions of the mid-Cornwall landscape, though it had breathed more sympathy into my soul and trained my æsthetic sense with a more tender mastery than all the pageantry of Nature. All my writings had been brooded out on the clay-dumps or in the still, terrifying depths of the deserted pits at nightfall or in the hush of Sunday, and my literary inspiration was as inseparable from their atmosphere as Emily Bronte's had been from the moors of Haworth. I had realized by this time the strange, unaccountable fact that my religion had been nourished by the clay-works, drawn by their grey, massive, ever-changing features towards the rude grandeur of a hermit faith. It was partly because I knew that I was not a child of the peaceful, teeming earth, the proud Mother, but only of the broken, ragged earth, the earth spilled out as gravelly refuse in a process of purification. I was thus dominated by a Christain symbolism that rejected all beauty. In my teen years I had preferred a bare chapel to an ornate cathedral; now in my twenties I preferred a rough claywork cuddy of rusty zinc to a chapel. It seemed that I could not get a setting simple and bleak enough to match the thoughts of God that possessed me. Like T. F. Powys, I had come to "have a terror of anything that is sound and whole."*

I always went to the most dilapidated claywork huts when I was most religious, reading my pocket Testament as I crouched

* *Soliloquies of a Hermit.*

on the splintered boards under the cobwebs, kneeling amid broken tools and scrap-iron and getting tar and mud on my trousers.

I knew that this mode of life was beyond the comprehension of the general public, and mother's advice led me to decide on a change of appeal in my future work. I had heard not long before of the new pilchard canning industry at Mevagissey, nine miles away on the coast—a "romantic" spot in the popular sense; and I became fired with the idea of writing a novel about the fisheries. Accordingly, on March 16th, I spent the whole day at Mevagissey, taking mental notes of the scenery—as much of it as was visible, for the place was blanketed in a clammy sea-fog nearly all the time. (Unlike most writers, I never took written notes or carried writing materials outdoors.) My deafness was, of course, a great handicap to me in gathering factual details for a novel. I could get no first-hand information, and returned home without even discovering where the canning factory was situated. During the next few days I tried to work out the plot of a story, very naïve and sentimental, but on the following Thursday the whole plan collapsed, frozen forever out of my mind as I saw Barbara's little bed being hoisted into the removal van outside our cottage.

My mother had known before I went to Mevagissey that Barbara was to leave us, but she could not bring herself to break the news until a few hours before Barbara stepped into the parlour, waved a bunch of flowers in farewell and passed—as it seemed—carelessly out of my life. In the general bustle and excitement she forgot even to kiss me good-bye, and I was left in a horror of desolation that lasted almost unbroken for five months.

During those five months I wrote, instead of the Mevagissey romance, a novel unlike anything I had ever planned or thought of: a village allegory which showed, from an erotic standpoint, the contrast between the Christ of dogma (the Lamb) and the Christ of ethics and idealism (the Son of Man). The Devil was introduced as an angel of light who supported the vicar in his attempts to apply the teachings of the Son of

Man and thus raise the moral standard of the village—all in vain, for the lechers and harlots were seeking the Lamb and when they saw it they were instantly converted, leaving the Devil and the vicar to sneer in impotent rage at "morbid mysticism." The book was a provocative and audacious piece of work, and I should never have dared to attempt anything of the kind had I been free to choose and think what I was doing. But the story simply flowed out of me without any conscious effort—an instinctive affirmation of the truths to which I had struggled and which were now being so painfully grafted into depths of my nature which no mere intellectual assent could reach. It is an odd fact that, although I have an excellent memory, I cannot remember writing that novel. As I look back to the summer of 1938 I can recall only a cloudy numbness, as if my normal mind were unconscious the whole time. It was certainly bruised and smothered: the diary entries consist only of prayers and expressions of theological belief, with no reference to external practical details except an occasional cry of poignant human grief: "Everywhere I look I see her"; "Tried to type, but could hardly see the keys for the tears splashing down"; and so on. This novel was therefore a unique product thrown up by the subconscious. The image of the "Lamb" first came to me immediately on waking one morning and was associated with a dream which faded from my mind before I was fully awake. Within a few hours I had written two chapters, which seemed to be given to me from an external source while my brain was dull and stupefied. The process was repeated. Day after day I came downstairs and wrote like one in a trance, having no coherent idea of what I was writing, yet struggling through black moods in which I was vaguely aware that a spiritual power of evil was trying to *prevent* something, trying to stop the agony of conviction in me from becoming creative for God. There were hours when an incubus of Satanic fury seemed to settle upon me and threaten me as it had threatened Luther and Bunyan. In the evenings I spent most of my time alone on Bloomdale claywork, sometimes kneeling on top of the dump or among knots of bushes along the pit-edge while the tears streamed down my cheeks. A tide of prayer that was both ecstatic and agonizing flowed in upon me from one quarter while a black tide of lust swirled in from another, so that my mind, submerged between the two battling currents, could not retain a semblance of its normal desires or movements. Each night I came in exhausted, went to bed and placed under my pillow the two little articles that symbolized all the sufficiency of earth and heaven that I had known: a handkerchief of Barbara's which I had found among a pile of comics soon after she left Goonamarris, and my pocket Testament, in which I had marked against suitable texts, the dates on which Barbara had been specially affectionate.

During that summer I read practically nothing but the Bible and the old Puritan books that had belonged to John Polmounter. One of these—Bunyan's *Holy War*—had some influence on my novel, emphasing the theme that God can triumph over Satan only where Christ intervenes. I was probably also influenced to some extent by the religious melo-dramas of Marie Corelli which had so deeply moved me in my adolescence. When I read the completed manuscript of my allegory in August the thrill of triumph I felt was not an artistic one; it was scarcely literary at all. I did not care so much for the book itself as for the proof it gave that I had not been deceived in believing that Barbara was leading me towards my true faith and work. When Evelyn passed out of my life my writings had become defiant and cynical, an admission that the beliefs with which I had associated her were false. Now with the loss of Barbara my sufferings were much more intense, but through them had flowered a vision that was unquestion-ably *real*, fitted to my temperament but having its roots else-where, in the authoritative creeds of the Christian Faith. Here at last was the pattern of Christian experience: first the accept-ance of a truth by faith, then the impact of some personal crisis that tests and vindicates the authenticity of the belief. Through the four years of Barbara's tender ministry I had been drawn towards the Calvinistic Gospel: now in the shock and storm I had learnt that no other creed was big enough either to explain the upheaval or to sustain me under it. It was a severe test that struck at the very root of Calvinism—the assertion of a special Providence ordering every detail of a Christian's life. When I entered 1938 I had looked forward to years of Barbara's companionship, had seen myself ripening under it even until she was in her teens, and had speculated much on the various phases of development that lay ahead. But in a moment that pattern had been irretrievably shattered, and the resulting questions were torturing. Had God's plan miscarried? Had a mere accident—the death of Rowse—deprived me of all further education, left me hopelessly floundering in the early stages of my emergence to normal sexuality? Before I lost Evelyn, Barbara had kissed me: provision had been made then. But now Barbara had gone, the weeks and months slipped by, and no other girl entered my prison-house to continue the human moulding of my personality. The actual predicament seemed to give the lie to Calvinism; yet under its stress I had produced my first Calvinistic novel. *This* faith could not be silenced, and I believed that it would yet reach the full height of testimony, Browning's height: "I, who saw power, see now love perfect, too."

It was the perfect human love that was defined or foreshadowed in my allegory—the love that renounces its place in Nature, enters a higher sexuality which has nothing to do with mere "racial instinct," and recognizes itself as "full-grown Dogma's offspring" (as I expressed it in a later poem).* The thrill of this regenerated passion I conceived to be eternal, and I was aware that on this point many Christians would disagree with me. Even C. S. Lewis, in his penetrating allegory of the religio-erotic relation, *The Pilgrim's Regress*, declared that "lasting passion is the dream of a harlot and from it we wake in despair." But the sort of passion I had apprehended—essentially Pauline in its anti-worldliness—could never be the dream of a harlot; it would be rather to the harlot a nightmare.

* "A Calvinist in Love." Published in *Penguin New Writing*, Autumn 1946.

The Christian and the unbeliever inhabit different worlds, and nowhere is the gulf between them wider than in sex experience which seems most common to all men. The thrill of being in love is short-lived for the worldling because it is for him a process entirely inside Nature and therefore soon burnt out. The Christian, however, cannot be burnt out in his love for a woman because he has already been burnt out in the stress of conversion; the life that animates him spiritually is no longer his own but Christ's. This divine life controls his sensuous reactions, so that the feminine glamour which is to the "natural" man irresistible is to the Christian physically repellent, while the unadorned simplicity which the worldling finds dull and unexciting is for the Christian an object of sensuous ravishment. When St. Paul forbade Christian women to wear jewellery or use artificial beauty aids he was merely recognizing the existence of this law—a law which the modern critics of Paul's attitude to sex seem never to have heard of. Christianity does not condemn the glittering fashions of sophistication because they rouse sexual desire but because for the Christian they paralyse it. He can love only as he is directed by the flame that has burnt out his natural bias towards tawdriness and corruption. The flame does not always burn with the same intensity; fluctuations of mood and feeling are an essential part of the discipline of life; but the vital heat is always there, always being replenished. If, out of prudery, he withholds his sex instinct from the divine fire he may at that point share the fate of unbelievers. This accounts for the failure of some Christians—Wesley is the chief example—who have made a mess of their marriages. In my allegory, and in most of my later writing, I expressed the Christian privilege as I had divined it through my strange contacts on spiritual and emotional borderlines. I do not suggest that Christians reach this level automatically; but I do insist that this is a fundamental law of Christian experience and not a pathological peculiarity of my own.

Admittedly, my circumstances forced me to feel these truths more intensely than they are likely to be felt in an average life.

The deaf, like the blind, become ultra-sensitive to the physical side of personality. Being unable to converse with anyone on the mental and spiritual planes, I learnt to *feel* the essence and outlook of a soul through the "atmosphere" conveyed by the body; and as my own soul was steeped in Christianity, shut up with its various tones and pulsations for months and years, I was naturally repelled by the slightest trace of an alien element. Practically all adult girls, even Christians, had some hint of this, some concession to the trivialities of fashion that would not have troubled a Christian man in the normal bustle of everyday life but which was enough to destroy all sex-appeal for me in my watchful stillness. This had prepared me for, and made inevitable, my attraction towards very young girls, the only persons in whom I felt the same clean spiritual atmosphere, purged of pride, vanity and ambition, as that in which I had been immersed for so long. I had first felt the tendency at Plymouth when contrasting the frigid, sophisticated adults with the lovely frankness of the schoolgirls who smiled and squeezed my arm as they passed me on the pavements. There had been more deeply revealing hints in my attachment to Barbara, especially after I heard of Evelyn's marriage; and the sudden wrench of losing the only human material that shielded me from worldly sexuality on the one hand and inhuman fantasy on the other flung me into a panic-stricken demand for an experience that would complete the revelation I had partially grasped. The beliefs which sustained that demand produced, as a by-product, my symbolist novel. Such phenomena are not uncommon in Christian history. Louis Cazamian, in his *History of English Literature*, wrote of Bunyan: "This keen force of perception is what comes to a believer from the stimulation of psychological life by faith." It is possible only where religion reaches a sort of feverish boiling-point of conviction, and is thus directly opposed to the whole policy of modern religious education in churches and schools, which aims at building up a cool, rational faith adapted to a scientific "climate of opinion." This leads completely away from any understanding of Christianity as a supernatural power; it explains the triviality of so much current writing on religion. Significant work in this sphere cannot be produced without a shock and upheaval. As genius apart from suffering is impotent, so talent under the stress of prolonged and violent anguish flames into genius. Thought becomes rhythmic and thus creates style under the fiery pressure of pain, not through mechanical coaching and study of text-books. The nature of the thought itself is conditioned by the degree of the mind's dependence on God; only an ultimate dependence can reflect ultimate truth. And that only comes through the collapse of every human prop—self-reliance, initiative, will-power—so that a man is driven to God not by his own choice but through the Divine bludgeoning and paralysing of every other desire— the position of Francis Thompson:

> "Naked I wait Thy love's uplifted stroke!
> My harness, piece by piece, Thou hast hewn from me,
>   And smitten me to my knee;
> I an defenceless utterly."

I know some Christian teachers, orthodox in other respects, deny that God ever acts in this way, ever *forces* a soul into His service. But being concerned with logical theories and not raw experiences, they are mistaken. At times when there has been no special strain upon me I have been conscious of my power of choice, and at such times I have freely chosen Christianity, whatever the cost. But at the turning points of my life, the crises that produced my novels and poems, God has never consulted my will. His providences have struck like thunderbolts, and the consequent movements of my mind and spirit, the creative movements, have been automatic, inevitable, uncontrolled and uncalculated by me.

The so-called Christian education of our age is directed more and more towards stiffening personality to resist these spiritual impacts. It has compromised with the ideal of contented worldliness, the desire for security, and has tried to justify this betrayal by dismissing religious sufferings as morbid. But if they are morbid then much of the Bible is morbid; the Book of Job ceases to have any universal significance and becomes a mere pathological document. It is hard to understand why the deeper notes of the Divine revelation should be regarded as morbid while the facile trills and squeaks practised by the modern churches are accepted as the only healthy parts of it. The great Christian leaders, from St. Paul to Spurgeon, have spent far more time in a spiritual wilderness under the terror of the Lord than in the socially acceptable atmosphere of Oxford Group house-parties. The modern Church has failed because its leaders know nothing of this terror. They would, indeed, be most anxious to affirm that they have avoided such spiritual experiences as Bunyan's, Kierkegaard's, Karl Barth's—or mine, for that matter. They have never felt the savagery of the Hound of Heaven tearing their harness from them, smiting them to their knees. And until they have known this elemental darkness and ferocity, which are fundamental in Christian experience, they are not competent to judge the "superstition" that alone can heal a soul after such wounding, much less to pretend that their own shallow theories are an adequate substitute for it. The "natural mind" must be broken before it will accept unconditionally the dogmas of that particular Super-nature which is redemptive. And that Super-nature now and then selects for its use a brain from which morbidities have stripped the normal human resistance: but not invariably, not often enough to oblige the materialist. Bernard Shaw's ridiculous contention that the Revelation of St. John could only have been written by a drug addict shows how short-sighted sceptics are in these matters. If apocalyptic religious visions came only to drug addicts like Francis Thompson the whole subject could be neatly pigeon-holed and dismissed; but they come with equal force to robust, healthy-minded men of the world like Browning, as well as to rough, realistic clay-workers' sons like myself.

One of the most remarkable facts of this period was the steady improvement of my health which had accompanied the buffetings of adversity. For nearly ten years I had been mauled and frustrated, wearied by unrelieved misfortune in every sphere of life. By all normal standards such a strain should have produced a nervous breakdown and left me a pitiful, shattered neurotic. But through it all I slept like a log for eight or nine hours nightly and had a good appetite, eating with stolid enjoyment except when I deliberately gave myself to fasting and prayer. The tendency to thrive on worry had long been recognised in my home as one of my chief peculiarities. Here too my experience contradicted popular rules and theories. On the physical side I think I owed this toughness to the simple countrified habits regarding sleep and diet which I had always practised. During my childhood I usually went to bed before eight o'clock, and no unimaginative dunce could have enjoyed more peaceful slumber. I thus reached adolescence with plenty of nerve-force in reserve. My habits remained practically unchanged right on into my twenties, except for that brief period when I sometimes burnt the midnight oil after returning from Nanpean. I still retired most nights between eight and nine o'clock, and was soundly sleeping at hours when many of my generation were draining their vitality in dance-halls. The exhausting pace of social and recreational life never touched me at all. Nor had I ever stimulated my powers artificially by drinking or smoking. It was fortunate that I was born and reared in a remote country area: had I been a town child I should probably have collapsed. And with this background of experience I regret the increasing tendency to mould and educate all children in the towns, hustling the most sensitive and primitive spirits from the solitudes to which they instinctively turn for nourishment. The medical service provided by the schools can never be an adequate substitute for an environment and a rhythm of life that create and preserve health spontaneously. These factors triumphed even in me, where the material could hardly have been worse. Throughout the fifteen years of my struggle for recognition I was not confined to bed with an illness for a single day, and apart from one or two attacks of toothache I suffered no physical pain at all between 1934 and 1947.

But this extraordinary stamina was due mainly to the

invigorating faith that came fully to dominate me through my attachment to Barbara. The religious spirit is essentially a spirit of healing, and all my afflictions had been received religiously—not, indeed, with meek resignation, but with the intellectual certainty that they were used by God, that He could remove them at any moment, and that their effect upon me was His responsibility, not mine. I have not in my whole life known the sort of worry common to the average man—the petty irritations of material affairs received from the standpoint of the materialist. I can well believe that that kind of fretful writhing under vexations traced only to *chance* would have made me as neurotic as most other misfits.

Richard Jefferies declared that he found strength for the burden of life through frequent "soul-draughts" of Nature-worship; but his pagan ecstacy turned out to be a mere symptom of his disease, the enfeebling intoxication of the consumptive. Something similar was true of D. H. Lawrence and Llewelyn Powys. Sensual mysticism boasts of its power to triumph over circumstances, to initiate men into the true "glory of life"; yet the only proof it offers is a final curse gasped in a sanatorium. It is the Christian with his stern theology and his rigid moral code who has the secret of real "soul-draughts" that overflow into the body. The exhilarations of looser creeds are temporary masks of corruption, and in unguarded moments their apostles admit the fact. "Miserable, slighted humanity," wrote Llewelyn Powys in a letter describing his amorous affairs; "their only consolation——, and God sends the pox!"* It is a revealing phrase and shows how untenable is the position of those who seek "strength through joy" in the pagan sense. They rail at moralists as life-deniers and enemies of Nature, while being driven themselves to turn against Nature because its laws are on the side of the moralists. (The Christian attitude is, of course, neither pagan nor simply moralistic. It divorces the sexuality of believers from the "racial instinct" that unites unbelievers, and is thus in one sense anti-natural; but in

* Quoted in *Welsh Ambassadors: Powys—Lives and Letters*, by Louis Marlow.

Christian marriage it sanctifies and preserves the only sensuous joy that even pagans really care for.)

I had been too well grounded in Christianity to be lured along the by-paths of popular revolt. I knew, too, that this false philosophy permeated most current literature, so I left it alone and—when my allegory had been finished, rejected by one publisher (during the Munich crisis) and put away in a drawer to await revision—turned with renewed concentration to the writings of the great Puritans: Bunyan's *Grace Abounding*, Spurgeon's and Talmage's sermons, and the *Journal* of Mrs. Fletcher, the early Methodist mystic. These books nourished me through the winter of 1938-9—these and the Bible. I had no other support, no relief in circumstances. My deafness grew worse; my total earnings for 1938 amounted to £4 2s.; and though Barbara paid me one or two visits they increased rather than lessened the burden. She was growing older, changing; the more active village life she was now living, with the deepening influence of school work and discipline, had blunted the qualities in her that had so appealed to me. I was flung back on God in an almost terrifying loneliness, plumbing "that depth of conviction which is so like despair."

At first sight it may seem odd that a twentieth-century novelist should find inspiration in Puritan theology; but it is not surprising when one considers that the chief thing being perfected in me was not an art but a faith. I was engaged in raw spiritual conflict, and I needed the counsel of Christians who had also grappled with these primeval terrors, not the "healthy-minded" modern ecclesiastics whose books would merely have assured me that I needed psychological treatment or that a social system which produced undesirable misfits of my type must be abolished. Apart from this aspect, it should be realized that to be unfettered, to outgrow sectarian boundaries and the prejudices and codes of one's class, to view localized forms of belief from the outside, does not involve any bias towards the current fashion of thought. An original and independent mind is not likely to remain content with the religious conceptions formally held by average minds, particularly in working-class backwaters; but it is a mistake to assume that it will necessarily gravitate towards something more modern. This idea arises from the attempt to equate the spiritual life with the intellect, and is another form of the heresy against which Karl Barth has been warring during the past twenty years—the heresy that there already exists in the human mind a "point of contact" at which the Divine revelation can be received and made subject to the normal laws of intellectual development, adapted and adjusted as the mind expands. This notion is a fallacy which the experience of every Christian refutes. My experience certainly refutes it. I have outgrown all the intellectual and æsthetic sympathies of my teen years, but none of the spiritual sympathies that were formed in me after the collapse of my natural religion. I cannot now read a single novel or philosophical work that I enjoyed during my teens, but the works of Puritan devotion that then nourished my spiritual life are as fresh to me today as they were when I was twenty. When the war came I turned in fifteen volumes of the *International Library of Famous Literature* for salvage, volumes that had lain unread in my cupboard for several years, but I kept the old theological books that had refreshed and edified John Polmounter long before I was born: I knew that I should need them, whatever changes took place in my general outlook. They are still abreast of my experience, always relevant and adequate. The reason is that these Puritan writers never tried to appeal to the human intellect and thus their appeal, once received by the spirit, remains unaffected by the ripening of intellectual and æsthetic taste. The idea that beliefs produced by the Christian germ of "eternal life" can be affected by science, or that science can be a source of "truths" by which the Christian knowledge of God "develops," is due to a superficial view of the nature of conversion. It is the old, arrogant error of assuming that "Truth" is something that springs up inside Nature in all sorts of unlikely places, thus enabling man to gratify his natural tastes on the pretext that he is "seeking truth", whether in Nature, art, or in the so-called "religious consciousness." The grafting I had undergone had made a final riddance of this heresy as far as I was concerned; it had shown me the bitter fact that, as Barth declares in his vehement *Nein!* (in reply to Brunner), Christian belief is "the realization of a Divine possibility, not of one that is inherent in human nature. Freedom to know the true God is a miracle, a freedom of God, not one of our freedoms." It confers on man the freedom to be orthodox, immune from the shifting currents of speculation that are released inside Nature by science and philosophy. I had found the personal bearing of Christian orthodoxy—that nothing but its concept of Divine revelation could explain, in the present, my detachment from contemporary fads of doubt and cynicism, or, in the past, the fact that all my fine idealism and poetic apprehension of "Truth" at Nanpean had merely proved the accuracy of the Calvinist claim that all natural knowledge of God is idolatry. This dogma, in its local and personal application, explained why I had lost Evelyn, and in its general bearing it threw light on many mysteries—the dissolute, tragic lives of "artists," the fact that the study of the beautiful, particularly in Nature, tended always to lead men away from Christianity, the failure of religious movements like the Oxford Group in which historic revelation was subordinated to personal "guidance."

I had followed the progress of the Group with interest for several years, and sympathized with its spiritual challenge to the average citizen who had to face general social problems, but I found its sleek, non-theological atmosphere repellent. A religion that functioned with polished ease in universities and hotels could have no kinship with the stark hermit-faith I was living, always against the background of clay-dumps and blasted rock. The landscape dominated all my tastes, reflected in everything from my religion to my clothes (for I liked to wear rough labourer's garb and to have my shoes muddy and my hands showing clay and tar stains when I sat down to write); and as no Oxford Grouper in plus-fours was likely to understand this peculiarity I should have made no contact with the Group at St. Austell—where it had some adherents—even had I not been deaf. My experience was too remote from the normal perceptions of spiritual life to be "shared," while "guidance" was useless when, because of my handicaps, I was totally unable to dash about the country in the bustling manner which was apparently the only correct response to such guidance. The whole movement was too superficial, too slick and cocksure to grip my interest for long. It lacked the authentic note of suffering which characterizes all genuine Christian revivals. These laughing crusaders did not look like persons to whom Christ had said: "Ye shall weep and lament, but the world shall rejoice." I remember being struck by Hardy's comment on these words, that "if 'the world' denotes the brutal and thoughtless merely, the text is eternally true," and I felt that the sternness and dignity of Hardy's conception was more truly Christian than that of some Oxford Groupers who tried to interpret life by the inanities of "I gotta wise old horsey."

The arrival of my militant Calvinism had no further effect on my literary work during 1939. The wave of sensuous dogmatism which brought me that symbolic novel had vanished: when I next wrote fiction it was in my old romantic narrative style—a sequel to the half-finished *Private Snow*. This too was refused by several publishers, the blows of rejection being almost the only incidents that broke for me the monotony of that year. It was the blankest year I have ever known, dragging on month after month in featureless misery. Apart from one day trip to Mevagissey in the summer, I spent the whole year inside my home or within a few hundred yards of it, as isolated and enclosed as if I had been behind barbed wire. During the previous two summers I, with other members of the family, had visited the Scilly Isles, but in August 1939 the war threat, the risk from lurking German submarines, was a deterrent. I had enjoyed the former trips, and did not feel a trace of seasickness on either occasion. I was, indeed, specially delighted and invigorated by the roughest parts of the voyage when the steamer pitched out beyond Land's End towards the open Atlantic. The dreamy loveliness of the isles as we approached them is an unforgettable memory, and the rugged scenery on St. Mary's, especially the bleak rock-formations on

Peninnis Head, was very close to my ideal of beauty in Nature, so far as Nature could be beautiful to me.

The chief event of most of the days of 1939 was the arrival of the newspaper which mother had just begun taking in, hoping it would help to keep me mentally fresh. I felt a dull sense of despondency about the world situation: hearing nothing of the excited talk about it that was going on all round me I could never really grip the issues or feel that I was moving with the general currents. I had been thankful for Munich, being desperately anxious to begin my literary career and knowing that the outbreak of war would indefinitely postpone success. But as the rejections began piling up as before I grew almost indifferent, fatalistic.

Barbara visited me again during that summer, but the only kisses I received in 1939 came from a Nanpean girl, slightly younger than Barbara, who called next door in August at Barbara's old home. I was still living in the afterglow of that unexpected touch of happiness when the war broke out, and this little human warmth prevented me from realizing at once the magnitude of the world tragedy. My mind had become rather like that of a prisoner-of-war—erratic, with no sense of proportion, receiving the slightest blessing of change with almost hysterical gratitude. The death of S. E. Burrow a few weeks earlier had depressed me; I had hoped and prayed that he might live to see that his belief in me was justified. But eight years had slipped away since he first drew attention to me in the *Cornish Guardian*, and he, like A. J. G. Hawken (who was already dead) had to pass out while I was still smothered in failure and humiliation. Frank Baron and John Rowland had not written to me for years: there was nothing more they could do, as my deafness prevented personal intercourse and friendship. It had been embarrassing to them to have to write so often expressing sympathy and regret at my lack of success. Yet, with the outbreak of war, it seemed more than ever necessary that someone with influence in the literary world should give me some practical assistance. I made one last bid with *Private Snow*, which I knew to be the best work I had done on the level of painstaking craftsmanship. The book was promptly declined—the thirty-seventh rejection that had been meted out to my novels—and mother agreed that I could get no further until someone in authority pulled strings on my behalf.

After talking the matter over, and praying much for guidance I decided to make an approach which mother had suggested in former years, but which I had hitherto regarded as an affront to my independence. Accordingly, I wrote in November to Sir Arthur Quiller-Couch, outlining my circumstances and asking whether he would be willing to read *Private Snow* and advise me what to do about it in wartime conditions. He was then at Cambridge, but courteously offered to give his attention to the manuscript when he returned to Fowey at the end of the University term. Just before Christmas I forwarded the type-script with much fluttering of heart, torn between extravagant hopes and black fears about the outcome of this venture.

In January, Q. returned the manuscript with a short letter of criticism, admitting that *Private Snow* had "a deal of power and promise, and should find a publisher," that the story was "well-knit and strong," but regretting that I had chosen to present characters who showed "habits of dirt, open lust and filthy talk." "I hope," he wrote, "your readers won't take this clan as representative of Cornish folk in general: though of course I know that the exposure of our common humanity 'without benefit of laundry like a rag on a clothes-line' is the vogue among novelists just now; and some Bloomsbury reviewers will smack their lips...." And so, because I hadn't written about the Cornish gentry, he had to confine his help to one or two technical hints, pointing out that in my descriptive passages there was "too much repetition of the Egdon Heath business." (I did not know what this meant until 1942 when I read Hardy's *The Return of the Native*.)

Mother and I were bitterly disappointed. Yet another venture, and still we were no further ahead. We had hoped for much from Q., having heard of his generosity to talented Cornish boys, his determination to give working-class youngsters of promise an equal opportunity of educational advance. One point we had overlooked—the obvious fact that all these children were normal school products while I was a wild Ishmael of the moors, untouched by such refined institutions. No Cornish school would be disgraced by my failure, so there was no particular reason why I should succeed. Q's refusal of active aid confirmed a view I had held for some years —that educationists—at least, those of a dryly academic type— are less concerned with the fate of the individual than with the prestige of a school.

It was obvious, too, from Q's letter, that my general attitude offended him. One of his comments had staggered me: his prophecy that the Bloomsbury intellectuals would smack their lips over my work. I had always thought that they were more likely to curl their lips over it. The fact that *Private Snow* dealt with a prostitute instead of a mayor would not make it more palatable to them than *The Mayor of Troy*, for I had introduced prostitution to point a moral—the "public mud" contrasting with the "private snow" of Christian love—and even to suggest original sin. I think it was this that Q. had detected, and it displeased him. He had no use for any author who would admit that there was original sin in his Delectable Duchy. Just after reading *Private Snow* he wrote an introduction to Charles Lee's *Cornish Tales*—because Lee had subscribed to the amiable fiction that "in Cornish village life the path of young man and maiden is so fenced about that straying is well-nigh impossible." I have no doubt that I should have received more encouragement from Q. had I been able to write in similar vein—with grateful acknowledgements to St. Austell County School. But the incident is an interesting sidelight on the weakness of mere idealism—the idealism that led Q. in his last fragment of autobiography, *Memories and Opinions*, to state that the goodness of human nature outlives the harshness of Christian dogma: an extraordinary judgment, considering what was then happening at Belsen and Buchenwald. That so kindly a man and so discerning a critic as Q. should treat me as a decadent who was best left to struggle alone outside the pale of a "decent-minded" community, is disturbing proof of the limitations of the educational system he represented. It shows, too, the pathetic inadequacy of genial philosophies of easy tolerance which must, perforce, greet art and literature with the cry of apostate Israel: "Prophesy unto us smooth things, prophesy deceits."

A month after Q. reported on *Private Snow* I went to Redruth to be medically examined by the military authorities. But I was not examined. Mother accompanied me and explained that I was deaf and had been blind, so after a quick glance at me the doctor filled in my exemption certificate, declaring that I was "suffering from complete blindness and deafness"—a statement that made me grin when presently I read it on Redruth station.

A significant incident of that day is that I saw Evelyn, with her baby, outside St. Austell station on my return—the first time I had seen her since that frantic evening six years before when I finally left the Phillips's. My mother stopped and chatted with her for a few minutes, and though I naturally turned away I knew from the complete absence of emotional turmoil that there was no possibility of my ever being ensnared again by the illusory values of an ideal world.

CHAPTER ELEVEN

Wartime Developments

As I spent the war years quietly at Goonamarris the continuity of my development was unbroken by the national upheaval. My life went on as an odd solitary pulsation, apparently separated from the general strain and sacrifice. Always I had seemed to be exempt from common stresses—exempt from scholastic pressure during childhood, from conventional religious and social pressure during adolescence; and now that a war had engulfed the world, shattering the pattern of life for millions, the unity of mood and theme in my experience was still mysteriously preserved. While my contemporaries were drilled and regimented, flung against new and bewildering backgrounds, I was left free to explore the particular by-path along which I had been led from infancy.

Yet my life and its problems were not really isolated from the deeper, spiritual movements of the hour. Although I could not "do my bit" in any material sense, I had some contribution to make to the common stock of ideas for which so many of my generation were laying down their lives. My peculiar education was not a sterile moulding of a detached ego; it was fashioning me to offer a challenge, and perhaps even a solution, to the general chaos. *Wilding Graft*, written during one of the darkest periods of the war, showed how directly and urgently a private drama might bear upon, and illuminate, the spiritual questions raised by widespread catastrophe.

It was fortunate that my deafness prevented me from being called up. To be a misfit in the Services—as I certainly should have been—is apt to be a grim business, possibly leading to a court-martial or a firing squad. Since my mental powers were entirely imaginative and creative, driving in remote depths of mysticism, they could never have been discovered in a general intelligence test. I should have been graded as of the lowest mental calibre, as incapable of assimilating factual details of military routine as of understanding the patriotic slogans that were supposed to inspire me. Had I gone into the Forces I should have fought, and possibly died, in the muddled, stolid, uncomprehending fashion that my father had done, groping in an alien world where I could not be touched by any spark of idealism, any sense of duty or nobility. I could never think or act under compulsion, or as part of a team. I should have felt always that perverse itch of revolt against authority which had made me slovenly and malicious at school and might have turned me into a traitor or a saboteur under the ruthless pressure of militarism. I was willing to help if I were allowed to do so with the savage independence I had always known. I was even willing to throw bombs at Nazis if I could do so in my own way and at my own time. But if I were told that I had ceased to matter as an individual, that I must act only as bidden by a group of brass hats to whom my personal vision meant nothing, my whole nature would have blazed up in frantic, hysterical protest: "I will not. I will not...." It is obvious, therefore, that but for my physical handicaps I should have become a tragic war victim in one way or another.

My general attitude to the war was neither patriotic nor pacifist; my Calvinism restrained me from both extremes. Like many young fellows of my generation I had included pacifism among my professed ideals, but my public references to it were vague and showed that I had not really faced the issue with an adult knowledge of human nature. The violent discipline which formed my religious faith had rid me of such sentimental illusions long before the war came. I had observed that completely orthodox Christians—those who believed in the Fall—were seldom pacifists. The apostles of non-resistance were for the most part idealists still entangled in the Victorian scientific dogma of evolution, believing that mankind had now advanced beyond the barbaric crudities of mass-slaughter. The Christian view of human nature made this notion untenable. War, and the ineffectual ideals of co-operation by which men tried to prevent it, were alike products of original sin. Power-lust was evil, but it was no more evil than the humanitarianism that sneered at orthodoxy. Both were symptoms of man's rebellion against God, and both must perish in the fires of spiritual conversion before there could be any hope of peace on earth. A man who has accepted this outlook can never fight for a flag or the independence of a State; he can only fight for a way of life in which people are free to be converted. And since for these reasons I could not realize myself as a British citizen— though I was very thankful to be living in England—I did not accept any official wartime safeguards except the identity card and ration books that were forced upon me. I was one of the few persons in the clay district who would have nothing to do with gas masks. I dutifully observed the blackout regulations when I was indoors alone during winter evenings, but I had no sympathy with the panic defence measures taken by most citizens. I was not callous or indifferent to the sacrifices these people were making; but the sacrifices demanded of me during the war were of another sort. The intolerable burdens I had borne during the peace—deafness and poverty—were intensified, and thus, deprived of an income and cut off from society, I knew all the frustrations of captivity without the alleviating sense that the Allied victory would restore me to normal life and prospects. The war meant for me five more weary years of literary struggle, a struggle now dwarfed to insignificance by the world drama. I felt smothered, impotent, and was astonished to find that, in spite of this, I continued to develop as a writer, becoming more firm and mature in all the veins of my talent—including the vein of humour. My last dialect tale was written for the 1940 issue of the *Camborne Almanack*, and was even more robustly slapstick than those I had produced nearly ten years earlier. Its climax reflected the fact that we had once suffered the inconvenience of a rotten stair in our home:

"Stamping down her feet wi' all her weight 'pon un ee gived away, an' next thing Mrs. Budge knawed her legs had gone right down through in the spence. A gurt stug o' pig's fat stood zackly in under, and she went plunk right in it while her hands laid hold to the banisters. . . .

" 'Thikky stair bin an' broke!' screeched Mrs. Budge, struggling to pull herself up through the hole. 'Come up an' 'elp me, caan't 'ee? I caan't git up. I caan't move me legs. Polly! I'm sinkin'. I'm in the pig's fat. Hale me out, caan't 'ee?' "

There was no suggestion here that I had yet learned to take life seriously.

Soon after I had revised *Private Snow* along the lines indicated by Q. I decided to enter it in a competition for first novels, and in May submitted the manuscript to the contest agent, Mr. Raymond Savage. My presence at Trethosa chapel a few weeks later, on the national Day of Prayer, was not entirely unconnected with this venture. I had never before prayed about my work in a place of worship, and thought—a little superstitiously perhaps—that this concession to average Christian practice might have some special potency. The villagers were surprised to see me slip quietly into the old pew in which I had listened to so many sermons during my childhood; they considered me very patriotic. I did, of course, pray about the war, but I was overshadowed by personal association that were bitter things while I was still a failure as a writer. The last time I had entered Trethosa chapel had been in October 1932 when I accompanied Evelyn and her parents to the Harvest Festival service; and a few months afterwards I had made that strange, fateful visit to Old Pound chapel where I had glimpsed the disintegration of the faith that had first set me writing. I felt bruised here again in a chapel, the patriotic hymns—the only parts of the service I could hear— breaking upon me as a vague, poignant reminder that my mood of helplessness and bafflement was spreading throughout the land.

Private Snow was unsuccessful in the contest, but the manuscript remained in London seven months, and this long respite from rejection slips gave me the opportunity to concentrate on the re-writing of its sequel. This was completed in December, and by that time I had become very anxious about *Private Snow* Daily news of the blitz on London was disturbing, and when I read of the great fire raid of December 29th I was horrified to learn that the premises of the publisher who held my novel had been burnt down. I entered 1941 with the paralysing fear, almost amounting to certainty, that my manuscript had been destroyed; and it was a genuine relief to me when, a week later, it was returned with not even a singed or damp page to suggest the inferno that had raged around it since it left Cornwall. And although this venture had failed it had an interesting connection with my ultimate success; for when in 1945 I was forced to fall back on *Wilding Graft* as an opening novel, I remembered that Mr. Savage was the only agent who had accepted *Private Snow* and so entrusted to him the marketing of the more mature work—with very fortunate results.

There had been several moves during the first year of war that contibuted to the education I dramatized in *Wilding Graft*. Some of them were bewildering, seeming to promise much and yield nothing. In 1939 Marshall Rowse's widow remarried; Barbara and her parents left Trewoon and settled at St. Dennis, and for awhile I was flooded with hope that Barbara would now be able to resume that emotional moulding which had been so strangely interrupted by Marshall Rowse's death. I formed the habit of strolling, almost every Sunday afternoon, up across the downs to the ridge overlooking St. Dennis, taking my pocket Testament and praying as I gazed across the fields to Barbara's new home that she would soon give me more happy "dates" to write in the margins. The hope was touched with a sense of ironic fitness, for Evelyn's brother Harry was still driving the milk van, coming from St. Dennis to Goonamarris daily, and Barbara could thus ride down to see me any Saturday in the very van that had taken me to see Evelyn eight years before.

But it was soon obvious that Barbara was not eager to take advantage of this chance of renewing our friendship. The brisk village scene, with its cinemas and concerts, seemed to have dulled her taste for the remote, bleak isolation of Goonamarris, where she could do nothing but chat with my mother, play with the dog Flush, and find me increasingly silent and awkward as my deafness worsened. The week-ends brought nearly always the sick disappointment of Harry coming alone: on one occasion I was so upset that mother went to St. Dennis and fetched Barbara down herself, though this did not mend matters, as spontaneity was the very essence of the help I needed. Gradually, reluctantly, I was forced to realize that for some inexplicable reason Barbara was no longer being used on the old sunny levels where she had hitherto instructed me. She spent two days with us in the first week of 1940, but was scarcely recognizable as the warm, impulsive girl who had healed me after the break with Evelyn. I was so distressed by the contrast that I could not go on with my work until, a few weeks later, my little Nanpean friend came again next door and romped with me for a whole morning in just the tender, affectionate way that Barbara had formerly done. This was the beginning of a vast entanglement and complication of my inner life, the root of the tragic disharmony I suffered during the war. Throughout that period my mental and spiritual approach to sex was clarified and given detail through contacts with several girls, none of them over fourteen; and try as I might I could not rid myself of the feeling that it would have been more seemly, more Christian, if all this education had come through the same girl. It is always hard to believe that God's way is best when it is contrary to our own; it is especially difficult to believe so when God's way is offensive to our moral sense—when we know that the course we wished to take would have produced a clear-cut, straightforward moral situation, while the course God has chosen and brought to pass is full of ambiguity, divided loyalties, and torturing questionings. Of course, my whole problem would have been brushed away like a cobweb had I been able to mix with adult girls, but they were to me an unknown species. I must either learn of feminine nature through girl-children or remain entirely ignorant of it, and thus incapacitated as a novelist, poet, thinker and, indeed, as a human being.

I had to face this issue alone, estranged by it even from my mother. Our home became darkened as never before by a cloud of misunderstanding, reserve, sometimes even recrimination. My approach to orthodoxy had been a strange one, and was so entirely unconnected with all that is usually understood by "religion" that mother felt it must be a form of self-deception. It seemed obvious now that I had been as much mistaken about Barbara as about Evelyn. The one inspiration was no more permanent than the other, so what was the point of saying that one was true and the other false? The failure of my work tended to confirm mother in her view that God was "displeased" with the contacts that inspired it. Thus the need of success became doubly urgent: nothing else could relieve the strain of poverty that was crushing us materially, and nothing else could convince mother that this phase of my teaching was "of the Lord" and thus relieve the tension that was stifling us spiritually.

The acute development of the problem, which was to make it a subject of comment, not only inside our home but throughout the village, began in June 1940, when our next-door neighbours took in a London girl evacuee called Irene, then within a few weeks of her eighth birthday—a little older than Barbara had been when she left that house, and in every way a complete contrast to Barbara. She came into our front room the next morning—a wet, stormy Saturday, oddly similar to that other fateful one on which Marshall Rowse had been killed. I glanced up from my desk to see this strange girl smiling at me from under a raincoat that was thrown over her head, partly hiding the dull brown hair. She was rather stout, with a general impression of heaviness in her features and movements: a slum child from Islington who conveyed to me very soon the raw, sullen atmosphere of the mean streets. Barbara, on the other hand, had been slim, light, full of airy grace, the sunny freshness of open fields and clear skies. Here was another phase of girlhood, another type—not so immediately attractive as Barbara, but revealing to me those smouldering undertones that had usually charcterized my imagined heroines and were thus instinctively within the range of my sympathies.

Irene came in to play with me fairly often during the early summer, though the friendship did not run as smoothly as the old one with Barbara. Irene was quarrelsome, impatient with me because of my deafness, and several times her sulky moods exasperated me and I became aware for the first time of a latent sadism in my nature. I was not alarmed by it; I had recognised the masochism which had accompanied the vague romanticism of my adolescence, and it seemed natural enough that as this perversion had been subdued by my stern dogmatic faith, original sin should try to counter-attack in the form of sadism. This is just the sort of idiotic thing Nature does when she feels the presence of Christ encroach on her territory. The urge was soon controlled, but it led to unseemly squabbles and caused some whispering among the neighbours. I was ruffled and unhappy, wishing more than ever that Barbara had stayed in that house, preserving a continuity of inspiration that was soothing, sympathetic, intelligent. Often in the evenings after a tiff with Irene I would wander with Flush up to Rosto-wrack Downs, looking down upon St. Dennis in an agony of yearning and bafflement—as bad as anything I had suffered at Nanpean. Affairs seemed to be perverse, bungled, lacking everywhere the master-touch which a Calvinist expects to see in the working out of predestination. The strain was essentially religious, not a superficial fretting at human choice or caprice: I knew that if the pattern was broken God had broken it and I could do nothing, blame nobody.

But in August came two developments that brought much relief. Barbara visited us again, and her mother told us that since leaving Goonamarris she had become moody and intro-spective, never wishing to play with other children but preferring to stay indoors and read—very much, in fact, as I had been during my childhood. The subject matter of her reading was equally peculiar. She spent hours reading the Bible and—an even greater offence at her age (for she was still only nine)—perusing love stories. Her parents were puzzled to know whence she could have derived such unusual traits. I made no comment, but I fancied she had got them from me, and was elated by the possibility. I had prayed much for Barbara from the time I realized how deep and essential was my debt to her, and it seemed that at least one aspect of the enigmatic change in her nature could be regarded as an answer to my prayers. I felt relaxed, restored to the old perspective; and the second development of August tended to preserve it. Through the death of a neighbour we took in two London girls, Pat and Doris, who had previously been billeted at Goonamarris. They came from a decent home in Stoke Newington. Pat was seven, Doris ten, and I realized at once that neither of them could complicate my emotional life. They were to me a completely neutral type—by which I mean a type that, even when mature, I could not possibly fall in love with. I could romp with them as I might romp with boys, treating them as little chums whose part in my "education" was purely negative. The presence of these girls in my home formed a new, daily background of companionship for which I was truly grateful after the loneliness of the past two years; it also eased the friction between me and Irene. We were seldom alone together, and when a squabble arose I could walk off and let the girls settle it between themselves. An even more helpful result of our taking in these evacuees was that they introduced me to two local girls who had lived at Goonamarris for a year, though I had not hitherto met them—Brenda and Sheila Snell. Brenda was then only five, and my friendship with her did not yield its full village flavour until after the war was over; but I still recall a lovely evening in the autumn of 1940 when she and Sheila, Pat and Doris strolled with me to Goonvean, and among the workshops and derelict farm buildings treated me as a convenient target for prickly teazels which I threw back at them, though in such a battle, one against four, I was not very successful in my counter-attacks. If John Polmounter's ghost still hovered around Goonvean he must have enjoyed the fun. It was exactly in his spirit.

These incidents of my life seemed trivial in comparison with the grim, epic drama in which my contemporaries had been engulfed. Some of my old school mates were in the Forces, overseas; others had joined the Home Guard and, with rifles and gas masks, kept tense vigils at nights beside local bridges and vital roadways where German saboteurs might be expected to strike. I felt very keenly my isolation from the massive texture of national defence; but I was never distracted for long from awareness of the stern challenge of the hour. I had only to step outdoors after nightfall and look upon the blacked-out countryside to feel the terror that was abroad, the sense of menace. I shared the common peril, even though I could not hear it discussed or do anything practical to avert it. The tension struck at me in visual images, night-pictures. Sometimes during that lurid autumn of 1940 we would stand at the bedroom window—mother and I, Pat and Doris—late into the night, watching the searchlights swooping along the coast from Falmouth; occasionally we caught the glare of fire where a bomb had dropped. Often I would come downstairs to break-fast to learn that the rest of the household had been kept awake nearly all night by the roar of Nazi 'planes, and our own intercepting Force based at St. Eval, passing overhead. Being deaf I never heard them and usually slept undisturbed, but sometimes I would be aroused by a light in the room and would look across from my bed—for I now shared the front bedroom as we were cramped for accommodation—to see Pat's or Doris' white scared face as she clung to my mother in the big double bed. I would know that Jerry 'planes were about, and would lie and wonder dully what would happen if a bomb fell near the house. Some bombs did fall in the district; a neighbour came in one day with a fragment of a bomb that had been found in one of Goonvean fields. I remained untouched by the general alarm, and still refused to take any precautions for my personal safety. An air-raid shelter had been dug beside Bloomdale clay-dump, but I never went to it except when the children used it as a camp during the daytime. The wail of the siren at Drinnick—so shrill that even I could hear it faintly if the winds were favourable—never induced me to seek cover. I was reckless, indifferent; I had always the feeling that I should not be killed. My Calvinism had given me an almost fanatical belief, not in myself, but in a Divine purpose for the individual life, a purpose fulfilled through the individual's acceptance of Christian dogma. I knew that from my earliest attack of blindness God had been preparing me for some bit of work in the sphere of ideas, and my reading of the Bible and Puritan literature had repeatedly assured me that, as Spurgeon says, "God has given no pledge which He will not redeem, and encouraged no hope which He will not fulfil." The emphasis here is on the Divine faithfulness, not on the human ego; the sense of God's integrity overshadows the individual and makes mere egoism impossible. I believed my vision was being perfected for artistic expression in fiction and poetry; I even believed that since the collapse of my romantic idealism at Nanpean, God had been preparing me for mature love. For these reasons I never doubted that I should survive the war, or that it would end in an Allied victory. When I expressed this conviction in a letter to the *Cornish Guardian* in June 1940, my old rationalist friend John Rowland protested against what he called my "unique revelation from an unspecified source." He questioned the relevance of spiritual factors in an armed conflict, and pointed out that our national Days of Prayer had been followed by disasters. The assured poise of my position was reflected in my reply, in which I dealt good-humouredly with "those whose self-appointed war work is a more tiresome stating of the case against religion" and the "superficial dabblers in religion" who had "mistaken their own wishes for God's will." Rowland had admitted that my Christian certitude was "exciting," and I expressed the hope that the Allied victory would "increase the decrepitude—if that be possible—of a system of doubt which is as false as it is un-exciting."

This letter is interesting not only because it shows the buoyant confidence that always irradiated my work when I wrote of my beliefs, but also because it reveals the maturing of my literary style—very different from the muddled, incoherent rhetoric of my pre-war letters. A similar ripening of faculty was apparent in my fiction, and I thought this a suitable time for a stocktaking of my literary progress. This disclosed that during the previous ten years I had written over a million words in novels alone, with another quarter of a million words in short stories, essays, Press controversies and verse. Of this mass of output only a tiny fraction had been printed: twenty-four short stories (all in Cornish annuals), three articles, seventy letters to the Press, and forty-four juvenile poems. My total earnings for this material amounted to £19 os. 6d. I had not sold a single manuscript in the open, competitive literary market. Yet after a decade of unrelieved failure I faced the wartime difficulties with a buoyant, publicly expressed faith in the efficacy of prayer.

It was a paradox that can only be understood in the light of my spiritual preoccupation with prayer during the past two years. My literary output in 1939 had suffered in quality because I was never able to concentrate upon the work itself but only upon the need of inspiration. My best energies were poured into prayer—prayer for Barbara, and also for some turn of events that would end my intolerable loneliness. Now in 1940 both prayers were in a measure, answered—that for Barbara in a mysterious way that deprived me of her inspiration, but the prayer for companionship very fully and unexpectedly granted in the coming of the London evacuees to Goonamarris. This evidence in the spiritual and emotional spheres encouraged me to have faith in other matters; and during the autumn and winter of 1940 I experienced a fresh wave of mystical exaltation that was in some ways similar to the one which had flooded me while writing my allegorical novel.

Almost every Saturday evening throughout this period I went to Rostowrack Downs while Pat and Doris were being bathed, climbed with Flush to the tip of one of the deserted clay-dumps and remained there in lonely vigil until darkness fell on the blacked-out village and Carne Hill became a blurred snout in the merging and softening of cold ragged clouds. There was drama in the twilight—intense spiritual drama, poignant, evocative. Vivid personal associations were here. I remembered that period twenty years before when every evening for nine months my mother and I had passed under these clay-dumps, I, a blind infant in a push-chair, down to the doctor's surgery in the same road in which Barbara was now living. Further north, under Carne Hill church, was Penrose Veor farm, where, in 1929, Evelyn had called me out of literal darkness into the spiritual darkness of romantic idealism. These 1940 vigils were very different from those of 1930 when from Bloomdale clay-tip I had watched Nanpean and dreamed of strange gods, nourished an undisciplined vision. They were, as I have said, more like the apocalypse of 1938; yet richer and more healthy even than that. The experience showed a marked advance in religious quality; the evil it encountered was no longer in myself but external. The dark sensual tide which had then risen and battled against the spiritual was absent now; there was peace, and a vast, co-ordinated movement of light and energy in the peace. It was a pure and unchallenged spiritual tide that not only flowed through my soul but thrilled and pulsed as a physical sensation, a liberation and freedom that were ecstatic; it even seemed at times to flood out over the landscape so that the moors and clay-peaks became to my vision "palpably fire-clothed." The sense of awe and wonder, the feeling that "the heavens had opened," weighed down upon me with such a deep and overwhelming joy that the tears would stream down my cheeks as I moved through the rain-splashed bracken or up the wet sandy slopes of the dunes into the evening mists.

Yet these experiences were not simply mystical; they were Christian, and the Christian is as much a misfit in the mystical world as in any other. I was not conscious of dissolving into, or becoming one with, any created thing outside myself. I still rejected the idea of Divine immanence in Nature, and remained an indifferent spectator of the moods of the earth, not fused with them but standing apart and throwing upon them a credal light under which they shrivelled away to nothing. The thrill of direct contact with Reality was produced not by sense impressions but by texts from the Bible which came to my mind so forcibly that they seemed almost to be spoken by an audible voice. The condition was similar to Bunyan's and had no kinship whatever with the intoxication of mystics who became aware of a "divine spirit" in the world around them. To the Christian, God is immanent only in

Christ and in the Bible, and this primary immanence is communicated to human beings exclusively through doctrinal faith. This conception seems a narrow one, but it is not so narrow as the vision of the independent mystic. The Christian has accepted something which is offered to everyone, and even a shallow experience of it, such as that of many in the Oxford Group, is used by God to transform other lives. Pure mysticism however, involves a tragic self-imprisonment, for its values and enthusiasms are repudiated not only by the mass of humanity but by God also. The mystic who has found some private point of view of which he can claim that "it is not orthodox but it is holy," knows that not even by prayer can his personal illumination be communicated to people with a different temperament. He is thus driven to a defensive and not very holy obsession with his own ego; he turns from heaven and from the world to the earth, and passes beyond morality in the sterile pride of a "life-lover." Elizabeth Myers, a typical modern mystic, followed Blake and Emily Bronte in her insistence that the key to Reality lies in "making importance of one's own self in total premeditated receptiveness to the earth and to life."* But even if this were true, it is obvious that to the average mind such language is no more intelligible than the Nicene Creed. It is certainly of less practical value, for the Nicene Creed can become a living force to persons of all temperaments, while it is doubtful whether anyone but a consumptive can attain the heightened sensuous consciousness which finds ecstacies in material trifles. This does not mean that purely subjective vision is without significance: it is significant for the imagination, and the Christian may extend imaginative sympathy and intellectual curiosity to modes of perception which he cannot admit to be adequate for the soul, which will ultimately be judged by the Christ of dogma. He realizes that all forms of relative truth may be fused with the Christian revelation, but not until they have fused with it do they become absolute truths, valid in eternity as well as in time. It is this realization that makes the Christian seem intolerant when he is not being

* *A Well Full of Leaves.*

intolerant at all as far as this world is concerned, but merely protesting that the temporal is not the eternal and that "Truth" must fit into Christ, not Christ into Truth. This protest may be made by those who are fully responsive to the "cosmic shorthand" of the natural scene. My indifference to Nature as a source of spiritual refreshment is very much a personal idiosyncrasy; it is not typical of all Calvinists, much less of all Christians. It was never shared by my mother, who was always sensitive to the presence of God in creation. I think the trait is due partly to my physical handicaps. For nearly half my life three of my senses—sight, hearing and smell—have not been normal. These senses being dulled, I was naturally stimulated to a defensive conviction that, after all, I was not missing much. This may explain some of my theological aberrations, my obsession with sex (the over-emphasis on the sense of touch), and the fact that these mystical experiences on Rostowrack were so alien to the usual mystical consciousness, so bleakly stripped of spiritual intimations from the soil.

The element of prayer was always focused, related to the practical issues of that sombre time. I often went to Rostowrack troubled about our evacuees' family in London. There were long silences to which news of air raids gave an ominous significance, tense periods when day after day the girls came home from school to be met with mother's tight-lipped admission that there was still no letter. It was poignant to receive their good-bye kisses as I set out for my walk, and to feel that they might be already orphans. Fortunately this fear was not fulfilled, and in September their mother was evacuated to Wales—a fact we did not learn until several weeks later. There was also the manuscript of *Private Snow* in London under the bombardment. I had no spare copy of the book, and if it were destroyed there seemed little hope of my going on with my writing. The urgency of my prayer was therefore very natural, and it was inevitable that, with my mystical faculty, I should feel a special assurance of the Divine protection as I watched each week close dimly over St. Dennis. The thought of Barbara down there in the village also made me deeply conscious of my need of guidance. Her interest in love stories did not lead her to be demonstrative when she came to Goonamarris, and thus my inspiration was split into two divergent parts—the spiritual aspect nourished by Barbara as an afterglow from 1938, while the emotional side was drawn increasingly from other girls, especially Irene. The irony of the situation, its fantastic remoteness from ordinary life, brought a continuous pressure of bewilderment and discord except during these hours on Rostowrack Downs when it became charged with a sense of Divine purpose. But I little guessed when I entered 1941 that before the year was out this stress would have produced a lurid drama at Goonamarris, revealing a village mentality of which writers like Quiller-Couch and Charles Lee were blissfully ignorant.

When *Private Snow* was safely returned I went carefully through it, and then through its sequel, and decided that it would be best to carry on the story into a third volume, making a claywork trilogy. Before my twenty-fifth birthday I had set to work on the third volume and was making good progress with it. I was also writing things of a very different sort which gave me more immediate happiness than the artistic stuff. These other things—and I admit the fact without blushing— were devotional papers which my aunt Bertha read at the Christian Endeavour meetings at Trethosa chapel. Their quality seems to have impressed the members, and in April I was asked if I would come down personally and read my next paper. The request caused me some trepidation; I knew that most of the Christian Endeavour members were teen-age girls, and these had been outside my world for so many years that I feared my thoughts might not be as devotional as they ought to be while I sat among them in the schoolroom. However, I accepted the invitation to speak on the last Monday in April. I spent the previous Sunday praying that God would keep a firm rein on my romantic impulses, and during the Monday afternoon I planted several rows of potatoes in the garden to develop a healthy mood free of sentimentality. In mid-evening, braced by the romps and good-bye kisses from my little girl friends, I strolled over to Trethosa with my aunt Bertha, the manuscript of my address in my pocket.

I gave this first paper as planned—a little nervous because of my deafness but not otherwise embarrassed. Nearly a score of young people were present, and listened attentively to my exposition of the forty-sixth Psalm—"God is our refuge and strength": a simple doctrinal talk with no literary frills about it. My contempt for culture and arid mental refinement, the student mentality, was clearly revealed in this first public utterance. I spoke as if I had never heard of literature—apart from one quotation from Browning—and for all I know some of the more educated persons present (my old school-teacher Miss Liddicoat was one of them) might have asked themselves in bewilderment how I could hope to succeed in the modern literary world if I had not yet got beyond this simple, old-fashioned piety. I certainly didn't talk like a novelist, and as the benediction was pronounced on that little gathering I felt that I would much rather be a "hot-gospeller." The actual experience of speaking as a Fundamentalist in public gave me a glimpse of the kind of thrill that lies in such work when done on the grand scale. It is a thrill peculiar to revivalism, and is unknown to the artist or the mere spreader of information and ideals. To me it would have been blasphemy to go into a Christian church and talk about philosophy and art, comparative religion and the "good life." Christianity, as I understood it, was distinct—rather terribly distinct—from all these things. And I had little use for them even outside the Church. I never could give my sympathy or support to adult, educative movements; I felt them always as intolerable fetters, encroachments on the simple gusto of living. With me Christianity came first, primitive secularism next, mere "spiritual values" and general "uplift" last of all. I often found myself in agreement with materialists in their contempt for "religion"; but I had been freed from "religion" not by materialism but by a theology—the doctrine of a supernatural invasion of the religious sphere, a Divine *reversal* of the weary human "search for God." I was thus in an oddly complicated position, and one in which I found myself closer to the average man than to the intellectuals: for even when the actual sphere of my interests was "highbrow," I approached it for the simple, immediate enjoyment, not for self-conscious mental culture. My dogmatic Christian insight made me unsympathetic to the trivial pleasures of the masses, but if I had to choose between such trivial pleasures and the dry technicalities of the "serious-minded," I should choose the pleasures every time. My attitude was that to which Browning came in his old age—the belief that true wisdom lies in "love allied to ignorance"—

> "in the claim for love that's gratitude
> For apprehended pleasure....Pleasure is,
> While knowledge may be."*

To *feel* the thrill of life and dogma, and to live, in the dull periods, on the memory of what they felt like—the touch of Christ on the soul, the girl's caress—I could admit no order of experience that claimed to supersede or modify such direct impressions. Most poets react to life this way; but most poets do not give papers containing nothing but Gospel platitudes. I had made a synthesis, and I knew which elements were fundamental.

Whether this enigma of my personality was felt by my hearers or not will never be known; for about two hours after we left the chapel tragedy struck in the district. A German 'plane, crippled over St. Eval aerodrome, jettisoned its bombs within earshot of Goonamarris. Several fell on Foxhole village, across the valley, killing four people and damaging thirty-seven houses. This sombre affair caught the local imagination, and my appearance at Trethosa was quite rightly ignored. Later in the year I gave two further papers at the chapel, but by that time I had lost something of my assurance because of the tone and trend of events at Goona-marris. A certain amount of talk was going about, and I wondered whether it had reached Trethosa.

These incidents did not show village life at its best, and but

* *Ferishtah's Fancies.*

for their bearing on the plot of *Wilding Graft* I might pass over them with a casual reference or charitably refrain from mentioning the humiliating fiasco. The episode was irrelevant to the main course of my life, an adventure in a by-path that threw an oblique light upon the subjects I wanted to write about—my spiritual grafting and the manners of the real Cornish villager.

It was a very tangled situation that had developed during the spring and summer of 1941, and not the least of its causes was the simple fact of the contrast between our home and the house next door. Our neighbours were a decent young couple with a typical, conventional working-class outlook: the wife having rather strict views on the training of children. Irene was not allowed to pull open drawers or rummage about as she wished to; she must not touch crockery without asking permission. She found these restrictions irksome after the freedom of slum life, and she soon observed that no such restrictions were applied in our home. Pat and Doris were ideally happy with us because they were given complete liberty to enjoy themselves and gratify any harmless whim. They often sat on the floor amid piles of comic papers that were strewn all over the chairs, sofa and carpets. They were free to explore cupboards, drawers and the bookcase. They could upset ink on my desk without being severely scolded, and knock the furniture about in happy romps—though mother was still a little anxious that her furniture should "look nice." I had tried to convince her that as long as a piece of furniture remains as it was when purchased it has no history and is therefore not worth looking at; that it only acquires a history through the scratches and stains which give it human associations that appeal to emotion and sentiment. Mother had not fully endorsed this doctrine, but she treated the children's needs with a loving consideration that made them passionately devoted to her. The mixture of simple piety and fun which she had inherited from her father was a revelation to them, and they were extremely well-behaved, never abusing the liberties we gave them. A lady expert in child psychology who accompanied the Nanpean batch of evacuees declared, after some talks with my mother, that she was a "perfect psychologist" in her approach to children. Actually she knew nothing of psychology, but she had a vivid Christian sense of values, and this, with my continual debunking of artificial conventions, had given her the wisdom and tact that were so much appreciated.

It was natural, therefore, that Irene should become a little piqued, envious, rather sullen in her billet. She began to beg mother to let her come in and live with Pat and Doris, where she could share in the fun which she so often heard going on on the other side of the wall. There was inevitably some friction through these repeated requests, and this was accompanied by other stresses. During the spring and summer of 1941 the strain of my "split inspiration" became very acute. Barbara called several times, but seeing other girls in the house she practically ignored me, and I was much agitated, dreading her visits instead of looking forward to them. A few times when she left the cottage without giving me even a smile in farewell—as frigid at ten as Evelyn had been at sixteen—I broke down and cried, and it was usually Irene who helped me to get back my balance and the freshness of interest to continue with my work. Everyone in the house, and the neighbours too, felt that something extraordinary was happening. The neighbours, of course, knew nothing of my old attachment to Barbara and the torture it was to have the Nanpean pattern in some degree repeated: they merely thought it prudent to keep Irene away from me as much as possible. Thus instead of returning to her billet from school she was often sent to her foster-mother's old home at Curyan; she began to spend the week-ends there, and I caught only brief glimpses of her sad, sullen little face. There were tragic conjunctions: visits from Barbara that desolated me—and Irene kept at Curyan, unable to help. The position became insufferable and led to hysterical outbursts on my part, sometimes in the presence of the foster-parent and other neighbours. Being unfamiliar with the latent peculiarities of my temperament these village folk took my violent behaviour very seriously. The result was that on October 8th I had to undergo a psycho-analytical test at Truro Infirmary.

My mother, of course, accompanied me, though the ordeal was a nightmare to her. She had aged much during that summer, grown haggard, her hair almost white. That the son on whom she had set her hopes and prayers should grow up to drivel into this nauseating mess seemed to be the very nadir of tragic irony for her. Where was God—the God of the fresh, clean life other Christians were allowed to live? Or were these the stern measures He had taken to show me the perils of the path I was following? We had both prayed desperately for deliverance, and it was now up to God, in that hospital consulting room, to vindicate our faith.

During the first part of the proceedings the psychiatrist asked my mother innumerable questions about my general character from childhood to maturity. He wrote down her answer, making a complete dossier of my psychological background and development. He then questioned me on general aspects of my taste and outlook, writing down his queries because of my deafness and handing the slips of paper across the table at which all three of us were seated. I was naturally somewhat flustered at this juncture, and I did not give very close thought to my replies. When he asked me who were my favourite authors, for instance, I mentioned Galsworthy and Hall Caine, both of whom had ceased to be my favourites years before. But it was probably just as well that I did not admit that my favourite author was T. F. Powys!

When this preliminary ground had been covered my mother was requested to leave the room and the psychiatrist proceeded to the main point of the inquiry. He told me that my friendship with Irene had aroused suspicion, and asked me what I had to say about it. I declared—more coolly now that mother was not present—that the friendship was innocent. I frankly acknowledged that I was fond of Irene, that I had kissed her, and was sometimes upset when she was kept away from me, but that there was absolutely nothing beyond this in our relationship. The psychiatrist probed deeper for abnormalities. Had I ever been homosexual? Was I troubled with frequent erotic dreams? Did I find obscene images accompanying my creation of imaginary heroines? To all these questions I replied simply and truthfully, "No." He did not refer to masochism or sadism, and I thought it unnecessary to mention these traits, as they had nothing to do with the charge. I was very relieved that he did not ask whether I had been in any way obsessed with other young girls. I was anxious that Barbara should be kept out of this, and that our old spiritual attachment should not be dragged into this murky by-path. It would be very difficult to explain to a psychiatrist what she had done for me, and what I still felt about her.

Throughout the last crucial phase of the examination I was quite calm and collected. I had read enough books on sex and psychology to give intelligent answers to the psychiatrist's questions. I knew what he was talking about, what he was trying to get at. As the minutes ticked by I felt assured that the cloud would pass—that it was, indeed, already passing. I could take an objective view of the situation, even enjoy it, seeing it not as a tragic débâcle but as just the odd sort of comedy a misfit was likely to run into. A touch of humour crept now and then into my admissions of the queer kinks in my character.

At length the long ordeal of psychoanalysis was over and mother, looking pale and weary, was summoned to hear the verdict.

The psychiatrist stated deliberately that his analysis, with the details she had given, had convinced him that I was innocent of the charge, that I was not the type of man who would commit that kind of offence. My mind was unusual but sound and wholesome, with firm moral control. He added—and I mention this as a mere factual detail—that there was no doubt that I possessed the mentality of a genius and was likely to show a taste for extreme simplicity which would be misunderstood by average adults.

These assurances lifted a great burden from my mother: we left the hospital feeling that God had overruled this squalid interlude and that there was some purpose in it. I was especially exhilarated—partly, I must confess, by the element of scandal and sensationalism in the crisis. A part of me—the least Christian part—could dramatize the event and make me feel like a sort of village Oscar Wilde. The real thrill was deeper—a sense of gratitude to God for this extraordinary deliverance and the encouragement it brought to strengthen my trust for the future.

The official confirmation of my "genius" meant little to me in comparison with the immediate human gains that resulted from my ordeal. Irene had remained stolid throughout the crisis; I never knew how much of it she comprehended. But she was still longing to share the comfort and happiness which Doris and Pat enjoyed; and events moved very rapidly towards the end we had all desired and which, only a few weeks before, had seemed utterly impossible. Irene's foster-father had been sent away to a war factory in Bristol, and early in October he asked his wife to join him. Seeing that further tension would be pointless, she became quite amicable. She assured us that she was glad I had no such tendencies as had been attributed to me, and she was now willing to let us take Irene off her hands so that she could go to Bristol. Within a week of my triumphal return from Truro, Irene was billeted in our home; her contribution to my "education" was assured. The tussle was over, and to mother's infinite relief it had made no general stir in the district. Goonamarris was a tiny and remote place, and a rumpus that was not reported in the newspapers could run its course there without being heard of two miles away. Everyone was preoccupied with the war, glum and tense about the Nazi advance into Russia, and had no thought to spare for the circumstances under which an evacuee girl had changed her billet.

CHAPTER TWELVE

The Mature Fusion

IT is no part of my business in this book to present a picture of what the world in general looks like "through a Cornish window," or anything of that sort. There are plenty of other writers who can supply such objective whimsy. Everyone knows what the world in general looked like during these war years; and an autobiographer's task, as I see it, is to give an honest account of something his readers would otherwise know nothing about—his own life. And if the whole of that life has been spent in a moorland cottage the writer will be wise to refrain from cluttering up his narrative with comment on world affairs. My view of the world was gained entirely through the newspapers: I spent an hour or two each weekday perusing the *Daily Mail*, and usually made a brief record in my diary of the current military situation. Even local events connected with the war were never personal impressions to me; I learnt of them only through the local papers or through my mother. I was oddly unlike most writers in my indifference to news values and dramatic colour. My mind remained, as it always had been rather sluggish; I was never alert, never curious to see or investigate any unusual occurrence. When Foxhole was bombed I did not even trouble to stroll over to the village and examine the damaged houses. During the blitz on Plymouth early in 1941 many people in mid-Cornwall climbed to ridges of the moors after nightfall and watched the lurid glare from the burning city, forty miles away to the east. Such a spectacle was inspiring to the imagination, and one would think it the very thing a sombre-minded novelist would wish to contemplate, seeing in it material for a thrilling story. But I remained stolidly within the cottage at Goonamarris, cutting myself off from such external drama, which had little appeal for me with my cloudy mystical obsessions. I wished my writings to have spiritual depth, and I knew that spiritual depth is seldom found in the work of writers who live adventurous lives. It was better, I felt, to be passive and watch the footsteps of God cross and re-cross the bit of mud and clay at one's doorstep, leaving each time a fresh line or twist in the pattern; to brood upon that, to try to interpret it and so get one of God's ideas complete, personal within oneself, not mixed up and blurred in the maze of irrelevant happenings outside. I had decided not to attempt any description of actual war incidents, and thus I fastened only upon the moral and spiritual issues. I was interested to read in the local papers that some women around St. Austell had been sent to prison for turning their homes into brothels, and promptly used the material in the closing chapters of my trilogy. I was gripped, too, by an account of some London women, evacuated to Truro, being jailed because they left their children unattended at Truro for several days while they made a trip back to London—an episode that proved very convenient to me in shaping the climax of *Wilding Graft*. I took a sternly Puritan view of the general laxity of the times; my diary entries frequently complain of the materialism reflected in the speeches of national leaders, especially Church leaders. The entry for November 2nd, 1941, is typical:

> "Read Jeremiah 8-10 this morning, and feel how true it is of England today. Why are people so blind, refusing to know and acknowledge God's judgment? "They have rejected the word of the Lord; and what wisdom is in them?" And "for judgment I will give their wives unto others"—what a deep unfathomable! As if *God's* is the predestinating will behind immorality—a destiny provoked by the abuse of man's free will. Logic is lost here, but I accept the truth—God help me to mirror it rightly in my novels, all in proportion."

This reveals the attitude of mind from which *Wilding Graft* derived its peculiar emphasis, a war book in which none of the characters play any part in the war, but work out its moral and spiritual implications in a remote hamlet where the peace-time routine of life is scarcely disturbed throughout the story.

To get the genesis of this book in true perspective it is necessary to realize that for several years I had been seeking

to embody in fiction the essence of the experience for which
Barbara had prepared me—the substitution of "grafted" faith
and love for the natural flowering of ideals and romanticism
which I had proved so disillusioning at Nanpean. I had
hitherto found it an impossible theme for a novel. There was
no adult counterpart of my experience, and a novel had to deal
with adult lovers. I had to content myself with praising the
"childlike" qualities of my heroines and attacking the spurious
"adult" outlook, and this had not proved very successful, as
my sympathies were not at all with the demure, Victorian type
of feminine innocent which the word "childlike" tended to
suggest. The very originality of my experience seemed to have
deprived me of suitable subject-matter for a novel: my imagination was wasted in exploring the possibilities of abnormal
relationships, all of which, if treated in fiction, would be
coarse parodies of the lovely thing I had known. Unusual
attachments between adults and children are rarely touched
upon by the average writer. In all my later readings I have
found only one instance of this theme—in T. F. Powys' *Unclay*,
which contains an account of a strange association between a
middle-aged man and a girl of nine. In Powys' hands it
becomes a very beautiful and spiritually significant thing, and
shows that frank appreciation of the girl-child as a sexual
being, "pagan and yet merry with God," which always
characterizes Powys' references to very young girls and is in
every respect identical with my own. This was another trait
of Powys' that enabled his work to relieve me of the sense of
being a literary pariah. I know of no other writer who dares
to depict young village girls as they really are, dismissing their
school life as an irrelevancy that is not worth mentioning,
and concentrating upon the deep, instinctive tendernesses that
are not supposed to exist by "nice" writers, though it is
certainly of these qualities and not scholastic ones that Christ
says: "Of such is the Kingdom of Heaven."

It was this perception in me which had caused all the friction
in my home since 1936. The mere fact of an adult writer being
inspired by children is not in itself unusual. Writers as different

in type as Wordsworth and Lewis Carroll drew some of their finest inspiration from young girls. But the resulting literary product was a direct and simple expression of childish influence; the reader could easily detect the child touch, unwarped and undisguised. Lewis Carroll was inspired by "Alice," and so he imagined her adventures in a fantastic nursery world. That kind of inspiration is so obviously innocent that no one, not even my mother, would have objected had my writings been so clearly in harmony with a child's mind. My peculiarity lay in the fact that, although I derived all my inspiration from young girls I never wrote anything that young girls could read. I kept child characters curtly out of my novels, and did not even write a poem about a child until I was over thirty. All the writing that Barbara had led me to produce was either about Calvinist dogma or about sex—topics never discussed in Wonderland, though they are gateways to the real Wonderland. The effect was so unlike the cause that I myself was baffled by it until I honestly faced the fact that my mind was, in its natural state, rather like D. H. Lawrence's: it turned everything into sex. There was also in it the "grafted" power which tried to turn everything into Christian sacrament and belief. A child's charm touched me as innocently as it would have touched a writer of fairy tales, but it soon encountered a wholly different medium, and by the time it reached my creative imagination it had gathered religious and sexual implications that set me writing about theology or about prostitutes. From the outset—that is, from the time my last fancies regarding Evelyn vanished in 1937—this activity had been wholesome—a fact which shows the vigour and discipline of my Christian faith, for I had every natural reason to hit back at life by producing another *Lady Chatterley's Lover*.

I had now, at the close of 1941, reached the point at which the processes of my inner life could be concreted in a novel with some fidelity to the truth. I had known the full range of experience which friendships with girl-children could yield— the heights of mystic vision through Barbara and the depths of vulgar scandal through Irene. In the calm enjoyment that followed my stormy tussle to get Irene billeted with us, the two elements gradually fused. There was a sharp personal urge, arising from the complex feelings of humiliation, triumph and renewed trust in the Divine purpose. My artistic powers had matured and was ready to deal with this complexity. Even the literary influence required at this juncture was provided, for in November, 1941, I won a book token prize in a Methodist Guild essay competition. I exchanged the book token for Hardy's *Tess of the d'Urbervilles* and *Jude the Obscure*, and a few weeks later bought *The Return of the Native*. I was thus saturated in the essence of Hardy's poetic fatalism at the very time when circumstances forced me to embody in a romance my own poetic Calvinism.

I finished my trilogy in December, and early in the New Year began jotting some notes of *Wilding Graft*. On February 2nd, 1942, I started writing the actual narrative, which came freely and needed little revision. I spent my Sunday afternoons strolling around Kernick and Meledor to check up my descriptions of the scenery. That around Meledor was entirely strange, for though I had lived all my life within two miles of the village I had not hitherto visited it. My geographical contacts, even within the clay area, were extremely limited. There are still, within three or four miles of my home, several villages I have never entered; even in St. Stephen's and St. Dennis there are streets I have never passed through. Of no man could it be said with less truth that he knows every nook and cranny of his own district. I had no interest, historical or æsthetic, in local beauty spots; all I wished to see could be seen from the clay-dumps around Goonamarris.

This habit of narrow concentration had always prevented me from giving much detail in my descriptive passages, except when I was writing about clay-works. I had to confine myself to a broad general picture of a scene, and try to convey its spiritual tone. I am still lamentably ignorant of botany and all other branches of natural history. The children had often come to me with some specimen of plant or insect life, and asked me what it was called. They thought I would be able to inform them like a schoolmaster, as I was clever enough to write books; but nearly always I had to confess that I didn't know. My indifference to Nature, my obstinate refusal to learn anything about her products—apart from the one product of human sexuality which could be aware of itself as redeemed from the fallen process—were remarkable traits in one who had always lived in the open countryside. Of the scores of flowers that bloom in our Cornish hedges I still do not know the names of more than half-a-dozen; among trees I can recognize only a few common ones like hawthorns, elms and hollies, while the colours and habits of various types of birds are as unknown to me as if I had lived all my life in the slums. When I mention any particular bird or flower I have to refer to the *Children's Encyclopædia* for details of its appearance, even though I may have been just within a few yards of the living original in one of Goonamarris fields. Such crass insensitiveness is rarely found in a poet: as I have previously stated, it is due mainly to my physical handicaps. But I must confess that for some mysterious reason I find it exhilarating. It renders me permanently immune from the heaviness, weariness and slackness of fibre which are bred by Nature-worship, as in Jefferies, Thoreau, Shelley, and preserves in me the rough, healthy texture of normal life. The *poison* of mysticism has gone out of me through my Calvinist faith—and partly, perhaps, through my ballast talent for commonplace vulgarity which prevents me from going too far in any direction. These traits have made me complex and contradictory—a poet who loathes the "poetic" world of illusion and ideals, a mystic who frankly derides all the popular forms of mysticism. I can grin in sympathy with the irreverent critic who chided Emily Bronte for writing of "celestial shine"—as if it were boot polish. I have no use for "celestial shine" myself; and when I read that mystics feel in tune with the Infinite, one with universal life, conscious of the essential unity of all things, and so forth, I have to face the terrible possibility that I am not a mystic after all. I have never felt like that. My spiritual vision is dogmatic, at once curt and exuberant; it makes me feel my separation, my eternal individuality that nothing can absorb or tone down into a flatness of integration with Nature. Even the pantheism of my teen years was of an oddly personal type, a sort of claywork pantheism that discovered God in a rusty waggon but still denied that He was in a flower. It was therefore impossible for me to handle natural background in fiction with the lyrical beauty and intimate tenderness of the pagans. Instead I developed to full strength in *Wilding Graft* the trait Q. had noted in *Private Snow*—a grim concentration on the "Egdon Heath business," worked out in a "clay-coloured monotony," as a publisher's reader afterwards said of it. I decided that such scenes as were not set on the clayworks should be placed, not in a lush pastoral retreat, but in a town; and my recent ordeal at Truro led me to select that spot with a quiet, ironic enjoyment.

The first pages of *Wilding Graft* were written in an atmosphere of tranquility, but this mood was shattered as I proceeded with the book. When Irene came in to live with Pat and Doris I had expected that all three girls would remain with us until the war was over; but at the end of February, 1942, Pat and Doris were suddenly recalled to London by their parents. I felt the loss very keenly, for though they had not inspired a line of my writing they had become associated with some of the main spiritual developments of my life—particularly those evening vigils on Rostowrack—and memories of them took on a new poignancy as I looked every day at their empty chairs, the cupboard where they had kept their toys, the discarded tins and bits of slate at the house corner where we had all squatted on stones so often and made mud pies in the sunshine.

Mother took in another evacuee almost at once as a playmate for Irene—a girl previously billeted at Nanpean, ten years old, but very small, a dark, shy orphan called Joan from Dulwich. Like Pat and Doris, she had no emotional significance for me at all: she moved about the house as a silent, remote shadow that could never "come alive" to me, never be known to me as a girl, so far did my deafness bar me off from normal perceptions of character. She was a fairly intelligent child, but my handicaps forced me to treat mental qualities as irrelevant, even non-existent as far as I was concerned. I could never notice whether a girl was backward or brilliant in the school sense, except for a certain sharpness and clarity in the clever type that moved me to repugnance, and a slow smouldering vitality in the dull sort (Irene was very dull, the despair of her school-teachers) that appealed. The only language that made a girl real to me was the deep, unerring language of the nerves, the mysterious vibrations of affinity conveyed by touch and having no relation to mental abilities or even to age. Adolescence made no difference here. If a girl's touch were blank or "dumb" to me in childhood I knew that she could never be emotionally valid for me. I have never been mistaken in this basic, primitive assessment of personality. These girls still return to Goonamarris on holiday, and I react to them in their mid and late teens exactly as I did when they were young children: they remain more shadowy and sexless to me than Irene was at ten, or Barbara at five. This fact convinced me that sex was not a mere biological function, but something that can be vitally active and compelling while the "racial instinct" is dormant. Everything depended on the type—and it had to be "the type untampered with." When the real nature became overlaid by conventionality—as it had done in Barbara since she left Goonamarris—the attraction vanished. And by this time I knew well enough why certain qualities and textures pleased me, while others, particularly those that made a girl socially popular, repelled. It was an expression of the fundamental bias that dictated all my tastes. Since I loathed smoothness and elegance in theology, literature and art, I could not admire these qualities in girls; the same demand for a certain roughness of fibre, the suggestion of violence, prevailed here too. It seemed an odd paradox that my Christian faith had drawn my sexual sympathies in a direction which, at first sight, appeared less spiritual than the one they had taken when controlled by poetic illusion. While I was bogged in the quietism of the mystic I could not find a girl who was refined and "ethereal" enough to suit me: when Evelyn upset chairs in scuffles with her brother at Nanpean I had suffered mental agonies of bewilderment and fastidious recoil. But as mysticism was replaced by faith my human sympathies broadened; I came to love noise, frolic and healthy vulgarity, as John Polmounter had loved them. Like him, however, I demanded these things in their innocent spontaneous form. I had been schooled through the transition by my romps with little girls, and the rough-and-tumble atmosphere I appreciated was that suggested by the sofa and the hearthrug: it was not that of the dance-hall or the sports field. I disliked as much as ever all forms of crowd excitement which harden gaiety into a habit, a mere social grace. My attitude was consistent with orthodox Christianity, which has always been associated with a certain noisiness that is not the clamour of "progress" or the shrill, nerve-racked hubbub of an "adult" world, but the childlike gusto of conviction, a quality too near to heaven, too wilful and wayward, to be civilizing. It was therefore inevitable that my creed should toughen my emotions as it did, and that by 1942 I could scarcely find a girl who was enough of a tomboy, sufficiently free from artificial dignity and reserve, to match the rugged vitality of my beliefs.

The misfit heroine of *Wilding Graft* was a reflection of all this. The so-called better type of girl was useless for my purpose. Only an undisciplined type can prompt the "stain of fire" that burns out a man's natural faith, whether through remorse—as might happen in a case of prostitution or adultery—or through an agonized conviction of moral rightness beyond moral convention, as in the actual case of Garth Joslin in the novel. The autobiographical element in Garth is in the record of his spiritual development, not in the external details of his love affairs: the account of Garth's courtship bears no resemblance to my frustration at Nanpean. Garth's apocalypse of prayer after Irma returned to London was, of course, derived from my mystical experience after Barbara left Goonamarris; but the character of Irma herself is more like Irene. It was Irene whom these villagers had tried to drive away from me, and who, in spite of their efforts, was now sharing the ups and downs of my daily life. I could not but speculate on what might have happened had Irene been a few years older. As she was only nine, I had to accept the incident as a temporary stage in my emotional training. It was certainly, on the human side, a big step forward from the point to which Barbara had brought me. I was forced to ask what might be the minimum age at which such a scandal could produce a permanent attachment, and decided that a highly sexed girl was capable of realistic responses when near adolescence. So in the original manuscript of the story, as accepted in 1945 by Mr. Savage, Irma was stated to be a mere child of twelve when she enjoyed her first embrace with Garth in the workshop. It was only after the book had been refused by several publishers that Mr. Savage suggested that the age of twelve might be "repellent" to some readers, and advised me to advance her age to fifteen. I did this with some reluctance, but no doubt the change made the novel more palatable to the general reader who knew nothing of the author's private life.

The experience of conversion attributed to Garth was unusual because it reflected my own—a very extraordinary one. But the book was entirely orthodox in its theological bearing. Nowhere in it did I suggest that sex can be a "point of contact" for the Divine revelation while it remains inside Nature. I was rather concerned to demonstrate the freedom of God in election—the freedom to *create* a point of contact at any level of the human personality—not only in the so-called higher levels of idealism and spirituality, but in the undisciplined instinct, a direct grafting into the life-blood of passion instead of into the cool bony structure of reason. This, however, does not mean that human feelings and sensations are more sacred than mere thoughts; it does not support D. H. Lawrence's notion of the essential holiness of the body. This heresy is possible only to writers who draw their inspiration from Nature —and I drew mine from the opposite source, Christian dogma. No experience, however thrilling, could inspire me until I had measured it by a theological footrule and found what doctrines it affirmed. Thus I approached my characters as an amateur theologian rather than a moralist. I conceived of Garth as

Browning conceived of his Caponsacchi ("Be glad thou hast let light into the world through that irregular breach"); and for the same reason. My experience was as "irregular" as Browning's, though my "breach" was involuntary.

Life always has to be simplified in a novel if one is to give the tale a coherent plot. I had to show Garth receiving the whole of his "grafting" through the same girl, whom he ultimately married. My own position in 1942 was nothing like so clear-cut; and my passionate desire that it had remained as clear-cut as in 1938 was probably one of the chief causes of the intensity with which I wrote. It might have been a very bitter book, for during the whole period of my writing it I was nagged by a general "contrariness" in circumstance, particularly by the ironic course of events at St. Dennis. Barbara's lapse into my own by-path of moody isolation seemed to have been short-lived. She had been persuaded to join a local children's choir, and nearly every week was travelling about Cornwall, taking part in concerts. The choir gained much popularity in the county and broadcast from the B.B.C. studio at Plymouth. This development was more humiliating to me than the village scandal I had been dragged through. Barbara had led me towards Calvinism, yet at the very time when I was expressing that faith in its mature form she was giving her support to the shallow worldliness which Calvinism so strongly condemns. The reports of the applause she was winning by singing in cinemas on Sunday evenings about fairs and fairies, were appearing in the *Cornish Guardian*—sometimes in the same issue as a letter of mine denouncing the superficiality of the hour and pleading for a deep religious response to the challenge. It was like a ghastly joke, and my inevitable reaction to it was to seek spiritual as well as emotional inspiration in Irene. This was not at all difficult, for Irene had altered much under the happy Christian influence of our home. She was no longer the sullen, shifty-eyed slum child who had lived next door, but a warm-hearted, trustworthy girl, becoming deeply interested in the simple religion my mother taught her. It was she now who stayed indoors and read the Bible—while Barbara was off at a concert; and when mother had given her some music lessons she spent hours in the evenings playing Sankey hymns and revivalist choruses on the organ, the sentimental tunes making a strong appeal to her emotional nature. The qualities that had once budded in Barbara seemed now to have flowered in Irene; yet Barbara's influence remained, and occasionally the old spell would reassert itself, pulling me into the peculiar fresh atmosphere, the feel of the *beginning* of things, the tang of 1937, which no subsequent experience with children could quite equal in vitalizing force. Barbara came to Goonamarris three times while I was engaged on *Wilding Graft:* the first two visits did not help much, but the third, in September 1942, surprised me, yielding the old magic I had missed in her for four years and quickening me with fresh confidence and zest as I tackled the final part of my novel. But there was still that choir, occasional items in the local paper about Barbara's proficiency in tap-dancing, which tended again to bring Irene close as the more congenial character. I was inextricably muddled, torn between the two loyalties, unable to resolve either because both girls were still children and the element of mature love did not enter into the dilemma. The only thing that could have broken the deadlock was the impact of a teen-age girl, with whom I could really fall in love; but there was little prospect of such a development. Of the various girls, playmates of our evacuees', who called at my home, only Brenda and Sheila Snell were vivid, real personalities to me— and both were younger than Barbara. I could do nothing but wait until the war ended and Irene went home, and see what happened then.

Although the strain of this emotional tangle was the most prolonged and exhausting, it was not the only worry that over-shadowed my life during 1942. Another source of anxiety was the breakdown in my mother's health. She was then nearly fifty, and the attritions of the past few years would have been a trial to any woman of her age. She was suffering badly from asthma, getting little sleep, and found the extra work of looking after the evacuees a severe strain on her vitality. Medical examination revealed an even graver trouble: she had developed a toxic goitre, and was warned that it was likely to prove fatal unless she had an immediate operation. Throughout the spring of 1942 we were all in a state of agitation and suspense while mother awaited the word to enter Devonport hospital. In June she was admitted, and fortunately the operation was successful, though for several days she was critically ill. I journeyed to Devonport to see her on the following Sunday, depressed by my first view of bomb-damaged streets, shells of houses and mournful heaps of rubble, feeling glum and tense in the hospital ward, having no cheerful news to help mother towards a quick recovery. She had to return to the same weary grind of poverty and frustration, and nearly a year passed before she regained her normal strength.

She still made whatever sacrifice she could to assist me in my writing. Sometimes she gave me a few shillings so that I could go to Truro and get more familiar with the city scenes of *Wilding Graft*. I spent hours wandering around the back streets and the Waterfall Gardens, and made brief tours of the cathedral, museum and art gallery, which I used as settings in the novel because I felt they were artistically right. I derived no personal pleasure from these contacts with dignified, cultural institutions. I always left the cathedral feeling as I had once felt at St. Dennis parish church—that if anything can kill Christianity it is ecclesiastical architecture. The oppressive æsthetic gloom of the surroundings, cold and ornate, was so obviously meant to arouse those natural instincts of reverence and awe which are more potent than any gross sins in destroying *Christian* reverence, that turbulent, untamed vitality of the new creation. In the art gallery in River Street I was even less at home, for this kind of sensuous appeal did not pretend to be Christian; it represented values that had always been antipathetic to me even when I was hankering after some sort of ideal beauty myself. My mother was much more sensitive than I was in this matter. She liked to enter such places and look at the "beautiful pictures." But I could hardly find patience to glance at them. The rarefied, subdued tone of these temples of art was so repellent to my rough virility that it was soon a torture to me to stay there. I had to hurry out, look at something ugly in the streets and feel myself again. For me as for T. F. Powys, "Art can very well keep shut up in a book... It is better," he says in *Soliloquies of a Hermit*, "to have a certain cheapness of ordinary and common things about, that one need never look at." That is the way of spiritual growth. While the soul is distracted by products of human pride, ambition or natural insight, it cannot begin to develop in a Christian sense. Art and culture do indeed help to develop a soul, but the soul that is nourished by these things is the natural one, not the Christian germ of "eternal life" which is grafted on to personality from outside Nature. St. Paul's vision of Christ "casting down imagination, and every high thing which exalteth itself against the knowledge of God"* is not a narrow perversion but a fact every Christian realizes when he feels the direct challenge of Christ apart from the symbolism and ritual of institutions that have increasingly pandered to the demands of art. There are certain assumptions underlying the technique of traditional art which are incompatible with the Christian view of man—assumptions of a human nature still proud and whole in dignity and innocence. It is an odd pardox that from an orthodox Christian standpoint modern "decadent" art is nearer the truth than the more classic and reputable forms. While I am repelled by the elegance and grace of the conventtional art gallery, I am an enthusiastic admirer of the revolutionary leaders of contemporary art. One of the first things I bought when success came to me was a book of reproductions of Picasso's pictures. They give me a deeper and more satisfying pleasure than all the Old Masters. Picasso's idiom is one which a Calvinist can understand—an idiom freed from the Pelagian obsession with "beauty" which saturated practically all European art from the Renaissance to the twentieth century. The savage distortions of Picasso's work arouse in me a sense of spiritual congruity similar to that which I derive from the fantastic swellings and angles of the clay

* II Corinthians, x, 5.

landscape. I am stimulated by the realization that Nature has not been allowed to reflect here the pride of its integrations, but has been invaded and broken down—the unchanging symbol of the activity of Divine grace. Thus creative modernity and Christianity unite in their rejection of the ideals and values of modernist religion. Both affirm that truth has no "sweet reasonableness" about it, but is a wayward, subversive movement of energy against the "dictatorship of common sense."

But while I could bring a theological appreciation to the work of modern artists I had felt in my own life the necessity of choosing between art and dogma. I had touched at Nanpean the fringe of the artistic tragedy; I had been warned that for me there could be no compromise. If I lived for my own personal vision of the created world, as the Van Goghs of art had done, I should probably share the fate of the Van Goghs. Safety for me lay in an unswerving loyalty to the general revelation of Christ, in fellowship with the despised rabble of believers whom He had promised to guide and bless.

My position here was so constant and comprehensive that it expressed itself in trifling matters as well as in the main choices of life. On one of these visits to Truro, for instance, I carried, besides my fare, a sixpence with which mother had told me I could buy a book. Smith's bookstall at the corner of Lemon Street was colourful with a display of Penguin reprints —sophisticated modern works of high cultural quality. But I scarcely lingered to glance over the titles: I strolled across to Jordan's second-hand bookstall, and purchased with my sixpence a tattered copy of one of Spurgeon's devotional works, called *Morning by Morning*. I still remember my walk home from the bus-stop at St. Stephen's that night. The moon had risen before I reached Goonamarris, and when I was half-way up Goonvean hill I climbed over a gate into a field, and there in the moonlight I opened Spurgeon's book and read the solemn and pregnant words: "The time of figs is not yet. The predestinated moment has not struck; but, when it comes, they (the elect) *shall* obey, for God will have His own..." The assurance sank deep into my soul, and I moved on up the moonlit, frost-whitened field to my home with a richer glow of poetry in my heart than I could have derived from a Penguin reprint of one of the classics.

This trait was too fundamental, too essential to my growth, to be dismissed as the deplorably bad taste of an uneducated villager. It is beside the point to say that a good education at a secondary school would have rid me of this execrable taste for pious platitudes. The aim of this book is to suggest the kind of originality, vitality and exuberant zest in life of which, I am convinced, modern "scientific" education is depriving thousands of young people. I do not mean that everyone would come to share my vision if they had the good fortune to leave school at twelve, as I did: temperament, physical handicaps and unusual workings of Providence have fashioned my peculiar outlook. But the younger generation cannot but be devitalized by a scholastic system which assumes that nothing is valid unless it has borne the scrutiny of science. It is very probable that nothing I believe or enjoy is compatible with the "scientific approach" to life; but that merely prompts me to ask why on earth it needs to be. If the historic creeds founded on the Incarnation of Christ have "become my universe that feels and knows" (as Browning expressed it), why submit that valid, palpitating universe to the laws of a cold, dry-as-dust world of analysis and speculation, worm-eaten with the squalid demand for "evidence"? I have no more use than the honest atheist for a faith that refuses to face facts and meet challenges, but for me the only relevant challenges come from life itself, not from a "climate of opinion," the mere atmosphere of scepticism bred in places like schools, laboratories and libraries, where people are least alive. The reality of a faith is tested by circumstances such as mine were at that period. Can it open up a way for a man when he is faced with humanly insuperable barriers? My reading had left me in no doubt that orthodox Christianity could do that. The biographies of such flamboyant crusaders as Spurgeon, Talmage and C. T. Studd, the cricketer-missionary, supplied ample proof that if only a man was orthodox enough to believe in miracles, they happened in his own life. The "natural" course of events was interrupted again and again by an Unseen Hand—the "Hand of Providence" which, as Talmage declared in his *Autobiography*, "is always a mysterious grasp of life that confuses and dismays; but it always rebuilds, restores, and prophesies." I had staked everything on that belief, and if my lack of formal education deprived me of the means of diluting that belief, I could only be thankful for the privilege

This enthusiasm for the more sensational type of Christian witness did not affect in the least my admiration for the contemplative mystic. When a man hates civilization as much as I do, he will welcome anything that challenges and repudiates it. He will dwell lovingly on the symbol of the pillar in the desert, the hermit's cave, and will be equally gratified to hear of revivalist "circuses" at which little girls toot trumpets for Jesus. My imagination was kindled by both extremes. I could project my inner life, see myself with Talmage on the platform of the Brooklyn Tabernacle, swaying vast crowds under the banner that was inscribed with the grandiose claim: "The Tabernacle his pulpit; the world his audience." And with an equally vivid sympathy I could picture T. F. Powys' red-brick cottage at East Chaldon, the solitary hermit life: often when I looked at our garden gate—an old wooden one that was falling to pieces—I was pleasantly reminded of Powys' fence which, year after year, he kept tying up with string, to the bewilderment of the villagers. I came even more deeply under Powys' influence during the war, particularly through my reading of *Soliloquies of a Hermit*. Its revelation of the undisciplined soul, the faith of mere *moods*, was very close to the workings of my temperament, and the prevailing tone of melancholy expressed the peculiar sense of isolation and perversity that still recurred in me at times, and to which I had found no parallel in other religious writers. It was the experience of "the dark night of the soul," and the loneliness it brought was that of the bruised spirit which turns away from life through excess of life and is forced to worship through a distorting element and feel the despair that comes of faith still held, even when mirrored as blasphemy in the contracted mind. I was most indebted to orthodox writers who could break the grip of this mood, but it was often a comfort to find the mood itself so beautifully expressed in Powys' work.

I felt, too, throughout this period, an odd sense of spiritual kinship with Hardy—not the bitter rebellion of *Jude the Obscure*, but the more wistful bafflement of some of his poems. Though he rejected the creed of normal Christians and I accepted it, I was more essentially in harmony with him than with them, compelled to realize "that with this bright believing band I have no claim to be." It is not really surprising that an orthodox Christian should feel like this as piercingly as an atheist. Much depends on temperament and circumstance. Here and there a Christian, toughened or warped by heredity, may be set in a spiritual wilderness apart, and while affirming the traditional faith, he may know it so intensely as *his* faith, the overwhelming personal impact of it, that the experience of gregarious Christians bewilders and repels him. Kierkegaard knew this isolation of soul no less than Hardy, and there remained in my own thought a stubborn, stinging vein of the existentialism of Kierkegaard. It did not affect my conviction that the ultimate Fact was external and knowable; I had no doubts whatever regarding the Christian revelation. But I felt that perhaps we did not need the churches any more, but only the church dogmas divorced from their ecclesiastical setting and rendered elemental by faith. This idea involved experiments in solitude and was not consistent with the atmosphere of fellowship. I was fully a believer, but a dark and wilful believer, overshadowed by the sense of evil I had derived from the Clemo's, and the knowledge of human impotence which my handicaps had forced upon me.

All these complexities and contradictions of mood were alike hostile to modern scientific materialism and rational theology. They assured me that, although "progressive" thinkers may try to gain their end by substituting a "historical Jesus" for the Galilean Mood, the priest-natures of the world will always escape, existing as mediums for the self-revelation of the Mood.

The original manuscript of *Wilding Graft* was finished in April, 1943. I had written the book at a steady pace, producing two chapters a month for fourteen months, and thought that at last I had attained to some measure of competence and reliability in my literary processes. This feeling, however, was short-lived, and was followed by a chilling fear that with *Wilding Graft* I had written myself out; that it was the last spurt of a creative life on the verge of collapse. During the remaining eight months of 1943, and the whole of 1944, I wrote practically nothing but revisions of earlier work. The pile of manuscripts lying uselessly in my drawers was depressing, yet I dared not submit *Wilding Graft* under wartime conditions, as this would probably mean its refusal by some publisher who would readily accept it in normal times. I tried to break the deadlock by entering *Private Snow* in a few more literary contests, but with no success. The long weeks of idleness, unlike anything I had known since I began writing in 1930, cast a shadow of frustration and futility over my whole life. My diary entries grew increasingly pessimistic. That for November 29th, 1943, is typical:

"This idleness is pulling me to pieces, and the monotony gets more horrible every day.... Day after day I spend hanging round the bookcase from morning to night, taking out book after book, dipping into it and putting it back—can't get interested. It's a travesty of life and gets me to hate reading and everything bookish, and that in turn paralyses me as a writer. God restore the true fire of me, or I shall be, like poor Thompson, "an icicle whose thawing is its dying."

The suspense in both my literary and emotional life seemed interminable. As the Japs overran the Far East and the Nazi armies swept through Russia to Stalingrad, I felt there would probably be years of this stagnation ahead of me. The prospect was grim, and drove me to a desperate, defensive treasuring of Irene's daily companionship. "I do feel *finished* and want my life to end with this friendship," I wrote on December 1st. The strain was aggravated at that period by severe attacks of insomnia: I was getting only three or four hours of sleep on many nights, and came downstairs in the mornings dog-tired, with no strength or heart to face the blank day. The attacks passed, however, before Christmas, and there was no subsequent recurrence of the trouble. But the daily attrition went on, and I found relief only in friendships and in turning my thoughts to the war, the tragedies that were striking at other households in the district. Some of my old school mates had been killed in action; a cousin of mine, Bill Julian, had been captured by the Japs, in Malaya, and interned in Java. Brenda and Sheila Snell's brother Reggie was also a prisoner of war in the Far East: they brought up the family's letters to him for me to type, and I felt a poignant contrast between the frolics in the room while I typed the message and the horrors of the camp where it would be received. In that camp Reggie Snell died before some of these letters reached it.

Brenda and Sheila were by this time very good friends of mine; they were in our home more frequently after Pat and Doris left us. They brought the authentic village tang, the tang of the soil, that was, of course, lacking in Irene. Sheila was now twelve—a dark solid girl, sometimes a little reserved but never "cold"; she liked to borrow our evacuee's books to read. Brenda, on the other hand, was an unpredictable tom-boy, almost as wilful and moody as I was and therefore very lovable—rather slim in those days, with a big laughing mouth and hair that was passing through various gingery shades from light brown to dark brown. It was a comfort to feel that these girls would still be near me when the evacuees had gone home, and the only hours of complete happiness I enjoyed were the hours when Brenda or Sheila added the sense of security and continuity to the friendships that were threatened by every Allied advance in the war. We often went out for rambles picking flowers—bluebells in the fields, wild lupins on Goon-vean clay-dump—or blackberrying in the summer, and on Saturday afternoons we would climb around the sand-burrows and clay-pits of Goonvean and Bloomdale. On fine autumn and winter evenings we frequently played hide-and-seek around the roads and garden until it became so dark that—being unable to recognize voices—I could not be sure which of the girls I had caught unless it happened to be Brenda. These contacts had become, not my recreations but the main events of my life, the only incidents that made a day worth dragging through. My abject poverty cut me off from all other diversions. Now that the Cornish almanacks had suspended publication I was receiving no income at all, and could make no move towards getting one; and despite the increased cost of living my mother's pension remained, until 1944, a mere pittance of 26s. 8d. a week. As far back as 1938 I had been forced to abandon free-lance journalism, because we could not afford to waste postage in sending out a mass of manuscript only to get them returned. Everything tended to cramp and deaden my imagination. I could not freshen my mind by taking frequent trips to St. Austell, I could not visit local cinemas or any of the outlying Cornish beauty spots that might have stimulated me. My deafness made me shun the villages where I was known—and not deafness only: I shrank from the superior glances of those who knew how my early promise had fizzled out. None of them guessed that I was still writing; and certainly I was no longer living the life of a literary aspirant. If continuous hard work was essential to success there was no possibility of my achieving it. After completing *Wilding Graft* I sat at my typewriter for only half-a-dozen hours each month, and most of what I tapped out was revision of existing work. Before the war I had written over a hundred thousand words a year, but in 1943 the total was sixty-three thousand words, in 1944 it dropped to forty-five thousand words, and in 1945 to twenty-four thousand words—no more than a really prolific writer can produce in a month. The situation seemed desperate enough, and my diary contained references to "fears that I'm outgrowing my work before it's published" and confessions that I had "grown reluctant, as if God has to push and pull me every step while I'm indifferent, without the will or desire to co-operate."

It was the lack of variety of human contacts, particularly contacts with men older than myself, that had brought me to this plight. Not since boyhood had I been able to chat with the old "characters" in the district. One of these, a shrunken, white-haired cripple called Johnny Bullen, had come to live in a bungalow near us in 1935. He had been a labourer at Goonvean when my grandfather was at the farm, and had a wonderful memory of claywork conditions in Victorian times. He was so crippled that he could only move one foot a few inches in front of the other, and the journey of less than fifty yards between his home and ours took him nearly ten minutes. But often when the weather was fine Johnny would hobble along the road to our garden wall and wait patiently until someone indoors caught sight of him and went out to gossip. My mother and aunt spent hours at the gate joining in his random reminiscences, listening to his anecdotes of the Polmounters, the Clemos and other families he had known. I would stay in the parlour, looking out through the window at the top of Johnny's cap almost motionless above the wall (for he could not move about or gesticulate), thinking what a store of information and incident I was missing because of my deafness. I was untouched, ignored by the currents of adult life around me.

But it was the neglect I received *as a writer* from the more cultured quarters in Cornwall that made the burden so heavy to bear. They could not, of course, have raised me socially: deafness and temperament prevented that; but they could have given my work its due recognition. Some of my most characteristic writing had already appeared in the Cornish Press, and a letter of appreciation, a passing reference in a public speech, would have shown me that I had friends and well-wishers in my lonely ordeal. But I found that nothing I wrote could arouse the slightest interest or response. My newspaper letters no longer provoked comment. Editors of new Cornish magazines, bent on encouraging local talent, never approached me for a contribution. I was surrounded by a stifling atmosphere, a whole community that obviously did not believe that I had a future.

It is against this background of general indifference that one must judge the bitterness I felt in 1944, when Cornwall

Education Committee launched the Q. Memorial Scholarship Fund. The public did not know that four years earlier Q. had read *Private Snow* and praised its "power and promise." Q. himself apparently had reasons for not mentioning to anyone his personal opinion of me, whatever it may have been. But my cup of humiliation was full when I noted the general response to the Memorial appeal. Local gentry who knew my plight well enough, and cast sometimes a pitying glance at me when they passed me in their cars as I slouched about the Goonamarris lanes, at once sent along fat cheques to the Scholarship Fund to enable poor Cornish boys to get a University education. Neither Q. nor any other educationist thought of launching a fund for Cornish misfits whose "schooling" is a raw, elemental grapple with life itself: I found myself left out of all benevolent schemes, not eligible. But I do not now regret the hardships and seeming injustices I suffered during the war years. They were most crushing when I wrote *Wilding Graft*, and if there is anything profound in that book it comes from the intensity of the strain, both spiritual and material, which I endured while writing it.

CHAPTER THIRTEEN

The Final Struggle

MY raw struggle in the cottage at Goonamarris was by this time matched by the grim transformation of the surrounding landscape. Preparations for the Second Front in Europe were very apparent in the district towards the end of 1943. I could no longer go to Rostowrack: the downs had been taken over by the military authorities and made hideous with long rows of tents in which several hundred Canadian troops were accommodated. Similar encampments were erected at Trethosa and on the moors beyond Nanpean, and were occupied by American soldiers, many of them negroes. A prisoner-of-war camp had been opened at White Cross, near Indian Queens, and Italian prisoners were transferred from it each weekday to various clayworks in the neighbourhood. Some roads became closed to civilian traffic, and after April 1st, 1944, when Goonamarris came inside the military zone that stretched ten miles deep across Southern England, the restrictions were tightened to such an extent that I became virtually a prisoner in my cottage. It was impossible to move anywhere without being bawled at by drivers of Army vehicles or challenged by sentries. There were American guards on the hill between Goonvean and St. Stephen's, and at many other points within a few miles of my home. One could not pass them without a permit, and because of my deafness I was quite likely to be regarded as a suspicious character by these officials. Life became very tense and uncomfortable: mother was turned back by the guards on her way to Trethosa chapel, and there was a lot of bother about identity cards and special permits when she went to Treviscoe post office to collect her pension. The whole atmosphere became heavy and morbid as D-Day approached: there was some panic among the villagers as the roads became lined with camouflaged guns and other equipment for the Normandy front—a tempting target for Nazi bombers. In May, 1944, long convoys began to pass through Goonamarris late in the evenings: we stood at the bedroom window looking down at the stream of lorries and field ambulances filling the road into the valley and up the opposite slope to Foxhole Beacon. Nothing like it had ever been seen in the district: we were fascinated, subdued, drawn breathlessly close to this sombre and titanic movement. It gave me a nightmare glimpse of the battlefields, and I wanted to turn away.

I remained in static depression amid the feverish activity, more than ever conscious of frustration, the apparent uselessness of my talent. My deafness almost drove me to despair of the future. The whole district was teeming with stories I could not get at. If I could have mixed with the troops and heard their conversation I might have found material for a new novel. But my imagination floated aimlessly in a mere atmosphere, unable to grip any factual detail that would set it working on a concrete, human tale. I knew, of course, the sort of thing that was going on in the surrounding villages: news of common prostitution and broken homes was frequently passed on to me by my mother. But I was too isolated to build up a realistic picture of the way such associations usually started and ran their course. I was also to some extent inhibited by a sense of humiliation and resentment towards local girls who had ignored me for over ten years but seemed more than willing to carry on with these foreigners. The Italian prisoners were the chief causes of scandal: with their feline grace and self-assurance they were irresistibly fascinating not only to the young girls but to many middle-aged women.

These Italians did not confine their charm to women, however; they were considerate and polite to all—even to me. The Allied troops paid no attention to me at all when they saw me in the garden or the roadway, but the Italian prisoners employed at Goonvean claywork became extremely curious. While awaiting their buses they would sit on the field hedge opposite our cottage and stare across at me as I lounged idly at my desk. There was much nodding and whispering, and on one or two occasions, when my mother happened to be outside, they strolled over to her and courteously asked whether that young man in there was a poet? Mother was surprised at their insight, but they assured her that anyone could tell at a glance that I had the peculiar "look" of a poetic or artistic type. Several of them came indoors to shake hands with me, and a few who could read English spent hours poring over my manuscripts. One sergeant whose home was in Florence told mother with dramatic conviction: "Florence is the place for him." Another prophesied that my work would be translated into Italian before his son was old enough to read it. They would cross the room and, without the least embarrassment, kneel at my desk and write their expressions of friendship and respect. I was touched by all this appreciation, especially as it came from enemy aliens, many of them still ardently pro-Fascist: I had never received such enthusiastic compliments from my own countrymen.

But these contacts brought to light many disagreeable traits that more than offset the pleasure I derived from Latin flattery. Some of these Italians were so proud of having met an English "poet" that they wrote about me to the girls they had carried on with around St. Erth camp before coming to White Cross, and the result was a nauseating revelation of shoddy morals and feminine effrontery. We received communications from these girls enclosed with love letters to the prisoners: would we kindly pass them on, as correspondence addressed to the camp was closely scrutinized? I felt like throwing their disgusting love letters into the fire, and the incidents hardened my attitude to something that was at times pretty near misogyny.

My own friendships with Cornish girls, even those under fourteen, were dwindling and fraying off all round. Barbara had not visited me alone since 1942: she had dropped in once in each of the subsequent two years while out for a stroll with her parents, but this added nothing to our attachment. Change and uncertainty still dominated all my relationships. In the summer of 1944 our Dulwich evacuee returned home; Pat came back to us, with her younger brother and sister, David and Rita. Their mother was dying of cancer, and within a few weeks of their arrival we learnt that she was dead. Mother had to break the news to the children—a heartrending task. As I noted in my diary, every turn in our lives brought us fresh suffering, personal or vicarious. Mother was deeply moved by the plight of David and Rita. They were good children, and I did what I could to cheer them, making a swing for them in the field beside Bloomdale clay-dump. But I was, by this time, rather tired of the child-world: I had been largely confined to it for ten years, and no longer responded to fresh contacts with the spontaneous pleasure I had known in my early twenties. When Irene came in to live with us in 1941 I had already learnt practically all that girl-children could teach me, and the later war years were very much of an anti-climax. The friendship with Irene had lost its power to inspire me during the last year that she was at Goonamarris. "It all passes, and the little Edens are barred from me one by one," I wrote in my diary. I was "tired of monotony, yet not ready for change;" awaiting a new creative touch from the faith that had outgrown its first emotional impetus and become a cold, unsatisfying matter of the will.

A peculiarity of my mental growth in these war years was the complete drying-up of my poetic vein. Apart from one or two ineffectual attempts at verse at the opening of my diaries, I had not written a single poem since 1939. It seemed that my "poetic phase" was a mere symptom of adolescence, and that verse was my natural medium only during the period of immaturity before I found my true medium in novels. I felt at times that my dogmatic faith had tended to repress the lyrical urge, and as my prosaic, realistic grasp of life since 1938 was in every way preferable to the sickly idealism that had been broken at Nanpean, I was quite content to feel that I should probably never write another poem as long as I lived.

I was therefore astonished when, early in February, 1945, I

came in from a stroll around Goonvean clay-work one Sunday afternoon and immediately wrote, quite effortlessly, some lines which I knew at once were the finest poetry I had ever penned. The poem was "Christ in the Clay-pit," the first contribution of mine to appear in a high-brow periodical,* and the product that set my mind to its mature, individual poetic rhythm. I brooded much on this "resurrection" of a dormant faculty, and began to realize that this too was part of the paradox of my Christian life. While I lived for poetry I wrote only doggerel; it was only after I turned my back upon poetry that I became a poet. I proved in the literary sphere the truth of Christ's words: "He that loseth his life for my sake, the same shall find it." I renounced poetry because it had meant for me the worship of strange gods, the cultivation of ideals that could never be reconciled with the curt brutality of the Gospel. I chose the bristling, harsh, barren world of dogma because it was the world of our Lord; and the result was that I began writing poetry of a quality that would never have been possible to me had I devoted myself to the beautiful, the ideal, the fanciful. The claywork symbolism, sensuous Calvinism, credal sexuality—all the idiosyncrasies of my writings—were produced through my renunciation of the "natural" vision of the poet. All poets are aware of the antagonism between Nature and dogma, but no poet, except by the grace of God, ever takes the side of dogma against Nature. His deepest instinct is to ally himself with Nature, to dispute the claims of a doctrinal revelation committed exclusively to the Christian Church. Yet it is only when a poet makes some concession, when he sacrifices some of the "pure" poetry within himself and develops credal sympathies—as Browning did, for instance— that he becomes really original. I had undergone this process to the extent of a complete reversal of sympathies which led me to write poems deriding the conventional poetic insights and usages. With "Christ in the Clay-pit" I had found the idiom that moved to its climax, perhaps, in "The Excavator":†

* *Orion* III. Published January 1947.

† Published in *Modern Reading 17*, May 1948.

THE EXCAVATOR

I stand here musing in the rain
This Sabbath evening where the pit-head stain
   Of bushes is uprooted, strewn
     In waggon tracks and puddles,
     While the fleering downpour fuddles
The few raw flowers along the mouldering dump—
     Ridge hollowed and rough-hewn
     By the daily grind and thump
Of this grim excavator. It shields me
From lateral rain-gusts, its square body turned
To storm-lashed precipices it has churned.

     I feel exultantly
The drip of clayey water from the poised
Still bar above me, thrilling with the rite
     Of baptism all my own;
     Acknowledging the might
     Of God's great arm alone;
     Needing no ritual voiced
In speech or earthly idiom to draw
     My soul to His new law.

The bars now hinged o'erhead and drooping form
   A cross that lacks the symmetry
     Of those in churches, but is more
     Like His whose stooping tore
The vitals from our world's foul secrecy.
     This too has power to worm
The entrails from a flint, bearing the scoop
     With every searching swoop—
     That broken-mouthed gargoyle
     Whose iron jaws bite the soil,
Snapping with sadist kisses in the soft
White breasts of rocks, and ripping the sleek belly
Of sprawling clay-mounds, lifting as pounded jelly
Flower roots and bush tufts with the reeking sand.
     I fondle and understand
In lonely worship this malicious tool.

CONFESSION OF A REBEL

Yes, this is Christian art
To me men could not school
With delicate æsthetes; their symbols oft
Tempt simple souls like me
Whom Nature meant to seal
With doom of poetry,
And dowered with eye and brain
Sensitive to the stain
Of Beauty and the grace of man's Ideal.
But I have pressed my way
Past all their barren play
Of intellect, adulthood, the refined
Progressive sickness of the mind
Which throws up hues and shapes alien to God's
Way with a man in a stripped clay desert. Now
I am a child again
With a child's derision of the mentors' rods
And a child's quick pain,
Loving to stand as here in outlawed glee
Amid the squelching mud and make a vow
With joy no priest or poet takes from me.

I cannot speak their language; I am one
Who feels the doggerel of heaven
Purge earth of poetry; God's foolishness
Laugh through the web man's ripening wisdom spun ;
The world's whole culture riven
By moody excavations Love shall bless.
All staining rhythms of art and Nature break
Within my mind, turn grey, grow truth
Rigid and ominous as this engine's tooth.
And so I am awake,
No more a man who sees
Colour in flowers or hears from birds a song,
Or dares to worship where the throng
Seek Beauty and its old idolatries.
No altar soils my vision with a lax
Adult appeal to sense,
Or festering harmonies' magniloquence.
My faith and symbol shall be stark.

THE FINAL STRUGGLE

My hand upon these caterpillar-tracks
    Bogged in the mud and clay,
    I find it easier to pray:
"Keep far from me all loveliness, O God,
      And let me laud
    Thy meaner moods, so long unprized:
    The motions of that twisted, dark,
    Deliberate crucial Will
    I feel deep-grinding still
Under the dripping clay with which I am baptized."

I could have written nothing comparable to that had I remained loyal to the inspiration that first came to me at Penrose and followed the normal course of development taken by working-class poets like Alfred Williams, the Wiltshire railwayman and misfit, whose protest—precisely because it was heretical—never took him beyond trite and commonplace Nature lyrics.

With the war hastening to its end I had to make some immediate move in my literary affairs, and being at a deadlock with my trilogy volumes I resolved rather desperately to cut the knot by starting off with *Wilding Graft*. In April, I approached Mr. Savage about the manuscript, and a month later posted it to him while at Newquay on my last outing with Irene and the other evacuees. I was fairly confident of its acceptance, as I knew that some tremendous forward move was absolutely essential to offset the loss of these friendships.

The war in Europe had ended on May 7th, and I was thankful, though my gratitude was complex and had in it some elements unshared by other Britons. Had the war lasted much longer I should have found it difficult to remain a patriot. The continual vilification of everything German was beginning to exasperate me. My prolonged isolation from the general mood had perhaps rendered me morbidly sensitive; at any rate, I had come to resent these gibes as one resents personal insults. They were directed against qualities which were supposed to be exclusively German, but which I happened to possess. My nature was very un-English, and had obvious affinities with the Teutonic character in its texture and outlook. (I was thinking of this when I gave the heroine of *Wilding Graft* the German name "Irma.") I had always shown the stolidity, the moodiness of the Teutonic strain, its clumsy sincerity, its belief in intuition and violence. My thoughts moved slowly and deeply, a grey undercurrent that sometimes grew black with melancholy and came to a standstill, or turned suddenly to lava and erupted with incalculable results. All this was part of the mentality that most British journalists and public speakers were holding up to ridicule, and by 1945 I had endured enough of their sneers and witticisms. The chorus of vituperation poured on Luther during the closing months of the war had strained my patriotic loyalty to breaking-point. Though Calvin had more exactly defined the creed which God had forced upon me, it was always to Luther that I turned for the human warmth and life-blood of that creed. Calvin's own personality, like Wesley's, was coldly logical and consistent, and I was too wayward and complex to feel much sympathy with the type. I did not like neat precision but turbulent energy, the *roughness* of truth which the German mind so perfectly apprehended and which was so alien to the decorous Anglo-Saxon tradition. Truth was to me not a thing of beauty and serenity but of storm and violence, a terror that could get its claws into a man's life and hold on until the blood flowed from the wounded and believing heart. It was Luther who had first introduced this intensity of Christian experience to northern Europe, opening the way for Bunyan and Kierkegaard, Spurgeon and Karl Barth, and thus for such elemental disciples as myself; and when I saw Luther's experience reviled in the interests of Allied propaganda, identified with the pagan violence of Hitler, my attitude hardened, became malicious and defiant. It was just another proof that my theological loyalties were supreme and that, if necessary, even my patriotic loyalty would have to be sacrificed to them.

It was, therefore, a great relief to me when the Nazi collapse freed me from this tension, though my circumstances prevented me from taking part in the general rejoicings. There was no "victory day" for me until my novel was accepted. I could not relax as others were doing: the sternest part of my fight for recognition was still ahead, and I faced it exhausted by fifteen years of failure and disheartened by the prospect of a return to the unrelieved loneliness of 1939.

At the end of June came the day I had regarded with such mixed feelings for several years, sometimes looking forward to it as the end of the epoch of child-friendships, the opening of a new, mature phase that would bring me the real love for which I had been prepared; at other times dreading it as an expulsion from the last of my "little Edens," with nothing but a grey inhuman wilderness beyond. But whether it meant release or tragedy, the hour was come. Irene and the three younger evacuees were returning to London.

In warm early morning sunshine we left the cottage and went out along the road to Nanpean, carrying the bulging suitcases. At Drinnick wharf came the good-bye kisses while we stood, a sorrowful little group, mother, Irene and the children weeping freely, I choking back my tears, hardly realizing the magnitude of the change that was breaking upon us. Only when I returned to the empty cottage at Goonamarris and saw the postman pass with still no news of *Wilding Graft* did the sense of loss close fully in, desolating me.

It had been evident before the war ended that Irene's influence was, spiritually, much more superficial than Barbara's, and this became even more apparent after Irene went home. There was no apocalypse of prayer, vision and creative activity such as that which I had known when Barbara left Goonamarris in 1938. The tears came, but they were barren tears; and the fact that, within a fortnight of losing Irene, I voted at the General Election, shows how different, how much shallower, was the spiritual experience her passing had brought me. Seven years of additional strain had left me too exhausted for another prolonged immersion in the mystical deeps. My instinct now was to protect myself by a stolid indifference to everything that would touch my emotions.

I received no vivid impressions on polling-day as I entered

the schoolroom I had left at the age of twelve and saw the ballot box standing just where I had sat so often at the rough, ink-stained desk, an alien among average scholars, dreaming and praying my way into a by-path. In that room I had struggled in vain to pass examinations and bewildered Mr. Pellymounter by admitting that my highest ambition was to tip sand on a clay-dump. My course of life since then had been incredibly different from anything I had imagined in those remote, shadowy schooldays, and nothing was yet settled enough for me to look back with wondering gratitude. I felt only the mystery and isolation of my lot as I put my cross on the ballot-paper and glanced through the high windows up at Trethosa clay-tip before slipping my vote into the ballot-box.

At first sight my voting for the Conservative candidate would seem to be one of the oddest things I have ever done. I was a proletarian and had suffered social injustices as few even among Communists had suffered it. The family tradition among the Clemo's was strongly for Labour, while the Polmounters were lifelong Liberals. I was the first member of either family to vote, in my lifetime, for a Tory Government, and it was to some extent, no doubt, a sign of my political naïvety. But considering my peculiar bias of temperament it was inevitable. Political programmes meant nothing to me, as none of the parties had any special plan for misfits. I was forced to judge a party by the spiritual tone of its propaganda, and even, because of my artistic kink, by its literary style. I was repelled by the crude materialism so apparent in the Socialist leaders, and by the flat, dry tone of their speeches. I loved the rhetorical phrase, the dramatic gesture—signs of a vivid, colourful personality that possessed the qualities of leadership because it was aware of its *difference* from the prosaic masses. Men who wrote and spoke like tenth-rate journalists were obviously not built on the grand scale or endowed with faculties that could fire the enthusiasm of the nation at its most critical hour of transition and renewal. I believed very firmly that, in the political as in the religious sphere, the world had reached a plight so desperate that nothing but sensationalism was *big* enough to save it. The tragedy was that this fact was realized and exploited by the wrong set—by the Communists in politics, by the spiritualists and heterodox cranks in religion. The situation demanded a militant and flamboyant conservatism in both spheres; and as Churchill was the only figure who represented this quality in politics I naturally gravitated towards his party, though I daresay I felt derisive of Conservatives who were mere gentry.

I never had any real sympathy with the Left. After the collapse of my idealism at Nanpean I had written several Press letters that seemed violently Socialistic, but as I have pointed out, this was part of a general mood of revolt and did not express a considered political view. When I came to think the matter through I found that I had no class-hatred because I had no class-consciousness. I was aware of myself only as an individual, an exotic prickly plant that had sprung up in working-class soil but caused as much bewilderment there as it would have done in a more refined strata of society. I had no special grudge against the gentry, the bourgeoisie. If I had been treated with neglect or contempt by certain sections in Cornwall it was not because of my working-class origin but because of my theological and sexual obsessions. If I had suffered active persecution it was at the hands of working-class folk who could not understand me and therefore thought me a nuisance. I had never, in the strict sense, been a working man myself, and I was no more capable of feeling the social stigma of poverty than Bunyan had been. My insistence on the supremacy of dogmatic spiritual values made my reactions very unlike those of an average proletarian. The men whose testimony to the power of faith had enabled me to overcome bitterness and escape despair—such men as Browning, Spurgeon, and Talmage—had all been wealthy, middle-class supporters of capitalism. The Left Wing prophets, from Marx to Laski, had no gospel for me; they offered nothing but the fettering sense of inferiority and injustice from which capitalist Christians had helped to release me. I may have been an unreasonable misfit, but on one point at least I was quite sensible: I wanted to be a happy man. I had not been "doped" into complacency; I had merely developed a sense of values that led to happiness—which the Socialist valuation of life did not. Its spiritual atmosphere was neither buoyant nor charitable, and it would be fatal for a man in my circumstances to risk being infected by it. My vote was a protest against a spiritual tone rather than a vote for a political programme. It did not matter in any case, for the Labour candidate got in with an overwhelming majority.

Mr. Savage had already advised me that, owing to the immediate post-war rush of business, he could not report promptly on *Wilding Graft*. The summer dragged on in silence. My worst fears about the emotional effect of the peace seemed to be fulfilled: neither Barbara nor any other girl came near the house, and the surrounding scene prompted memories so poignantly that I could hardly bear to go outdoors. I was forced into an ever-narrowing circle in which my life threatened to run completely down and stop.

On August 7th the cloud of futility suddenly swelled out and covered the whole world horizon. News of the atom bomb, the possibility of a general disintegration of the globe, brought a brief, chill feeling that it did not matter whether I succeeded or not. I say "brief"; for while Hiroshima burned Mr. Savage was dictating a very long and enthusiastic letter to me concerning *Wilding Graft*. He offered a few suggestions for improving the book, chiefly relating to ecclesiastical and topographical details of Truro, which he knew far better than I did, as his father had been a Canon of the Cathedral for many years. He seemed quite confident of being able to place the novel with a first-class publisher, and when I mentioned to him my peculiar physical and economic disabilities I knew from the warmly sympathetic tone of his handwritten reply that in him I had found not only a business partner but a true and understanding friend. The collapse of Japan, the coming of final victory, appeared to promise some return to normal conditions, and I felt that, after all, the world would probably last long enough for me to taste a measure of success, a personal vindication of a faith that would make me thankful to have lived on the planet for thirty years or so.

But again the weeks slipped by in silence and I lapsed into depression; September and October passed without incident, each morning bringing a further sick disappointment as the postman went by with still no news of *Wilding Graft*. And when the news came, early in November, it shattered the hopes that had buoyed me after Mr. Savage's acceptance of the manuscript. He reported that the book had been refused by two publishers and enclosed a letter from the latest firm who had declined it. This admitted that it was "very nearly an excellent novel," but as it would not appeal to a wide public it was not acceptable under the abnormal conditions left by the war. I was greatly discouraged by this verdict, for I had known all along that it was the limited appeal of my work rather than technical defects that had brought upon me the unbroken run of failure even in normal times; and as I could not write "popular" stuff I still seemed to be facing deadlock, even with Mr. Savage's support. I told him frankly that I was "down and out until some publisher has faith in my work," and commented in my diary: "I really am exasperated and feel things must be forced to a crisis." In mid-November I submitted one of my trilogy volumes to Mr. Savage. He reported at once that it confirmed his belief in my work, and I took fresh heart, thinking that perhaps both novels would be accepted to give me some real uplift for the New Year. While awaiting success I wrote several love poems, including "A Calvinist in Love"—the first love poems I had written since 1938. I was cheered by their mature, individual flavour; but on Christmas Eve a letter from Mr. Savage informed me that *Wilding Graft* had again been refused and that he was laying it aside and starting off with the earlier novel after the holidays. It was a gloomy Christmas in our home, the crushing sense of failure added to the loneliness, the poignant memories of the wartime Christmases. The strain produced another attack of eye trouble; sometimes my sight became so fogged that I could not move about the room without feeling my way. It was the first threat of blindness I had suffered since that fateful Christmas twelve years earlier, when Evelyn last visited my home and left me, tormented and half-blind, amid the wreckage of a false faith. My Calvinism was being tested even more severely, but there was no sign of it becoming a wreck. Before I entered the New Year my sight was normal again and my spirits rose. I could even feel a thrill of triumph as I considered the poems I had written in November, especially one entitled "The New Creation," in which a Christian husband admits that his faith has blotted out for him all the beauty of Nature—but only to reveal a higher, eternal order of beauty in which creation and redemption are one.

THE NEW CREATION

If you were Nature's child
I could not love you, for I shun
Corrupted trees and flowers which the sun
Kindled in disobedience. Neither wild
Nor tender are the hills, but stained with seed
Still shadowed by the serpent, while
Streams rasp of ancient guile.
Like evil spirits the winds speed,
Or grope like blinded bawds
From brothel-teeming clods.
The hostile sea now slinks from cliffs
Whereon the new Law's hieroglyphs
Pronounce its tides unclean.
All Nature stands obscene
In hideous disguise:
No loveliness remains even in the skies.
Hell snickers in the chatter of a starling
And fleers in each sunrise,
Because one Eastern tale
That makes creation pale
Is known to me and true.
The Christian nightmare holds me, darling—
Creatively, as I hold you.

Now, you are not one of these—
Not one with earth and Nature's powers.
For He Who fashioned creeds when tired of flowers
Remade you through His stern theologies.
Limbs, breasts and hair were naught to me
Till cleansed by baptism they grew womanly
Beyond the waiting worm
And opened love's true term.
Your female rhythms, free now from what they seemed,
Surge lonely: nowhere in the unredeemed
Unconscious heat of beast or natural man
Is this pulsation, hunger, ecstacy,
This Galilean ban
On weariness and lack
And sad inconstancy
That follows beast and man at mating call.
The dark waves of the Fall
Rebound from these, thrown back
By witless instinct or by mortal pride.
You only in my sphere dared take His side,
His vows that bind,
Submit and know a birth beside His Tree
That made you lovable so that you find
You are with child by me.

It was to this Divine incubus of "a Christian nightmare" that I owed my freedom from the sadness of the poet's dream, and that stern grasp of reality which I expressed in my first diary entry for 1946: "Stevenson was never further from Christianity than when he said that to travel hopefully is better than to arrive. To the Christian the arrival is so tremendous a manifestation of the grace of God that it is worth while paying one's price towards it by travelling in despair." Something of this outlook is implied in Kierkegaard's philosophy and in the work of modern Calvinists like Barth and Niebuhr, but I had reached it independently before I read any of their books.

Early in February Mr. Savage reported another rejection, and it became obvious that the only way to break the deadlock was for me to revise *Wilding Graft*. The manuscript was returned just after my thirtieth birthday, and within a few weeks I was cheered to receive the first practical encouragement I had known in high literary quarters during my fifteen years' struggle. Through Mr. Savage's introduction some of my poems were read and praised by Major John Grey Murray and Peter Quennell, and two of them were promptly accepted—"Christ in the Clay-pit" by *Orion*, "A Calvinist in Love" by *Penguin New Writing*. Spurred by this success I soon finished the alterations to *Wilding Graft*, and when at the end of May it was again submitted to a publisher I felt that the impasse had at last been broken.

But once more there were hitches and delays, weeks of torturing suspense: though the monotony was relieved in June by a new little girl friend, a seven-year-old Londoner called Iris—a slim, vivacious brunette, a cousin of our former evacuees, though very unlike them—who came down on holiday for a week. To me who for nearly a year had been cooped up with two elderly women, my mother and my aunt Bertha, untouched by a girl, the fresh companionship brought a revival from emotional asphyxiation. In July, Iris returned again, with her cousins, and for a month I tried to escape altogether from the racking worries and frustrations of my literary life. I was especially glad to renew my friendship with my old Goonamarris playmate Brenda, whom I had seen only once since the evacuees left us. She was by this time a well-grown village girl, nearly twelve, and her occasional presence helped to balance the mere childishness of my romps with the London group. I spent practically every day playing with them, picking berries, climbing around sand-dumps, digging out sites for camps which they made with old scraps of corrugated iron, carrying the girls about on my back and letting them tie me up with string and fasten me to field gate-posts to be publicly viewed as a captured bandit, and other frolics of this undignified sort. I spent memorable days with them— mother, of course, accompanying us—at Porthpean beach, Mevagissey, and at my cousin Bill Julian's farm near Roche, to which Bill had just returned after three years' captivity under the Japs in Java. His account of the gruelling experience would have been very stimulating to me, and might have given me material for a story; but I could hear nothing of it; I was barred out from the adult world wherever I went. I had to content myself with sharing in Iris' pranks, getting behind doors and barrels from which we could defy the pigs that chased us up from the field through the drizzling rain, and later scrambling over Roche Rock, racing up the iron ladders to the hermit's cell and crawling among the pillars at the summit, eighty feet above the bleak spur of moorland.

For our Mevagissey trip we had finer weather, and the long afternoon was one of drowsy, nostalgic beauty. It was the first time I had visited Mevagissey since 1939, "and we went boating in the same fishing smack," my diary records, "Iris lying in my arms, her yellow coat over her head to keep off the sea spray." I kept the bus tickets of the Mevagissey trip—Iris' and mine—for many months thereafter in my breast pocket. My Calvinism had not made me less of a sentimentalist, and I was very grateful for the fact: it disproved the popular notion that a "terrorist religion" dries up all human tenderness. I was aware of a new wave of vigour and a fresh perception of the fundamental conflict of sympathies that had always made ambition impossible to me. The diary entry for July 25th reveals what had become my chronic state of mind:

"The girls to Newquay—free to read a bit and pull up my intellect; yet only in Powys is there a true reflection, for I, too, find the "children playing under the shade of God" my only contact with Joy. Everything adult disappoints me and I grow more and more sick of it, feeling that to lie among the buttercups for an hour and look at Iris and Brenda and eat orange-peel which they throw at me—as last Saturday—is indeed "of more value than everlasting life," in Powys' sense of the phrase—i.e, everlasting worldliness and sham."

This sense of the intellectual life as a sham and a form of worldliness was probably a defensive reaction from the continuous set-backs I had suffered; and another of these rebuffs fell amid my infantile happiness like a bombshell in early August. The publisher to whom Mr. Savage had last sent *Wilding Graft* had raised great hopes by expressing "enormous interest" in it in June, but he now decided not to take it unless I re-wrote the closing chapters, which showed Garth and Irma hiding from Griffiths in Irma's billet at Truro—only to learn that he had already left the city and disappeared. This climax was said to be so feeble that it let down the whole story. Collapse again seemed to be inevitable; but after praying much for guidance and discarding a dozen false ideas I hit upon a more appropriate ending which closed the novel at Meledor instead of at Truro. Very reluctantly I gave up several days of my precious friendships in order to write the new sequence. The revised manuscript was posted back to London a few days after Iris and her cousins had returned there late in August, and I was left to wait, fortified by the memories of the holiday.

The chief event that gripped my imagination in September was not the Nuremberg trial of Nazi war criminals—which had become so boring that it was no real contribution to the peace—but the centenary of Browning's marriage. Newspaper items about the celebrations, and the articles in the literary and radio journals, moved me deeply. I set apart the anniversary day, September 12th, as a day of special meditation and prayer, reviewing the past decade in which I had so oddly combined the robust faith of Browning with the "bird in a cage" existence of Elizabeth Barrett. I read the Browning love letters, the *Sonnets from the Portuguese*, and Browning's personal love poems, remembering the thrill with which I had first read them in 1935, the conviction that had come so vividly through the humanizing touch with Barbara. In the enthusiasm of that dawn of hope I had named my little dog Flush, believing that he would live to see something similar to what his namesake had seen in the darkened room at Wimpole Street. He was now eleven years old, getting very stiff in his limbs so that I had to carry him most of the way when I went out for my evening walks: standing upright in my overcoat pocket he would often lick the tears from my cheeks as I stumbled around Goonvean claywork after dusk, plumbing depths of wretchedness and dereliction that made me feel more like Francis Thompson than like either of the Brownings. I was burdened to recall the strange moves Flush had seen in my home, touches from various girls, each of whom in turn had "lifted me from this drear flat of earth where I was thrown"— only to let me fall back to it again as she grew older and turned to more normal companionship. I was tired of this trick of God's by which He alternately raised me and cast me down on the immature, uncomprehending wave of childish caprice.

This renewed immersion in the Brownings' poetry stimulated my own poetic vein, and at the end of September I wrote six poems. Three of them were about children—the first of the kind I had ever written; the most characteristic of them, "The Token," describing the way in which Brenda had given me some orange peel in one of Goonamarris fields in July, shows that I was aware of the reactions and processes by which I had mastered the psychological problem of my twenties.

THE TOKEN

A shift of His mood brings an hour's relief
    From the cloudy pressure of grinding grief,
This hammering grief that kills all worth
    In woman's bounty and gifts of earth.

No woman again, no flesh mature,
    With the serpent rhythm in its tidal lure;
But He drops amid my hermit pain
    The old thrill purged of creative stain.

In a field on which the sand-dump spilt
    A vomit of gravel where grasses wilt
My ice-world broke for an hour of flame
    With one who shared it in childish game.

We romped in the sun, but the warmth I felt
    Came only from her as she tried to pelt
My face into smiles with orange-peel.
    She skinned the fruit with her teeth—would steal

CONFESSION OF A REBEL

Close up, undeterred by the threatened smack,
    Her hand curled tightly behind her back,
Her hand clenched warm on the missiles broken,
    Growing soft and moist with her blood's shy token.

She would pull and push till my face was free,
    Then snuggle closer and shower on me
Those trivial tools of her childish freak,
    Splintered from Nature mature and sleek.

No symbol here to adjust, adapt,
    Be fogged and bogged by: beauty lapped
So calm her childhood's nakedness,
    I needed not mask its frank caress.

She is the real: I taste and see
    Her girlish magic, unflinchingly:
Unstripped to Nature's evil core,
    She shows her bounty of sense the more.

Each scrap of yellow peel she flung
    Lay fierily on the turf, a tongue
Speaking of bliss I dared not name
    Till I saw in her the new way it came.

With hints like this I can bear His shade,
    Nor fear His jealousy's blasting blade
Back under the cloud: here His eye shall see
    I am purged at last of idolatry.

Shall I praise Him again when, as Nature's foe,
    I emerge to deride its creative flow,
Hating flesh and flower when ripe for seed,
    But for sex, bare rind, feeling love indeed?

The position of a man deprived of adult love and forced to keep his creative flame alive through contacts with young girls, can scarcely be a dignified one; but I had never cared for dignity anyhow, and as I was not a thwarted idealist I had not become either pathetic or neurotic. I knew that my emotional life had been arrested, that it had remained for over ten years at the child stage: in such circumstances my attitude to sex might easily have become sentimental and infantile. But my modern realism, Christian dogmatism and downright working-class honesty had combined to forestall the Freudians by enabling me to say with buoyant, frank beauty what they would have said with solemn nastiness. My attitude to women was negative because I had had no dealings with them, but my approach to sex was fully positive and receptive. This was another triumph of my Calvinist faith, for during my teens when I was free to mix with women my sex technique had been entirely negative, dominated by the urge to "escape" to romantic idealism. But since 1938 I had felt no desire to escape—there was nothing to escape to. The doctrine of total depravity had shown me that my highest ideals were as much a product of original sin as my grossest lusts, and for a man who has accepted this view there can be no fastidious recoil from his so-called "lower" nature. The only tension I felt was a theological one, the uncertainty as to whether a playful mood in a near-adolescent girl confirmed the dogma of original sin or the dogma of election. The whole experience had illuminated for me the essential Christian teaching about sex, which is so completely misunderstood by modern critics of St. Paul and Puritanism. I expressed in this poem the Christian hatred of the merely biological urge of sex that is inside Nature, and affirmed the "converted" sexuality that is redemptive, credal yet not spiritualized. The sexuality of the new creation is as much a physical thrill as that of the old, fallen one, but its ultimate aim is to make male and female "one flesh" not in order to reproduce the species but to touch realities beyond normal consciousness and transmute them, by faith, into elements of the body of Christ. I think this is what D. H. Lawrence was after, but he missed it through the stupid modern habit of rejecting the orthodoxy which is the only key to it.

The last and best of this batch of poems, "The Excavator," was written on Saturday, September 28th, and was to some extent prompted by the trial of Neville Heath, the sadist murderer. Throughout that week, I, in common with most other English people, had been engrossed in the neurotic and morbid symptoms of modern life embodied in that young man—only a few months my junior. His tragic destiny showed what an unbalanced sexual temperament could bring a man to if it was divorced from Christian faith, nourished on the values and sanctions of "progressive" morality; while my life and work brought increasing proof of what a power for good a potentially dangerous mental kink might become if surrendered to Christian discipline. This brooding on sadism in relation to moral and spiritual beliefs moved me deeply, and the resulting poetic testimony was thrown up without any conscious effort. The reference to the excavator

> "Snapping with sadist kisses in the soft
> White breasts of rocks, and ripping the sleek belly
> Of sprawling clay-mounds...."

is obviously a reflection of the evidence at Heath's trial.

When this poetic urge subsided there came a lull, a brief final test, and then deliverance. The publisher at whose request I had altered *Wilding Graft* again refused it, but he recommended Chatto and Windus as a firm likely to be interested, and within a fortnight of Mr. Savage's handing them the manuscript, they made an offer for its publication. The struggle of nearly two decades, involving fifty-three rejections of my novels, including seven refusals of *Wilding Graft*, was over, and I found myself, an uneducated villager, set incongruously among the most brilliant intellectuals of the day.

I was relieved for Mr. Savage's sake as well as my own. I had given him more trouble than any other author for a good many years. He had been fighting my battle in London for fourteen months, interviewing publishers and their readers, doing his utmost to persuade them of the quality of my work, and it was humiliating to feel that I was wasting his time, that his belief in my powers had possibly been misplaced, over-enthusiastic. Chatto and Windus' acceptance vindicated his faith, and with characteristic foresight and consideration for my difficulties he set to work to make this success yield me the maximum encouragement. He asked the firm to be especially generous in the advance they paid me on account of royalties; and the firm's response was such, that for the immediate future at least, I could feel that I was no longer a financial burden to my mother.

The magnitude of this sudden turn in my affairs seemed like a miracle to mother and me: it was certainly a miracle that I had won through as an uncompromising Christian. Material success might reward a handicapped atheist if he persevered long enough; but the work with which he emerged would not make pleasant reading. It was the spiritual tone of my accepted novel, its sober and considered statement of the triumph of Christianity over the "modern mood," that led my mother and me to feel that this was scarcely a natural fruition. Mother was deeply moved by my dedication of the book, in which I acknowledged my debt to her faith. She was no longer troubled about the strangeness of my experience; she could only note with amazement and thankfulness that it had produced the very quality of belief which she had prayed I might know, and which, during my early teens, had seemed so foreign to my poetic, idealist temperament that I could never honestly accept it. Her life had been full of exceptional trials, but she was spared the obvious trial that old-fashioned, pious parents of "clever" children are usually doomed to suffer—the pain of watching her son grow increasingly contemptuous of her religion. She had often shared my dismay when manuscripts written and submitted in prayer were refused, but she had said that her suffering would be far greater had I succeeded as a sceptical, pagan, or even a Modernist writer. Now, at last, I had broken through the barriers—as a Calvinist.

My achievement naturally caused much bewildered comment among the neighbours. I was so entirely unlike their mental picture of a literary man. To them a novelist was a very superior gentleman who dressed smartly and spoke correct English, which I had never troubled to do. There was also my cottage home—not at all the sort of place a novelist would be expected to live in. It was a beautiful irony that at this time our dwelling was in a more dilapidated state than ever before. The back bedroom window had been smashed in the September gale and was patched up with cardboard; the drainpipe had been broken and hung forlornly, dripping water down the side of the wall; the wash-house adjoining was rickety, its zinc roof full of holes; and we had no gate. All this delighted me: success against such a background, so far from making me feel ashamed or humiliated, took on an added relish; I felt an infantile, exuberant joy in the oddity of things. It fitted my role; for I had known all along that I was certainly the oddest writer Cornwall had produced. The others were brilliant school products who said and did what they had been trained to say and do, and were thus able to fill responsible public positions outside their books. But I had never been trained to say or do anything, and so my moods and actions were incalculable. I could champion Nietzsche and D. H. Lawrence—and then give a Gospel address in a Methodist schoolroom. I could experience mystical raptures—and then alarm honest villagers by acting hysterically in order to get a little girl to play with. I spent hours climbing around the clay-dumps with little girls on my back, or tumbling about with them in fields—and then strolled indoors, muddy and dishevelled, to write with sphinxish gravity a chapter of a novel. No school-sponsored talent ever led a man to behave like this: the village folk knew that well enough, and I had never hoped or tried to gain their under-standing and respect.

In the surrounding villages where my personal peculiarities were unknown, the arrival of Cornwall's "new novelist"—as the local Press described me—aroused a more normal and sympathetic response. These people knew I had paid a heavy price—a price that made my hair turn grey before I was twenty-eight—to prove what I had set out to prove: that creeds rejected by most of my contemporaries as dead super-stition could still enable a man to find his place in the world, despite the most grievous handicaps, and that the claim of the schools to be indispensable to intellectual development, and to success in literature, is nonsense. (This does not, of course, apply to the various branches of business and science, or such professions as law and medicine: there the specialized technical training of the schools is obviously essential. I am speaking only of creative work for which misfits are particularly well adapted.) I had proved also the value of those qualities of independence and individuality that were threatened by the bureaucratic Socialist State; but at the same time I was grateful for the magnanimity of a Socialist Government which allowed mystical writers like myself a fair chance, and left us completely free and unfettered to write and publish our (to them) unhelpful and irrelevant propaganda. I knew that in Russia such writers would be liquidated, and almost for the first time in my life I felt proud of being an Englishman.

I was also proud of being still an undiluted villager, though for years I had felt myself to be something of a stranger in my own birthplace. The present inhabitants were persons I had not met before being sealed off by deafness, and thus Goona-marris itself had become an unknown world to me, full of strange faces, voices I had never heard, human dramas of which I had only a remote, fragmentary knowledge. All the old inhabitants who had known me during my childhood were dead or dispersed; some of the cottages had changed hands twice since I left school. Our house was, in fact, the only one in the hamlet still occupied by the tenants who had lived there during my infancy. Captain Grigg's grocery store, where I had bought so many sweets and biscuits, had closed in the 1930's, the house being taken over by the Snells just after Brenda was born and the shop turned into a living-room. Barrakellis farm was also under new management: my old friend Colly Bullock had gone to Plymouth to live with his son and, though over eighty, had become a leader in a back-street mission-hall. Mr. Treverton, whose gramophone had so fascinated me as a boy, still survived at Nanpean, but I had lost touch with him, as with Colly, from the time I grew deaf, and my success, if they heard of it, probably meant little to either of them.

I was in no position to celebrate my triumph; my life had to go on its lonely rut as before. None of my girl friends were with me to share the thrill of success, and only one of them—Brenda, who was with me on the day the proofs arrived—was to freshen me during the long interval before the book was published. The only visible indication that I had passed from apprenticeship to a measure of fruition was that the walls of our front room became adorned with the portraits of Browning, Spurgeon and T. F. Powys—the three men whose spiritual affinities with me were most obvious. I had no portrait of Hardy; and in any case my debt to him was æsthetic rather than spiritual; my break with his philosophy was now complete. The ravings of Jude were totally irrelevant to my experience. Hardy's bitter protest on behalf of working-class intellectuals was proved to be a misjudged and ludicrous by-product of unbelief, with no reference to the facts and possibilities of such a predicament when controlled by strong and unfaltering religious conviction.

My general feeling of gratitude did not overlook the human agencies that had helped me forward. I wrote to A. Browning Lyne of the *Cornish Guardian*, thanking him for the encouragement he had given me during the years of struggle by printing the letters and poems that had brought me into touch with S. E. Burrow, Frank Baron, John Rowland, and other stimulating personalities. In response to this, Lyne printed a generous appreciation of my success in the following issue of the paper (November 7th, 1946). 'After much thought and prayer—for I always prayed about everything—I sent a copy of it to T. F. Powys with a letter acknowledging my great debt to his work, the "fortitude and sympathy" I had drawn from it. I hardly dared hope for a reply, for I knew from my own reactions that we village mystics are inclined to be suspicious of any approach from strangers. Powys, then seventy-one, had also been idle and silent since 1934. But a few days later I was thrilled to see the Sturminster Newton postmark on an envelope which the postman handed me over the garden wall. It contained a charming letter of congratulations and good wishes. With characteristic whimsical humility Powys wrote: "I am cheered to know that these stories of mine have influenced you, and, in a tiny way, helped in your success". His help had certainly not been "tiny"; and that letter of his more than compensated me for the absence of any congratulations from my old schoolmasters and literary friends.

About a month after the acceptance of *Wilding Graft* I was mildly shocked to hear of the death of Mr. Phillips, Evelyn's father. A pathetic old man, nearly seventy, deaf and blind, he had died at Truro Infirmary after a short illness. The event jolted the half-forgotten memories of my visits to Nanpean thirteen years before; they seemed strangely bitter-sweet now in the light of my success. They had their place in the pattern: the bafflement I had suffered at Nanpean had broken the natural faith and pride of the misfit in me. It had shown me that the vision that was in me by nature was derived not from some sphere of ultimate Reality but from the Fall. What had begun as a mystical apprehension which I considered far more reverent and beautiful than orthodoxy had crumbled in less than five years' testing: it had disintegrated in a welter of blasphemy expressed in the language of Billingsgate. So much, then, for what Wordsworth called "natural piety"—the complacent enjoyment of the insights and spiritual thrills that could be found inside Nature. I needed something more revolutionary —something which could not be provided by the modern churches with their intolerable belittling of Christianity, their continual squalid attempts to pull the Faith inside Nature where it could be examined and approved alongside the arts, philosophies and religions of fallen man. How, indeed, could I turn even with respect to churches that offered me something less than a religion when my nature demanded something more than a religion? And what could be more than a religion except the basic Christian creeds which affirmed realities beyond Nature and beyond the "God" of popular theism? So I had questioned in 1936; and the answer had come, prompt and unmistakable. The flame had struck in the silence, pure radiance in its infantile pre-war phase, smouldering and confused in my wartime friendships, kindling towards maturity in my post-war contacts with Brenda—a progressive grafting

that was God's reply to Nature's abortive effort at Penrose.
It was not yet complete, and those touches of it which involved Christian fellowship were still to come—through Eileen
Funston, a girl whom I first heard of a few weeks after
Phillips' death. But I saw the process clearly now, brooding
upon it while my mother was at Nanpean cemetery looking at
Evelyn across her father's grave. I knew that it was this alien
sting of orthodoxy that had sustained me during the later years
of my struggle—this and not my own will or a "divine spark"
inherent in my humanity, not even the inspiration of the
Christian ethic; and in learning to welcome that wayward
supernatural power I had unconsciously been fitting in at
the one point in the universe where to fit in is to be saved.

THE END